Development Against Democracy

Development Against Democracy

Manipulating Political Change in the Third World

NEW EDITION

Irene L. Gendzier

Introduction by Robert Vitalis
Foreword by Thomas Ferguson

PlutoPress
www.plutobooks.com

Originally published 1985 by Westview Press as *Managing Political Change: Social Scientists and the Third World*

Reissued 1995 by The Tyrone Press as *Development Against Democracy: Manipulating Political Change in the Third World.*

This new edition published 2017 by Pluto Press
345 Archway Road, London N6 5AA

www.plutobooks.com

British Library Cataloguing in Publication Data
A catalogue record for this book is available from the British Library

ISBN   978 0 7453 3729 6   Hardback
ISBN   978 0 7453 3728 9   Paperback
ISBN   978 1 7868 0145 6   PDF eBook
ISBN   978 1 7868 0147 0   Kindle eBook
ISBN   978 1 7868 0146 3   EPUB eBook

This book is printed on paper suitable for recycling and made from fully managed and sustained forest sources. Logging, pulping and manufacturing processes are expected to conform to the environmental standards of the country of origin.

Typeset by Stanford DTP Services, Northampton, England

Simultaneously printed in the United Kingdom and United States of America

Contents

Acknowledgments

I am grateful to Pluto Press and to David Shulman, Commissioning Editor, whose editorial guidance and support have been unique in my experience. His continuing interest in this project over an extended period of time, made its reprinting possible.

The critical responses offered by anonymous readers made a difference. So did the support of friends and colleagues, including Thomas Ferguson, Zachary Lockman and Robert Vitalis, and Nathan Citino, whose works on the political economy of oil, money and power, Middle East studies and International Relations, have long been sources of inspiration, as was the work of the late Marilyn Young, who was among the first to encourage me to reprint *Development Against Democracy*, so that her students could finally find a copy of it. Noam Chomsky, provided judicious criticisms of an earlier edition, and was enthusiastic about its reprinting. And finally, I am grateful to my husband, Assaf Kfoury, whose steadfast support was an indispensable element in the completion of this and many other projects.

Foreword

*Thomas Ferguson**

Irene Gendzier and Pluto Press are to be congratulated for many reasons, but the most compelling is probably their exquisite timing. As this updated reissue of her classic appears, the Trump administration is bringing out a new edition of its own: a rerun of U.S. foreign policy's past heedless embraces of authoritarian regimes, penchant for secrecy, and reckless overconfidence in the power of military force.

The sometimes disorienting mix of muscular rhetoric, deliberate efforts to look "unpredictable," and almost casual talk of "boots on the ground," bombings, and the need for new strategic poses is eerily familiar to analysts who lived through the period Dr. Gendzier writes about with such nuance and verve. I certainly remember the department spaces I was enjoined from entering as a young assistant professor at MIT, for want of the requisite security clearances, even as many authors Dr. Gendzier discusses here repaired to them to work, study, or visit. But younger scholars and a new generation of Americans who never experienced the Cold War mostly do not know this history. They are mostly unaware of the close interactions between many major works of Comparative Politics, International Relations, and American foreign policy or the intense coordination among many protagonists with all manner of government and major foundation personnel. They have little or no conception of how thoroughly broad psychological themes pushed out serious discussion of political institutions and economic analysis.

Researchers working on this period report that documents once available have disappeared, even as some new archival materials open up. Irene Gendzier's splendid book is not the last word on its subject, but it is indispensable for anyone trying to understand how theory and reality related to each other then (and since). One might doubt whether understanding this past will be enough by itself to prevent us from making the famous second move from tragedy to farce—the basis of American economic and political power is so much shallower now than in the age of High Cold War.

* Thomas Ferguson is Professor Emeritus at the University of Massachusetts, Boston.

Development Against Democracy remains, alas, startlingly contemporary. Many of the doctrines it discusses live on in second or third generation versions whose deep structures are only occasionally apprehended. The ease with which these constructions combine with ideology and poor empirical methods to become instrumentalized is breathtaking; Irene Gendzier's fine study merits a wide readership from a new generation of readers.

Introduction

Robert Vitalis[*]

Thirty-five years ago, on June 6, 1982, Israeli forces invaded and occupied southern Lebanon. Its army and air force laid siege to the capital, Beirut, with the objectives of destroying the Palestinian Liberation Organization, then headquartered there, and installing its Maronite Christian clients in power. I had returned to the United States that summer, where I was a PhD candidate in political science at the Massachusetts Institute of Technology, specializing in the "political development" of the Middle East, and had taken a two-year leave of absence in Cairo. Through friends in Cambridge, I made contact with a small group of mostly academic activists that had constituted themselves as the "Ad Hoc Emergency Committee on Lebanon" and as a result found myself handing out leaflets to subway commuters one September evening at the Harvard "T" Station with one of the committee's founders, Boston University professor Irene Gendzier.

I didn't know it then, but, Gendzier had been considered a rising star in the relatively small U.S. Middle East studies field, back in the 1960s. A historian with a Columbia University PhD, she taught in BU's history and political science departments. Her first book, a scholarly monograph published in 1966 and based on her dissertation, was a critically acclaimed biography of the exiled nineteenth-century Jewish-Egyptian nationalist writer, Yaqub Sanua. She wrote on Arab-Israeli affairs, on "Palestine-Israel," in her ahead-of-its-time formulation, and on North Africa for the private, Washington, DC-based Middle East Institute's house organ, the *Middle East Journal*, which served as the main professional outlet prior to the founding of the Middle East Studies Association in 1966. Gendzier was elected to MESA's board of directors in 1974, but by then her profile and research program had changed, like many others affected by the U.S. wars in Southeast Asia, and she soon resigned in protest of the association's ties to the Central Intelligence Agency and other parts of the national security state.[1]

She published her next two books with trade rather than university presses. *A Middle East Reader* (1969), an edited volume for which Gendzier

[*] Robert Vitalis is professor of Political Science at the University of Pennsylvania.

supplied a critical introductory essay, provided non-specialists with an understanding of regional developments following Israel's defeat of Egypt and Syria in June 1967 and its takeover of the whole of Jerusalem, the West Bank, and Gaza. In 1973 Pantheon published her path-breaking *Frantz Fanon: A Critical Study*, the first such account of the thought of Fanon, the Martinique-born, French-trained psychiatrist and revolutionary philosopher who had joined the Algerian National Liberation Front. At the same time, sharp analyses of Israel's settlement policies, of the 1975–1976 Lebanese civil war, and of the beginning of U.S. force projection in the Persian Gulf appeared under her byline in the *Nation* through the last half of the 1970s.

When I met her in 1982, Gendzier was working on revisions of the book you hold in your hands. As she notes in her new opening chapter, it began as a study of the effect of social scientists' fascination with what they dubbed "modernization" or development theory on her own field of Middle East studies, seemingly, as an outgrowth of the criticisms she had raised behind the scenes at MESA. You'll learn more about the so-called theories in the pages to follow. The project though grew bigger, the targets more numerous, as Gendzier dug deeper into the history of the key figures and their auxiliary roles in the violence that the Truman, Eisenhower, and Kennedy administrations unleashed across Latin America, Africa, the Middle East, and Asia.

She was indicting some of the biggest names in the social sciences, many of whom clustered in the Boston-Cambridge area. I had taken seminars with a couple at MIT, and experienced first-hand their contempt for the critics of their intellectual enterprise and refusal to teach or otherwise engage with them. As Gendzier herself notes, by the 1970s these theories had come under withering attack from various ideological and geographical quadrants. I remember one of her own putative comrades, by then rising in the ranks at MIT, wondering aloud to me why she was still bothering with the topic. Many others told her the same thing.[2] They all missed the point. The puzzle for Gendzier is why, despite the withering criticisms, the ideas and, more important, the support for authoritarianism and militarization in the name of "democracy" that these ideas rationalized proved so resistant to change? That question is as relevant today, after more than a decade of failed son-of-modernization "nation-building" and "democracy-pro-motion" theories and policies in Afghanistan, Iraq, Egypt, and elsewhere, as it was in 1985, when she published *Managing Political Change: Social Scientists and the Third World*, the book's original title, reissued ten years later as *Development Against Democracy*.

Thirty years later, *Development Against Demo*cracy would appear to have been ahead of rather than behind the times. The first edition received laudatory reviews by important thinkers in history, sociology, and education, even as the main professional journals for the development theorists she dissected—*Comparative Politics, World Politics, Economic Development and Cultural Change,* and the *American Political Science Review*—ignored it. Coincidence? More likely, it is confirmation of Gendzier's view of the highly ideological enterprises that operated behind the facade of disinterested "scientific" expertise. A great deal more confirmatory evidence has since been amassed, because, starting in the 1990s, PhD students in diplomatic and intellectual history, in science and technology studies, and in anthropology began to work with newly accessible archival sources for the same era that Gendzier covers, where *Development Against Democracy* is now recognized as a foundational text for the study of the *history* of development and modernization as ideology and policy.[3]

Three of her findings impress me anew upon rereading the book thirty years later. First, she shows that the early modernization theorists were first and foremost producers of what Joy Rohde calls "militarized knowledge" for the national security state, in the form of contract research, that they later repackaged as "theory."[4] In the case of the MIT scholars, who advised on counterinsurgency policy through their CIA-funded Center for International Studies, created in 1951, they were only constituted as a political science faculty in the early 1960s as the university administration acknowledged the ethical problem that the close ties with the intelligence agency posed. These entanglements and the compromised nature of scholarship that Gendzier and others identified are never part of the practitioner histories of theory building and of research ethics that professors teach their graduate students today.

Second, she shows that the theories ostensibly derived from in depth knowledge of the peoples of the Middle East, Latin America, Asia, and Africa were in reality deeply-held conservative beliefs—fears actually—of mass participation in politics at home in the United States. There is a seamless transfer of these fears and projection onto so called "underdeveloped," "traditional," societies of their preference for elite guidance (management, manipulation) of citizens, not least through policies of exclusion. She might have gone further.

That is, third, Gendzier argues that the modernization theorists turned to explicating the alleged multiple psychological and cultural deficiencies of Egyptians, Burmese, Indians, Nigerians, and others in order to resolve the paradox at the heart of their ideas about development: A project that in the name of democracy supported intervention in the domestic politics of newly independent countries, the backing of military rule, and the suppression of unrest, insurgency, and, worst of all, "revolution." The latter followed, quite predictably, from the deepening U.S.-backed investment in capitalist enterprise, oil complexes, plantations, and the like, across the so-called "Third World," but American political scientists reached instead for old ideas about what the critic John Hobson identifies as the "defective agency" of so-called non-Western, non-white peoples.[5]

The social sciences in the United States were concerned with the putative inferiority of others, Black peoples above all, long before the government began to champion Point IV and successor development programs in the ex-European colonial possessions. Around that time, it became common to define as "racist" those who believed in and advocated for the biological basis and hence immutability of inferiority, which were in fact the grounds for segregation, anti-miscegenation statutes, and the like at the close of the nineteenth century. But historian Ibram Kendi asks: What about those who instead traced Black inferiority back to environmental causes—"hot climates, discrimination, culture, and poverty"?[6] Post-World War II social science was replete with strategies for reducing "behavioral inferiority" over the long term through programs of education and uplift that would lead to "assimilation" and "adoption" of white cultural traits. As an example, Kendi points to the landmark 1944 study *An American Dilemma* by the future development economist Gunnar Myrdal. But professors at Harvard, MIT, and elsewhere had been promoting policies of "race development" for the world's inferior peoples from Harlem to Hawaii and beyond decades prior to Myrdal's Carnegie Corporation-funded project. That formative epoch in the history of the theory and practice of development had been forgotten by the time Gendzier had begun her research, and it needs to be recovered.[7]

The University of Michigan's Joy Rohde, one of those younger historians following in Gendzier's footsteps, underscores one of the unintended consequences of the effort to delegitimize and disrupt the classified research programs at dozens of university Institutes and Centers across the country. The Pentagon and allied agencies are still at it, but the role of universities and university faculty have long since been eclipsed by the vast expansion of literally thousands of private "security firms, consulting agencies," and other organizations doing classified work on counterterrorism, counter-insurgency, and, yes, democracy promotion and nation building.[8]

Since writing *Development Against Democracy*, Gendzier, too, turned to declassified government records in writing about U.S. imperialism in the Middle East. She came out with an important study of Lebanon (*Notes from the Minefield*, 1997), and in 2015 published a radically revisionist account of the U.S. decision to recognize Israel in 1948 (*Dying to Forget: Oil, Power, Palestine, and the Foundations of U.S. Policy in the Middle East*). Her commitment to countering the liberal orthodoxies that rationalize the exercise of domination is unwavering. She is surely right about the unself-conscious recycling of modernization theory by old and new scholars alike in the 1990s, toward the same ends, and with predictable consequences: secrecy, waste, corruption, death, and destruction, all in the name of democracy. These ideas live on, not because they are true, but because they have served the powerful so well for so long.

June 2017

I

The "New Look" in Development Studies

The pages that follow constitute a guide to postwar studies of modernization and development. The times are different but the revival of programs dedicated to the export of democracy serve to remind us of the earlier approach and the urgency of examining its roots and legacy. At stake is understanding theories and policies based on elitist concepts of democracy with their profound suspicions of participatory democracy that were aimed at the global south but reflected the interests of ruling elites in the U.S.

According to a well-known typology of development studies, the field evolved in three stages: the first in the aftermath of World War II; the second following the collapse of the Soviet Union and the end of the Cold War; and the third, inspired by the events of 9/11.[1]

What of the present? Far from signaling continuity, the emergence of populist movements across Europe and the United States in 2016–2017 marks a phase of widespread contestation of the politics of globalization and immigration in a disordered world. Absent from the latest edition of development theories is consideration of the uneven consequences of unchecked neoliberal policies and the impact of technological change. Misinterpreting the roots of alienation of those excluded hardly dispels the problem. On the contrary, it promotes attempts to control the manifestation of discontent through pseudo-scientific programs that mask the objective of controlling dissent and assuring social control.

This too is reminiscent of the earlier, "classic" phase of modernization and development studies, further reinforcing the urgency of confronting its roots and legacy.

First published in 1985 under the title, *Managing Political Change: Social Scientists and the Third World*, the present work was originally destined to be a study of the impact of theories of modernization and development on the growing field of contemporary Middle East studies. That objective was soon overtaken by the study of its impact in the social sciences, and more particularly in political science, international relations, and Third World studies. The title of the second edition (1995) was changed to *Development Against Democracy: Manipulating Political Change in the Third World*, in order to avoid the mistaken impression that the purpose of this study was to provide a manual for political manipulation. Aside from the change in title, however, its objective and underlying premises with respect to the limits of elitist views of democracy and their influence on modernization and development studies remained constant.

The New Look in Development Studies

Despite the underlying similarity that marks the old and the new views of development and modernization, some contemporary scholars maintain that there has been a significant change in the field. Joseph Morgan Hodge is among them, as his widely-recognized survey of development studies demonstrates.[2] According to Hodge, this is a product of increased emphasis on a comparative, interdisciplinary and global orientation that deepens our understanding of development, while additionally freeing it from the past focus on U.S. experience.[3] While the emphasis on an international-ist approach is admirable, marginalizing U.S. experience is not, given its centrality in postwar experience.[4] Its marginalization serves to divert attention from the role of development and modernization policies in the broader context of U.S. foreign policy in the global South.

According to Hodge's typology, Development studies evolved in three stages, the last of which resulted in,

> a truly global and transnational history of development, one that brings together the literature on late colonialism and decolonization with the new international history of the Cold War, and that offers a more diverse, refined, and historically-informed reading of international development.[5]

Hodge interprets the first phase as "part of an internal disciplinary critique, written from the inside with the intent of reforming rather than radically overturning the structure."[6] His reference to *Managing Political Change* in this context is misplaced, as the intention of that work was— and remains—to expose the anti-democratic character of elitist democracy and the extent of academic collaboration in the manipulation of political change.

The second phase of Hodge's chronology follows the end of the Cold War. It was marked by the triumph of neoliberal reformers who saw "greater market integration as a development alternative."[7] The third phase represented an awakening of, both policy makers and scholars to the realities and rising instabilities of the new, post-Cold War order which gave rise to the movement for the renewal of empire along with the ideology of American exceptionalism and its unique role in exporting democracy.[8]

Many policy analysts, Hodge writes, were persuaded that the events of September 11, 2001, "pointed logically toward a new U.S.-led imperialism designed to bring stability and democracy to the world's insurgent zones."[9] The logic was used to justify the operations of British as well as French empires that envisioned their roles as part of a civilizing mission. Hodge relied on the writings of the neoconservative trio of Niall Ferguson, Michael Ignatieff and Francis Fukuyama, to bolster his arguments. Fukuyama, Hodge pointed out, not only emphasized the urgency of state building, but culture and "social trust" in economic change, themes that were dominant in Development studies of the 1960s.[10]

What was striking in Hodge's account was the omission of critical analysis of neoliberal policies in generating poverty, inequality and the conditions conducive to dependency, as Frederick Cooper remarked in his comments on Hodge's text.[11] Hodge's omission was not a unique trait. With few exceptions, it was characteristic of conventional analyses of development. Cooper's observations, on the other hand, were part of a broader critique that included the works of economists as well as members of the IMF who, in 2016, openly questioned whether "instead of delivering growth, some neoliberal policies have increased inequality, in turn jeopardizing durable expansion."[12]

Years before the appearance of the widely heralded work of Thomas Piketty, *The Economics of Inequality*,[13] economists including Joseph Stiglitz argued in favor of replacing the "Washington Consensus" with one embracing "a focus on the living standards of people and the promotion of equitable, sustainable and democratic development."[14]

The World That Was

The world in which modernization and development studies arose was marked by the graveyards of World War II and the collapse of European colonial powers, the Cold War and in 1949, the Chinese Revolution. The U.S. emerged in this global arena as an icon of political and economic stability bent on assuring its hegemony. The environment it faced was one of disastrous postwar economic conditions across the European continent and the adverse conditions facing newly independent states of the Third

World. The combination aroused deep concern among Washington policymakers who feared the risks of economic collapse and its potentially destabilizing effects.

Washington's preoccupation with the fate of recently decolonized states and those struggling for independence was inseparable from the protection and projection of U.S. interests across Middle East, Latin America, Southeast Asia and Africa. U.S. officials responded to movements for reform and revolution in these regions with counterinsurgency policies designed to neutralize and undermine radical activists.

Michael Klare reminds us that "between 1960 and 1970, the United States spent $1 billion to overcome insurgent threats to the existing order."[15]

Rooted in the "visionary globalism" that characterized postwar American ideology, modernization and development policies assumed the U.S. capable of restructuring both "the United States and the globe in ways that would ensure American centrality in world affairs."[16] In the postwar framework, James Peck observed, "modernization offered a compelling internationalist vision, a bold globalism promising not only freedom but also development and well-being for the poorest nations."[17]

In his remarks on the "Foundations of Social Change," Kees Van Der Pijl observed that early versions of modernization and development policies could be traced to the post-World War I period when international studies "were recast as a direct extension of Anglo-American open nation-state building, a process in which client governing classes are given the keys of a state on the condition they leave the door open."[18] The works of major contributors to Development studies such as Gabriel Almond, Sidney Verba, Lucian Pye, Samuel P. Huntington, Edward A. Shils, Daniel Lerner, and W. W. Rostow, among others, confirmed Van Der Pijl's interpretation.

Almond and Verba's *The Civic Culture* alone warrants recognition as a work that influenced the dominant approach to political development, including its vision of political participation as a threat to the existing social and political order. "The need for elite power," they wrote," requires that the ordinary citizen be relatively passive, uninvolved, and deferential to elites."[19] Their analysis applied to the examples of Western European states, the U.S. and Mexico, but it was applicable to other constituencies, according to Huntington, Crozier, and Watanuki, in their work on, *The Crisis of Democracy*.[20]

W. W. Rostow achieved prominence with his publication of the

"Non-Communist Manifesto" [that] envisaged the "developing" nations as passing through similar stages of development, out of tradition-bound poverty, through an industrialized modernization overseen by the US, the World Bank and the IMF, to mass-consumer prosperity.[21]

Vivek Chibber later observed that Rostow's Manifesto addressed "capital's universalizing mission," according to which "Europe showed the developing world a rough picture of its own future."[22] The prosperity that Rostow's Manifesto promised was unequally shared in the Third World as in the First, where the inequality reproduced through the institutionalized racism against Afro-Americans made a mockery of the claims of development. Institutionalized racism was not foreign to domestic politics or to the foundations of international relations as a discipline, as the recent work by Robert Vitalis has starkly demonstrated.[23]

Major foundations played a critical role in funding and propagating Development and Modernization studies. By 1952,

the Rockefeller Foundation and the Carnegie Corporation had contributed several million dollars to the creation of international studies centers throughout the country. As early as 1948, one of the most influential of such institutions from the point of view of Development studies, the Social Science Research Council (SSRC), turned to area studies considered to be "vital to national interests and to intercultural understanding."[24]

Those focusing on the Middle East were among them. It is useful to recall that "from the early 1950s into the 1970s, modernization theory was the dominant paradigm in U.S. area studies in general and Middle East studies in particular, informing a mass of research and writing on political change, economic development and social transformation, and interacting with Orientalism in complex ways."[25] However widely its influence on different disciplines varied, "overall it certainly functioned as the 'big idea' underpinning a good chunk of US social science research about the world in this period."[26]

The "dominant paradigm" fueled interpretations that served as apologies for intervention and the politics of repression aimed at intellectuals and political activists committed to movements of secularism and democracy. Daniel Lerner's study, *The Passing of Traditional Society: Modernizing the Middle East*, a work which was considered by social scientists as an effective response to Edward Said's influential study, *Orientalism*, provided the template for the reductionist interpretation of Middle Eastern states and societies. It contributed to promoting a monolithic view of contemporary

Arab states as stuck on sectarianism and unprepared to jettison traditional habits in favor of modernity.[27]

The critical literature on contemporary North Africa and the Middle East offers a very different body of evidence, whether on the modern history of Egypt, Tunisia, Algeria, Gaza, Palestine, Lebanon, or Saudi Arabia.[28] Primary sources of U.S. foreign policy are similarly at odds with the outlook expressed in Lerner's *Traditional Society*, insofar as they disclose extensive political and economic interests guiding U.S. policy.[29] Those records, however, also serve to confirm how U.S. officials viewed the relationship between development and foreign policy.[30]

Exporting Democracy: True Believers and Cautious Realists

The end of the Soviet regime and the accompanying Cold War undermined the ideological justification of development and modernization policies that had long been publicly rationalized in terms of containing the USSR. Neither the policies nor the studies that legitimized them, disappeared. They were reincarnated in the form of democracy promotion, which some advocates claimed had been their original intent in the postwar period, as did Sean M. Lynn-Jones, editor of *International Security* and Harvard University's Belfer Center Studies in International Security. In his view, following World War II, promoting democracy was "America's next mission."[31] It was an approach that captured the "idea of divine chosenness, and the political conviction that the new republic of liberty was decisive for world history."[32] Reminiscent of Henry B. Luce's vision of "The American Century," it was adopted by supporters of the "Project for a New American Century" in the 1990s.[33]

The campaign to promote democracy rapidly gained the support of U.S. academics who were "quick to pick up the scent of democracy promotion as a vector of bringing open nation-states under Western global governance."[34] By 2004, "approximately $2 billion per year (roughly half from public and private sources in North America and half from largely public sources in Europe)" was devoted to projects related to democracy assistance.[35] "By 2005, it had reached the level of ritual," as Chomsky wrote in *Failed States* (2006).[36]

Writing in 2012, Thomas Carothers, head of the Carnegie Endowment for International Peace and its Democracy and the Rule of Law Program, and a prolific and critical writer on the subject, similarly held the view that democracy promotion had long been part of U.S. foreign policy. It was further encouraged in an international environment where, according to Carothers, the U.S. and its allies faced no serious rivals.[37]

In 1983, the National Endowment for Democracy (NED), "was instituted as the 'overt', public arm of Project Democracy, in which the CIA and the NSC handled the 'covert' arm."[38] The *Journal of Democracy*, edited by Larry Diamond of the Hoover Institution, became a recognized resource for the democracy export agenda. According to Diamond's position, "democracies possess unique virtues. They do not indulge in politics of ethnic cleansing or use weapons of mass destruction against their own populations or those of allied democracies. In addition, they offer favorable investment climates and honor international treaties."[39]

Diamond conceded that the U.S. and other democracies were in need of reform, but he had little to say about the history of ethnic cleansing conducted by the U.S. against its own indigenous population; or the history of supporting terrorist groups to undermine left-wing movements, including democratically elected regimes, as in Latin America, the Middle East and Southeast Asia; or the sale of weapons of mass destruction, as in the case of the U.S. to Iraq, prior to the 2003 U.S. invasion.

In a rejoinder to David Forsythe's criticism of the "democratic-peace proposition", Sean Lynn-Jones, derided the claim that "democracies sometimes have sponsored covert action or 'state terrorism' against other democracies."[40] Ignoring the impact of "US actions in Iran in 1953, Guatemala in 1954 and Chile in 1973," Lynn-Jones claimed that since the states targeted had "dubious democratic credentials," the U.S. could not be accused of intervening against democracies.

In 2000, Thomas Risse, professor and chair of international politics in the Department of Political and Social Science at the Free University of Berlin, offered another defense of the export of democracy along the lines of Diamond's work. As Risse argued, "liberal democracies not only rarely fight each other, as the 'democratic peace' argument correctly claims, they form security communities that effectively reduce the security dilemma to insignificant levels and exclude the possibility of great-power war among them."[41]

Thomas Carothers, who had served in programs of "democracy enhancement" in the State Department under President Reagan, eventually became director of the ambitious and well-funded Carnegie Endowment for International Peace and its Democracy and the Rule of Law Program. In that capacity, he offered an approach that endorsed a cautious realism that did not eschew the contradictions of U.S. foreign policy, observing that the U.S. benefited by operating in an international environment where it had few serious rivals.

In many respects, Carothers' prolific output on democracy promotion is unique, in that is has been accompanied by a critical strain against the hypocrisies of U.S. policy. He has not been reluctant to point to the conflict between the formal objectives of U.S. policies that claim to promote democracy and the priorities of U.S. policy that undermine them. But he has also consistently stopped short of confronting the significance of the contradictions involved.

Carothers situated the prodemocracy movement in U.S. policy in the context of the dramatic changes affecting Eastern Europe, Latin America, Southeast Asia and the USSR from the mid-1970s to the 1990s. While the political trends in these regions differed, Carothers discerned a dominant trend "towards more liberal and often more democratic governance," which rendered their transformation part of a global phenomenon. Carothers found S. P. Huntington's description of the "third wave" of democracy, particularly apt.[42] But he appeared to find some deeper solace in other connections between current developments and the modernization and development policies of the past.

Indeed, Huntington's book by the same name furthers Carothers that the dynamism of this wave had effectively buried "deterministic, and often culturally noxious assumptions about democracy, such as that only countries with an American-style middle class or a heritage of Protestant individualism could become democratic."

Carothers was convinced that the bipartisan appeal of rule of law programs was enhanced by recognition of their "reassuring roots in the formative 'modernization' period of political and economic development work of the 1960s."[43] The reassurance offered by such roots was that the stabilization of sociopolitical systems which was an inevitable feature of modernization, would not lead to increased popular participation. Instead, in accord with the "formative 'modernization' period" of the 1960s, there would be support for "limited, top-down forms of democratic change [that] did not risk upsetting the traditional structures of power with which the United States has long been allied."[44]

In a volume co-authored with Marina Ottaway that dealt with the Middle East, Carothers admitted that "the new democracy imperative for the Middle East," was "driven not by a trend toward reform in the region, but by the West's own security concerns."[45] Washington's so-called "soft diplomacy," as distinct from its militarization of policy, meant that the

U.S. was soft on dictators when such policies coincided with U.S. interests irrespective of its impact on the society and state concerned.

Hence,

> as urgent and serious as the prodemocracy imperative appears to many in the US policy community, the stubborn reality remains that the United States has other important security-related and economic interests, such as cooperation on antiterrorism enforcement actions and ensuring secure access to oil. Such interests impel it to maintain close ties with many of the authoritarian regimes in the Middle East and to be wary of the possibility of rapid or unpredictable political change. Given the strength and persistence of these other interests, it is not clear whether the new prodemocracy impulse will result in a fundamental change of the long-standing US support for authoritarian and semi-authoritarian friends in the region or simply end up as an attractive wrapping around a largely unchanged core.[46]

In so far as Iraq is concerned, Carothers' candid assessment of the G. W. Bush administration's fraudulent claims demonstrated that "the notion that democracy promotion plays a dominant role in Bush policy is a myth" devised after the invasion to cover for the justifications for the invasion.[47] Carothers did not fail to admit that for many U.S. policy appeared to be "self-serving and profoundly hypocritical. America's own recent violations of the rule of law and human rights only complete this picture."[48]

Washington faced a choice and a risk, he concluded, in "expending real political capital that up to now has been used in the service of economic and security interests. This is the key choice facing the United States with respect to promoting democracy in the Middle East."[49] For the U.S. to implement the policies of democratic reform it claims to favor, a "significant change of course—away from decades of support for political stasis and from deep attachments to particular rulers," would be necessary.[50]

Carothers continued to insist that "democracy promotion" was at the core of U.S. foreign policy although he conceded the difficulties it faced. He was no less straightforward in debunking the "fads" of democracy campaigns, including those involving the "civil society craze in the 1990s," or those focused on the rule of law.[51] The civil society concept was misused, he argued, with unrealistic expectations in addition. As for the rule of law, Carothers admitted that "despite the many rule-of-law programs now under way, we actually know troublingly little about what we are doing in this domain."[52]

In 2002 Carothers was prepared to admit that the so-called "transition paradigm" to democracy had failed. The key elements that had come to play a central role, such as,

> political party development, civil society strengthening, judicial reform, and media development almost never conform to the technocratic ideal of rational sequences on which the indicator frameworks and strategic objectives of democracy promoters are built. Instead they are chaotic processes of change that go backwards and sideways as much as forward, and do not do so in any regular manner.[53]

Without hesitation Carothers thus demolished the underlying framework of development programs. In the process, he called attention to the criteria according to which democracy promotion operated, which was based on the calculation of U.S. interests. Erasing the pretense of significant differences on this score between the administrations of George H. W. Bush, Bill Clinton, and George W. Bush, Carothers underlined their common exploitation of the democracy paradigm.

> All of these administrations ended up making democracy promotion the rhetorical framework of their foreign policy. Yet, at the same time, all three pursued what might be described as a semi-realist policy in practice: Where supporting democracy in another country or region was consistent with U.S. economic and security interests, the United States stood up for democracy; but where policy makers saw strong economic or security reasons for staying on friendly terms with authoritarian or semi-authoritarian regimes, Washington almost always downplayed its democracy concerns.[54]

Unlike Hodge's survey of the third phase of development studies, with its apology for the renewal of American empire, Carothers offered a blunt description of U.S. foreign policy following September 2001, in which he exposed Washington's ties with repressive regimes, observing its justification in the wake of the terrorist attacks. In the process, he confronted G. W. Bush's Undersecretary of State, Paula Dobriansky, who claimed that the Bush administration "always strikes the right balance between democracy and security," pointing out that since the terrorist attacks of September 11, 2001, the Bush administration has sought closer ties and enhanced security cooperation with a host of authoritarian or semi-authoritarian regimes—in Algeria, Bahrain, China, Egypt, Jordan, Kazakhstan, Kuwait, Malaysia, Pakistan, Qatar, Uzbekistan, Yemen, and even Syria.[55]

The grim mood that pervaded Carothers' edited volume, *Promoting the Rule of Law Abroad: In Search of Knowledge*, revealed his alienation from conventional supporters of democracy promotion. Describing "democracy promotion and support for market-based economic reforms," as the "twin imperatives that have come to dominate contemporary donor thinking about political and economic development," Carothers was candid about the results.[56] He admitted a "loss of global democratic momentum," and he conceded "problems of western political credibility, and the rise of alternative political models [that] are making it a more challenging task than ever."[57] Under the circumstances, Carothers called for a "broader notion of democracy, one that encompasses concerns about equality and justice . . ." while staying well within the parameters of state-building.[58] Carothers' willingness to confront the internal contradictions of the promotion of democracy stopped short of breaking with the "paternalistic and neo-colonial overtones that cling to the development industry—and which is in turn subordinate to a deeply inegalitarian global establishment."[59]

End Notes

The "new look" in development studies did not break with the "paternalistic and neo-colonial overtones" of past Development studies. It was singularly indifferent to the critiques of its foundational premises with respect to elitist forms of democracy and the manipulation of political change. Claims of American exceptionalism and the promotion of democracy export, were not the only indicators of a revival of earlier Development studies.

The program of the "Next Generation Social Science," announced by the Defense Advanced Research Projects Agency (DARPA) in the fall of 2016, is reminiscent of some of the work on psychological warfare and propaganda by political scientists such as Harold D. Lasswell and Daniel Lerner.[60] The newest generation of programs follows in a long tradition that includes the contribution of psychology and the social sciences to the military from World War II through Vietnam and after.[61]

In the mid-1960s the role of the behavioral sciences in foreign policy was the subject of investigation by the House Committee on Foreign Affairs. The latter issued a report on "Behavioral Sciences and the National Security" that was presented before the House of Representatives at Hearings on "Winning the Cold War: The U.S. Ideological Offensive."[62] As the authors of the report pointed out, "what they [behavioral sciences] tell us about human attitudes and motivations, and how this knowledge can be applied to governmental undertakings designed to carry out the foreign policy of the United States—has been of keen interest to our Subcommittee."[63] Defense Department officials, including the head of research and development in the Department of the Army, indicated that his division was looking for "improved performance in counterinsurgency, military assistance, unconventional types of warfare and psychological operations through social and behavioral science studies of methods for predicting the reactions of indigenous troops and populations in foreign areas; and other studies as may be needed for direct support of stability operations."[64] Some fifty years later, the focus of comparable research by the military deals with "the ability of positivistic social science to provide scientistic recipes for controlling and managing the trajectories of social change and economic growth on demand in various 'developing societies.'"[65]

In the fall of 2016 DARPA announced a program titled, "Next Generation Social Science."[66] The goal of DARPA's research was "to probe what unifies individuals and what causes communities to break down into 'a chaotic mix of disconnected individuals.'" The Next Generation Social Science (NGS2) program will seek to harness steadily advancing digital connections and emerging social and data science tools to identify "the primary drivers of social cooperation, instability and resilience." The above project was designed "to build on the ability to link thousands of diverse volunteers online in order to tackle social science problems with implications for U.S. national and economic security."

The program and its funding are designed to appeal to university researchers and advanced students capable of making use of the most advanced "social and data science tools," an option that holds out the possibility of significant research as well as support at a time of increased financial vulnerability for students and universities.

Where, then, are we with respect to the new look in development studies and its relation to democracy?

The times are different but the revival of programs dedicated to the export of democracy serve to remind us of the earlier approach and its underlying world view. Yet the origins and significance of this connection have been ignored, both in the media and in academia. Partisans of past and present theories of development share a common view of the risks of popular democracy and the urgency of manipulating political change in order to contain it. The consequences of globalization that were not evident in the earlier period, and those of the uncritical celebration of market economics that has been a feature of the old and new looks of development studies, can no longer be hidden. The ravages of inequality and the demands for social justice and political freedom cannot be denied.

The new look in Development studies does not address these questions. For the most part, the authors who contributed to the earlier literature of Development and Modernization studies did not address issues of inequality and the demands for social justice, save when they feared that their expression might serve as the trigger for a broader instability that would endanger U.S. policy.

What does it mean to reproduce the uncritical legacy of Development studies in this environment? The answer lies in the re-examination of that legacy and its consequences as an act of consciousness raising and resistance.

2

Making Connections

Stating the Problem

Development and *Modernization* are terms that evoke powerful images.* They speak to the collective aspirations of people throughout the world for a life of meaning and dignity. They inspire the hope that what the rich nations have achieved, the poor may one day obtain. They address the desire for social, political, and economic reforms that moves people in the most disparate of lands. Who can be against Development? Who can oppose what Modernization promises?

Reality has not matched the dream or the promise. Policies of Development have become suspect. Modernization has intensified poverty, social conflict, and the very conditions it was meant to alleviate. What does it mean, then, to speak of Development or Modernization? For the past two decades there has been an ongoing debate about what Development has accomplished, about why the process has been implicated in underdevelopment and de-development. The debate has been intensified as conditions in the Third World** have become more acute. Studies on economic growth repeatedly point to the distinction between growth and development. The gross national product (GNP) increases. But the standard of living for

---

* Development and Modernization are capitalized throughout this text to refer to a specialized body of literature. It is a literature produced by academic theorists who adhered to a common view of sociopolitical change and the appropriate means of explaining it, both of which are examined in the pages that follow. I refer to this common view, central to Development doctrine, as the conventional interpretation of Development.

** The term *Third World*, used throughout this book, is unsatisfactory and requires explanation. Originally employed to describe states outside the major industrialized capitalist and socialist centers, it was associated with countries marked by widespread poverty, illiteracy, and the existence of largely agricultural economies with a limited industrial capacity. The term is now used to refer to states that are, in fact, dissimilar with respect to their political, social, and economic conditions; the danger of reductionist explanation is to be found in this reality. In fact, the heterogeneous character of the states so classified precludes a usage that seeks to explain their condition. The term as used here, then, refers to those dissimilar states and societies that were the avowed objects of studies on political change and its implications. It is used in the descriptive sense only.

men, women, and children, hidden in statistics that neatly adorn textbooks, declines. U.S. policymakers extol Development in terms of democracy, yet they support authoritarian regimes that manipulate social and political change.

For many, terms like Development and Modernization have lost their meaning. They have become code words. They refer to policies pursued by governments and international agencies that enrich ruling elites and technocrats, while the masses are told to await the benefits of the "trickle down" effect. For many, Development and Modernization are terms that refer to a politics of reform designed to preserve the status quo while promising to alter it. And for many, social scientists who have rationalized the interests of governments committed to such policies are accomplices in deception.

Neither theorists of Development nor policymakers engaged in such projects concur in this outlook. For the most part, they view their different tasks as difficult to accomplish. Conditions in the Third World are repeatedly alleged to defy the kinds of improvements formally intended by Development policies. The problems, according to this perspective, are economic, political, and cultural: an inadequacy of resources, a pervasiveness of instability and corruption, and a persistence of habits antagonistic to change. For ordinary people in the United States, the issues appear to be no different, save that they question the value of assigning generous sums to foreign governments while economic problems on the home front are aggravated by the lack of such resources.

What can one make of this impasse? Why the continuity of public support for Development policies that seem doubtful in terms of their stated purpose? Why the reproduction of explanations that seem to contradict their terms? Conventional theories of Development—and Development policies—have been challenged from a variety of sources. Social scientists in agreement with the underlying premises of Development theories have pointed out their shortcomings. Left-wing scholars have exposed their theoretical flaws and empirical weaknesses. They have noted the extent to which such theories are defined to suit capitalist interests while, in practice, promoting neither capitalist nor other forms of development. And events in the Third World itself have challenged both the validity of explanations based on Development theories and the policies associated with them.

Yet for a majority of working scholars and students, and for a large number of educated lay persons, the premises of conventional explanations of Development remain valid. The impact of radical, left-wing research has been uneven. The challenge issued by a minority of prolific scholars, by no means in agreement on an alternative approach to development, has not altered the agenda of the majority of students and scholars. For this latter segment of the public, events in the Third World often appear to confirm rather than to contradict conventional explanations of political change. Civil wars, disturbances, and revolutions are read as signs of internal weakness, as proof of the lack of rationality that dominates Third World politics. This approach is found not only in the United States. There is an international group of scholars and students in solidarity with the conventional way of interpreting sociopolitical change that conforms to their interests.

Looking back at the critical literature produced by liberal and radical scholars in the 1960s and 1970s, we find that attention was indeed paid to existing explanations of change, if only to identify their weaknesses. But as critical scholars became increasingly preoccupied with the search for alternative interpretations, they abandoned the critique of Development doctrine. Persuaded of its blatant defects, they assumed the genre to be not only bankrupt but defunct as well. Mainstream scholars, on the other hand, were often unprepared to concede the validity of such criticisms. For them, the importance of the attack on Development theories was of doubtful validity. Its relevance to their own empirical research was skeptically viewed. Arguing from entirely different perspectives, then, radical critics and exponents of Development theories in effect jointly recommended that the inquiry into the limits of Development theories be sharply curtailed.

For defenders of the genre, Development theories were capable of being reformed. Hence, the problem was worthy of continued consideration. For critics of the genre, the failure of the very same interpretations in question was so blatant as to undermine additional efforts at their reconstruction. What both such reactions overlooked, however, was the extent to which the assumptions underlying Political Development theories and interpretations persisted. On the level of policy, and in the general approach to political change in the Third World to be found among scholars, the educated public, and the media, it was by no means clear that the views identified with Political Development studies were defunct.

What are the reasons for this situation? What conditions support it? Unlike those who consider the question closed, I argue that it is imperative to reconsider the significance of the body of literature pertaining to Political Development. Furthermore, I maintain that it is the classical period of Political Development studies that deserves particular attention, since this formative period defined the limits of the analysis of political change in ways that continue to affect us. Reconsidering the genre of Political Development studies, then, is not equivalent to writing an obituary for a dead intellectual form. Rather, it is an effort at demystification, at the uncovering of the intellectual and political coordinates of the interpretation of Political Development.

The viability of conventional interpretations of Political Development rests on their congruence with foreign policy and, on a different level, with the prevailing interpretation of political change and political order. The former has been documented in critical studies of Development that have lost none of their relevance. But the foreign policy connection is not the only key to the explanation of the viability of this literature and approach. The sense of familiarity evoked by Political Development studies rests on other foundations as well. The view that they reflect the common sense of politics and social change strikes at a deeper root of this connection.

Interpretations of politics and society that were codified in Political Development theories were the product of a particular vision of American society. Forged in the period of the 1950s and early 1960s, this vision was expressed in debates provoked by national and international developments, from McCarthyism to the cold war. Trends in the social sciences were affected by this climate. Revisionist theories of liberal democracy that were crafted by a generation of postwar political scientists reflected the conservative response to democracy and mass society implicit in such theories. And from this source came the political vocabulary that became the language of Political Development studies. Applied first to analyses of contemporary U.S. and Anglo-Saxon political systems, the revisionist view of liberal democracy was then extended to analyses of Third World states, where its apolitical view of politics, its elitist bias, and its pessimism about mass-based social and political movements colored the interpretation of Third World Development.

The deconstruction of Political Development theories and interpretations, then, involves not only the defining of foreign policy but also the identification of a normative view of domestic policy. It involves situating Development studies in a broad context that includes the convergence of Development doctrine with foreign policy and the convergence of the same doctrine with a conservative definition of democracy. Out of this combination issued that managerial view of political change that Political Development studies represented.

Origins of Political Development Studies

Academic interest in problems of social and political change in the Third World coincided with post-World War II U.S. foreign policy. It was in this period that Development policies were put on the agenda and that academic consultants were invited to turn their attention to its analysis. Funding for policies and studies related to Development increased accordingly. The form assumed by the academic interest in Development policies, deeply molded by foreign policy interests, was influenced by other historical experiences. The emergence of fascism, Naziism, the impact of Stalinism, the response to the Depression, McCarthyism, and the cold war were all factors that affected the discourse on Development among academic students of the field.

For liberal theorists who became engaged in the study of social and political change in Third World countries, the years after 1945 represented a time when newly independent nations in Africa, Asia, Latin America, and the Middle East were becoming industrialized or semi-industrialized states. Modernity was envisioned as a "syndrome" of changes that included industrialization, urbanization, the extension of literacy, education, and the media. But it was also assumed that improvements in economic conditions would lead to the emergence of more democratic regimes. Further, it was assumed that such regimes would be immune to the temptations of neutralism, socialism, or communism. Results proved otherwise. In less than a decade, early students of Political Development began to voice their disenchantment with the course of Third World change.

Modernization, an increasingly popular area of academic study, was now increasingly viewed with suspicion as a process that led to instability. The dilemma was neither trivial nor temporary. It lay, in fact, at the very source of the Development process, thus provoking an ongoing debate among scholars as to the meaning and political implications of Development policies and studies. The problem dogged those committed to conventional interpretations of Development who simultaneously supported the expansion of capitalist market systems and democratic political institutions while rejecting the nature of the historic connection between them. For students of Political Development, the emphasis was placed firmly on the question of political change and the most efficient way of steering Third World regimes around the dangers of widespread instability and possible radicalization.

By the late 1950s and early 1960s, when studies of Political Development began to appear, the study of economic growth was already well under way. There was a considerable modern literature dealing with Europe and selected areas of the non-Western, nonindustrialized world.[1] By the late 1960s a specialized branch of development literature concentrating on the problems of contemporary Third World states had come into existence as well.[2] Those interested had access to a variety of interpretations, as the works of the following suggest: Irma Adelman and Cynthia Taft Morris, Dudley Seers, Keith Griffin, T. W. Schultz, Michael Lipton, Arthur W. Lewis, Hla Myint, Paul A. Baran, Benjamin Higgins, Gunnar Myrdal, Raoul Prebisch, and Albert O. Hirschman, among others.

For many conventional students of political change, however, this literature remained outside the scope of legitimate study. Its relevance to the understanding of the dynamic processes at work in the development process was generally ignored, regarded as foreign to the more specific interests of those concerned with state and nation building. Evidence of a false "separatism," to use Macpherson's term,[3] this approach reflected a more coherent position than initially appeared to be the case. It was the product of an intellectual orientation marked by an antimaterialist bias, justified in terms of disciplinary differences and specializations. For all of their formal commitment to a social science, most scholars of Political Development were fearful of crossing the boundaries of economics, unless it was to reach out to a compatible interpreter of change—as in the case of W. W. Rostow, for example.

The reference is not a minor one. Rostow was the economic historian whose work had the most obvious appeal in the circle of Political Development scholars. His commitment to the production of an anticommunist manifesto coincided with the orientation that dominated Political Development studies. His conception of the evolution of Third World societies confirmed the outlook of Development theorists who shared an evolutionary bias and a Darwinian approach to the interpretation of progress. That Rostow's work was severely criticized by economists who expressed reservations about the validity of his analysis did not affect his supporters among Political Development scholars.[4] It was less his economic view than his social and political outlook on Development, after all, that recommended him for support in this milieu.

The milieu in question was primarily that of professional political scientists (although contributors to Political Development studies included sociologists, whose influence was more extensive than their actual participation in the disciplinary effort suggests). Reference to this discipline is a useful reminder of the context from which Political Development studies emerged. Rooted in the revisionist interpretation of liberal democratic theory, the Political Development theories of this period (late 1950s to late 1960s) shared the same outlook with respect to the nature of politics, the dangers of mass society, and the reliance on personality and psychology, as well as culture, in their interpretations and rationalizations of political change. These traits were essential elements in what became the doctrine of Political Development, the conservative interpretation of political change at the core of Political Development studies. They informed accounts of political change that characterized the first decade of Political Development studies, which were marked by the publication of Lerner's *The Passing of Traditional Society* (1958) and Samuel P. Huntington's *Political Order in Changing Societies* (1968). And they persisted in subsequent accounts of Third World change written on the basis of the same premises.

In spite of this common adherence to the conservative, elitist interpretation of democratic theory that informed conventional interpretations of Political Development, no single theory of political change emerged from this group of like-minded scholars. This point merits underlining. Doctrinal support resulted in a widespread consensus, but it did not yield a singular theory of Political Development. Those most often cited as among the major contributors to the foundations of Political Development studies, such as the following list of scholars, are also recognized as having produced distinct approaches to the analysis of social and political change: Gabriel Almond, David Apter, Leonard Binder, James S. Coleman, Karl Deutsch, S. N. Eisenstadt, Samuel P. Huntington, Joseph LaPalombara, Harold D. Lasswell, Daniel Lerner, Max Millikan, Lucian Pye, Edward A. Shils, Sidney Verba, and Myron Weiner. As later discussed in this text, scholars of the field have been classified according to a variety of schemes—namely, those labeled as social process, functionalist, and neo-institutionalist approaches to political change. These classifications represented stylistic rather than substantive differences in the interpretation of political change.

The same may be said regarding the different products issued by policy-oriented as opposed to more historically or theoretically inclined scholars. At bottom, a common view of the contemporary world and a common understanding of the perils of mass society and democracy accounted for a coherence that overshadowed obvious differences. This was true in the work of the Social Science Research Council's Committee on Comparative Politics as well, a group that, under the direction of Gabriel Almond and Lucian Pye, contributed significantly to the definition of Political Development as a legitimate field of study.[5] The major series on Political Development sponsored by the committee in the years between 1963 and 1978 is discussed at some length in the coming chapters of this book.

Development Theories and Interpretations Under Attack

Within a decade after the emergence of the field, Political Development studies came under attack.[6] Liberal and radical critics called for revisions in the field, exposed its weaknesses, and demanded a more systematic study of Third World development. Those sympathetic to its purpose rejected the dualism of conventional interpretations—that is, their tendency to categorize societies in terms of "traditional" as opposed to modern forces. They supported a more historical orientation and called for a more stringent analysis of the liberal policy underlying theories of Development.

The criticism from radical sources was more comprehensive. It posed a greater challenge, focusing on the ethnocentric and apologetic character of Political Development, its ahistorical and conservative bias, and its failure to make sense of what had transpired in the Third World before and after colonialism.[7] Conventional interpretations of Development, such critics argued, neglected to explain the kinds of changes that had taken place and those that failed to occur.

The spectrum of views was wide, including those of Marxist, non-Marxist, and nationalist-oriented scholars dissatisfied with the method and purpose of such conventional interpretations, as well as the conclusions to which they led. Some took their inspiration from studies produced by members of the UN Commission on Latin America, where the work of Raoul Prebisch figured prominently in this connection. Others attempted to use the Latin American experience as the basis for more general hypotheses on Third World development. Economists, sociologists, and political theorists who contributed to this effort included Samir Amin, Jairus Banaji, Paul Baran, Henry Bernstein, Fernando H. Cardoso, Ernesto Faletto, Manuel Castells, T. Dos Santos, Andre Gunder Frank, Celso Furtado, Geoffrey Kay, Ernesto Laclau, James Petras, Anibal Quijano, Bill Warren, and Immanuel Wallerstein.

United in opposition to the conventional approach to Development, these theorists were considerably less united in defining alternative explanations.[8] From the perspective of conventional Political Development studies, however, their impact was considerable. It represented an epistemological break that was recognized by students as shattering accepted explanations of Third World transition. Committed to challenging interpretations of Development that they found wanting, dependency and postdependency theorists moved the inquiry into Third World development in hitherto unexplored channels. They furthered the investigation of the social and political changes occurring in the Third World, while at the same time situating them in a global context. In the process, they reopened the question of capitalist development, which was central to conventional Development studies.

Uneven and incomplete, radical critiques did more than generate controversy about the evident limits of conventional Development studies.[9] They launched an investigation into the historic as well as contemporary meaning of socioeconomic development in a manner that continues to compel attention among those concerned with the conditions of Third World states as well as those of the First. With the exception of a minority of students and scholars, however, and with due recognition to differences between fields, the radical critique fundamentally altered neither the conventional approach to the analysis of political change that dominated universities nor the discourse of the educated public.

At the same time there were other kinds of events that undermined the conventional way of looking at political change. Throughout the Third World, in Africa, Southeast Asia, the Middle East, and Central America, the prevalence of anticolonial wars, liberation movements, and post-independence struggles combined to challenge postwar U.S. foreign policy and with it some of the more deeply rooted assumptions about the nature of Third World societies. In Latin America the meaning of the Alliance for Progress was opened for reconsideration, while the scandal associated with Project Camelot alerted students to the place of Development studies in counterinsurgency planning. In Southeast Asia, the Vietnam War scarred generations of Vietnamese, Laotians, and Cambodians, while its repercussions in the United States marked the late 1960s as a period of turmoil and domestic instability.

The same period witnessed an inquiry into the political uses of social science research. In the nation's capital as on academic campuses, the question of Vietnam was intimately tied to the conduct of research and the study of Development. The alleged neutrality of social science research was exploded before the evidence of complicity between well-known scholars of Development and political change, and the policy planners in charge of the military operations in Southeast Asia. Although some denied and rejected this connection, others advertised its importance, thereby deepening the public admission that counter-insurgency and Development doctrine were mutually reinforcing. The effects of this and related controversies generated by the Vietnam War and its domestic impact extended to universities and their constituents. Concerned scholars organized to protest, first in caucuses in various national associations of scholars, then in the formation of alternative journals, and, most important perhaps, in the large-scale inquiry into existing and alternative approaches to social and political change in the Third World. If Political Development studies were sparked by postwar U.S. foreign policy and the need for a cadre of domestic experts, the war in Vietnam generated the conditions that opened the door to widespread support for counter-Development studies, in the form of dependency and postdependency studies. But the protest was contained. Some fields were affected more than others, notably Latin American, African, and Southeast Asian studies.

In such a field as Middle Eastern studies, the crises of Latin America, Africa, and the Far East were viewed as irrelevant; yet at the same time there was a palpable fear among some scholars that its disruptive effects might extend to their own field of study. To judge by the scholarship on contemporary Lebanon and Iran, long regarded as exemplars of the positive approach to Modernization and Development, whatever questioning was provoked by the experiences referred to earlier was inhibited in the case of the Middle East. In both areas, Lebanon and Iran, the support for the elitist interpretation of political change was a characteristic of contemporary political analysis. As the civil war of 1975–1976 and the Israeli invasion of Lebanon in the summer of 1982 shattered the illusions of the prewar civil order, so they did away with the satisfaction of conventional interpretations of Lebanese society.[10] The inability of such interpretations to make sense of internal forces that were in conflict was not only a function of their inherent complexity. It was a reflection also of the irrelevance of such interpretations to the functioning of Lebanese society.

Iranian studies were not better served. Until the events leading to the fall of the shah in the winter of 1979, the political literature on Iran focused on the benefits that Modernization had brought at the hands of the shah and his political elite. Social and political movements were viewed with suspicion, that is, in roughly the same manner as the shah himself viewed them. With the fall of the shah and the evident collapse of a U.S. policy based on his active and compliant presence, the conditions for a reconsideration of scholarship on Iran came into existence. Even then, policymakers who criticized academic analyses of Development reproduced the assumptions of Development doctrine that had limited their effectiveness in the first place.[11]

The response was not unusual. For a large number of readers and followers of Third World developments, foreign policy failures were read as confirming the weaknesses of Third World leaders and their regimes, much in the manner invoked by Development theorists. According to such reactions, the instability of Third World states was a function of excessive politicization, insistent pressures for participation that were dangerous to "moderation" and stability, and the presence of large-scale movements bent on overturning the existing leadership. Little attention was focused on the reasons for such movements and for the evident dissatisfaction that existed. In a popular and seemingly spontaneous expression of the behaviorist reflex, the symptom generated more interest than did its underlying causes. The result furthered the tendency on the part of political analysts and academic students of politics to reduce matters of political conflict to personality and culture—a deviation with deep roots in the prevailing mode of interpreting political change. Such an outlook, reproduced in analyses of South Africa, Latin America, and the Middle East, did not stem from a confrontation with the peculiar realities of those regions. The origins of this approach are to be found in a more proximate experience. It was not the Third World but a particular interpretation of politics in the First World that lay at the root of this way of seeing political change.

Liberal Democratic Theory, Its Elitist Interpretations, and the Study of Political Development

Earlier critics of Development studies were not indifferent to the connections noted previously. They emphasized the apologetic aspect of Development theories in relation to foreign policy, but they did not ignore the effects of a conservative reconstruction of social and political reality on the interpretation of Third World change. From the mid-1960s on, scholars interested in and critical of mainstream interpretations of Third World Development began to emphasize the connection between such interpretations and trends in the social sciences (Willner, 1964; Mazrui, 1968; Bodenheimer-Jonas, 1970; Hopkins, 1972; O'Brien, 1972; Ocampo and Johnson, and Frank, in Cockroft, Frank, and Johnson, 1972; Macpherson, 1972; Kesselman, 1973; Tipps, 1973; and Packenham, 1973).[12] Collectively, the criticisms of these writers pointed to the impact of an elitist, pluralist, equilibrium model of political change and its antidemocratic tendencies. Although not all of these scholars agreed with the radical theses on the limits of such interpretations, most supported the view that the dominant interpretations of Development left much to be desired.

More remains to be said concerning the connection between Development theories and contemporary political science. More can be explained with respect to the origins of Development studies and the contemporary interpretations of the liberal democratic theories that informed it. This was not only a matter of academic interest. The investigation of such features of the cold war as the conferences of the Congress for Cultural Freedom that were held in the 1950s have special meaning for students of Political Development. These conferences offered a laboratory in which to experiment with different approaches to Third World issues. They provided a forum for academics who were engaged in the ideological battles of the cold war and who played major roles in the foundation of Political Development studies. Exponents of the revisionist interpretation of liberal democracy that issued into the elitist interpretations of political change, they transferred these to the analysis of Third World societies.

It is the elitist interpretations themselves that hold the key to the nature of Political Development theories and the more general orientation to political analysis to which they gave rise. Although elitist interpretations of political change have been intensely debated since the 1960s, most critics of elitist and pluralist theories did not turn their attention to the implications of this literature for the analysis of Third World societies. Primarily concerned with American politics and the impact of neoconservative political thinking on the analysis of liberal democracy, they were less interested in the results of an export of elitist views.[13]

Theorists of Political Development, on the other hand, included some of the active interpreters of elitist theories of democracy. To reread the works of Gabriel Almond, Sidney Verba, Lucian Pye, Samuel P. Huntington, Edward A. Shils, and Daniel Lerner from this perspective is instructive. The origins of their conservative interpretations of Third World politics are, in fact, closer to home than the Third World societies about which they wrote. Speaking the language of revisionist interpretations of democratic theories, their analyses of Political Development represented the justificatory theories of contemporary capitalist expansion. Set in historical perspective, Political Development theories, as extensions of contemporary liberal democratic theories, share a common historical origin. They reproduce the contradictions that have historically beset liberal democratic theory—those at the root of the tension between the commitment to capitalist development and democratic change. A reconsideration of the theories of Political Development from this perspective, then, assumes the task of coming to grips not only with the relationship of "politics to markets"[14] but with the justificatory character of such theories as well.

That theorists of Political Development were committed to the interpretation of Third World change in a manner compatible with the expansion of capitalism is beyond controversy. That many of the same theorists were committed to the proposition that capitalism and democracy were historically linked in Western experience is also beyond question. What made this conviction problematic were not only the objective difficulties of Third World change, but also the implicit view of politics and society contained in the dominant paradigms of political change adopted by Development theorists.

Much as earlier theorists of liberalism had done, contemporary theorists of Political Development confronted the fact that "a market society generates class differentiation in effective rights and rationality, yet it requires for its justification a postulate of equal rights and rationality."[15] Stated in different terms, the proposition was a commonplace in discussions of Development. It conveyed the tensions that characterized capitalist development and its interpretation in justificatory theories as seemingly far apart as those of early liberalism and late theories of liberal democracy and their extension in Political Development theories. Caught between their support for a form of sociopolitical change that conformed to their interest and supported their world view and the recognition that it generated precisely the instability that they feared, theorists of Political Development responded by relying on the elitist, pluralist, equilibrium model of political change that most effectively satisfied their concerns.

The choice was not random. Its roots in the conditions that gave rise to liberal democratic theory recommended it for contemporary consumption. Further, its ambivalence between a formal support for democracy, equality, and participation, and a subtle undermining of such commitment through interpretations that were managerial in nature corresponded to the ambivalent positions of Development theories.

The choice offered no respite, however, from the inherent contradictions that beset theorists of Political Development. These emerged in their nearly interminable debates on the meaning of Political Development and on its relationship with democracy as opposed to economic growth. They led some to argue in favor of severing such a connection, while others rejected the implications of such a break. They furthered the tendency, found in the earliest expression of liberal theory and magnified in contemporary American social science, to rationalize class differences and the resistance to preferred modes of social change in psychological terms. The conformist aspects of such an approach belie its alleged intellectual challenge.

Above all, theorists of Political Development adopted a justificatory scheme that proved to be simultaneously self-serving and self-defeating. It corresponded to their world view, to their understanding of politics and society, yet its identification with a politics of tutelage was scarcely designed to be acceptable. Its formal commitment to democracy was at odds with the elitist approach to politics and political change. Its endorsement of equality and participation was not matched by an implicit support for a politics of obedient consent. Prepared to jettison the connection between Development and democracy, theorists of Political Development recognized that maintenance of a permanently ambivalent position was preferable. At stake was a view of politics relevant not only to the Third World but to the First as well.

A Reader's Guide

At the root of Political Development discourse lies an interconnected series of relationships. Uncovering them exposes the different historical, political, and intellectual experiences that are synthesized in conventional interpretations of Political Development. What follows is an attempt at the same kind of deconstruction—that is, one in which the relationship of Political Development studies is traced to policies, to domestic considerations, and to disciplinary tendencies. No attempt will be made, however, to compare Political Development theories with Third World "realities," an entirely different project; nor is there any attempt to synchronize the present investigation with the vast literature on other aspects of Development studies—Economic Development in particular. The underlying argument of this book is that an internal critique of the literature of Political Development sheds light on its contradictions in a manner that explains the arbitrary limits of the approach. These contradictions are disclosed in the linkage of democracy with elitism and in the formal support for democratic forms of social and political change with their management and manipulation. Looking inward, moreover, serves to underline another objective of this exercise—namely, to demonstrate the extent to which theories of Political Development are to be defined not in terms of the Third World, but in terms of their correspondence with a particular view of politics and society in the First.

In Chapter 3 of this text, entitled "Discourse on Development," something of the official interest in Development policies is introduced. The background of such policies in postwar foreign policy is outlined. And so is the changing character of the official description of the meaning of Development policies, thereby permitting one to trace their evolution from economic to social and political programs of change, in which formal support for democratic change was endorsed. Discussions and recommendations by various academic consultants before the Senate Foreign Relations Committee are of particular interest because they demonstrate the links that existed between the official and the academic translation of Development projects. More specifically; such texts—and those discussed in the following section—disclose significant differences in terms of the rationalizations of policy. Where programs of Political Development were integrated into military aid programs and counterinsurgency programs, policy-oriented students of Political Development played important roles in precisely this justificatory aspect of interpreting Development.

It must be pointed out, however, that the discussion of the official view of Development as policy is not meant to be an investigation into the effects of implementing such policies. Nor is there a comprehensive analysis of postwar foreign policy in the Third World, where Development programs served to further U.S. interests.

In Chapter 4, "Transparent Boundaries," there is a discussion of the relationship of government to policy-oriented academic students of Political Development in a number of specific contexts. The report in the same chapter entitled "Behavioral Sciences and the National Security" provides important information on the subject, as does the discussion of Project Camelot. Similarly, the support by policy-oriented specialists of the introduction of the military in Development projects, and of the more general definition of the purpose of Development policies in the context of foreign policy, offers useful insights into this connection. More subtly disclosed than the conclusions of the aforementioned report, it is relevant to the elaborate outline of the map of Third World change to which policy-oriented Development specialists contributed. Such efforts were not free of the contradictions ascribed to the academic interpretation of Political Development theories. The conference on the implementation of Title IX, held in 1968 at MIT, to which a number of Development scholars and government officials contributed, reveals such contradictory aspects of Development in an overt way.

If the emergence and timing of Political Development studies were a function of postwar foreign policy, such a policy does not by itself explain the nature or support that Development studies generated. To understand the roots of that support and its appeal, it is necessary to consider the domestic base of the analysis of Political Development. Accordingly, Chapter 5, entitled "Defining the Parameters of Discourse," considers the domestic climate in the 1950s—in particular, the impact of McCarthyism on liberal intellectuals who were to be active both in the discipline of political science and in the production of Political Development studies. It also considers the place of the Congress for Cultural Freedom in this context, a connection that has not previously been drawn and one that is useful in unearthing the prehistory of Development studies in the cultural cold war. Falling between the academic formulas in which Development studies were articulated and the cold war ambience that influenced them were certain public events—such as the debates on the nature of mass society—that deserve attention. A prominent feature of intellectual exchange throughout this period, these debates exposed an approach to the issues underlying the analysis of contemporary American society, the nature of advanced capitalism, and its bearing on social and political movements such as fascism that proved to be important to the interpretation of Political Development.

The transfer between such intellectual controversies, the language in which they were expressed, and parallel developments in the academic discipline of political science are traced in Chapter 6, "The Academic Translation." Given that the production of Political Development studies was an academic enterprise, that it emerged from academic disciplines and the particular trends to which they were subject at the time, the connection between intellectual controversies and academic developments is critical to this study. The relevant changes in the discipline of political science were those that resulted in the articulation of the conservative interpretation of democratic theory. And what has been insufficiently underlined in critiques of Political Development studies is not only the general affinity between the literature of Development and a conservative social science, but the coincidence between the former and the emergence of elitist interpretations of democratic theory, to which major scholars of Political Development contributed.

These connections are central to this investigation, which brings together works long regarded as symptomatic of the conservative mood in the analysis of democratic theory, with the extension of such a theory and its particular characteristics to the discussion of Political Development. The critique of liberal democratic theories is here joined to the critical reappraisal of Political Development theories. The significance of this rereading emerges in a consideration of some of the key texts in the field. Works that have customarily been read as examples of current trends in the analysis of Third World politics appear quite different when read as illustrations of the approach to domestic politics. Their striking affinity to the revisionist interpretations of democratic theory suggests the basis of the coherence of Political Development literature.

These samples of early "classics" of Political Development not only illustrate the conservative trends common to political analysis; they also disclose the deeper problems inherent in revisionist interpretations. These are studied in Chapter 7 of this text, entitled "The Impossible Task of

Theories of Political Development." What makes this task "impossible" is its internal contradictions; these contradictions, in turn, are a function of the origins of liberal democratic theories as well as their contemporary versions, which Political Development theories extended to the interpretation of Third World Development. To write in terms of "deceptions," "false promises," "impossible tasks," is not to accuse individuals of falsehood and deception. It is the *interpretations* and not the *interpreters* who are central to this investigation, since what they articulated in their definitions of Political Development has become the currency in which many other students of the field discuss its conditions. And so the favored solution to the "impossible task of Political Development," the search for psychological explanations of political choices, the investigation into the peculiarities of political cultures and their responsibility for the failures of Development—these significant paths are also widespread phenomena in contemporary social science that find particular meaning in analyses of Political Development theorists.

What the reliance on psychology and culture offered was an interpretation that justified undermining the support for Political Development in terms of participation. And the latter, the most feared and most central of subjects in the analysis of Political Development, is also the key to understanding the limits of the prevailing approach. It is the interpretation of participation, intimately tied to the accepted interpretation of politics, that explains the transformation in Political Development from a literature formally designed to explain Third World change to one that prescribes a strategy for its containment. The result constitutes a pedagogy directed against the oppressed, to invert the intention of Paulo Freire's text.

It is perhaps useful to underline a number of problems raised by this study. One such problem has to do with the question of generalization. The risks in generalizing about a literature as vast as this one are obvious. By identifying the theorists of Political Development whose works are analyzed in particular detail, we may avoid some of these risks. But there is an additional problem: Many of those cited as exponents and/or contributors to Political Development studies in some capacity have changed their own interpretations of the subject over the intervening years. Since the focus is on what I argue continues to represent a prevailing view of politics and political change, the emphasis is on the interpretation rather than on the individuals per se. Recognition of such changes is important nonetheless.

It may also be said that the discussion of Political Development abstracted from the more comprehensive interpretations of Development produced by economists, sociologists, and anthropologists is fundamentally problematic. There are significant parallels in these fields. Well beyond the parameters of the present study, such an expanded investigation of the entire academic enterprise of Development should be pursued by scholars interested in and capable of dealing with so extensive a repertoire. Related to this effort is another compelling subject, the reproduction of Development doctrine outside of the United States, among European social scientists and Third World scholars. This issue obviously merits attention; it also does away with the suggestion that what is involved is to be defined in national terms. There is, in fact, an international group of Development scholars committed to a similar approach to the analysis of political change whose works deserve similar investigation.

Finally, it ought to be stated by way of introduction that the approach of this work is largely historical in character. In part an intellectual history of ideas, it is also an effort to map out correspondences and contradictions in modes of explanation that affect political analysis. In this context, the primary sources are those works on Political Development that constitute the basis of this study. Not their relationship to policy nor their relationship to the individual biographies of the authors themselves, but their illustration of a deeply grounded way of perceiving the problem of political change—this is the material that constitutes the subject under study. What such a study contributes to, however, goes beyond the sources themselves to the larger question of the role of intellectuals and the reproduction of ideology.

3

Discourse on Development

Putting Development Policies on the Agenda

Long before the term *Development* made its regular appearance in discussions of U.S. foreign policy, its economic and political dimensions were integral aspects of post-World War II American geopolitics. And long before it was fashionable to talk in terms of the Third World, policymakers were concerned about the economic potential and political instability of regions considered indispensable to U.S. economic and strategic interests. The notion of Development, as an expression of policies designed to channel social and economic change in the Third World, emerged in roughly the same period as U.S. policymakers reassessed their position in the non-Western and non-industrialized worlds of Latin America, the Mediterranean, Africa, the Middle East, and the Far East. Out of this reassessment came a succession of policies and projects that reckoned with the international balance of power and with the situation of newly independent states. These states, their aspirations, and their anticolonial sensitivities imposed a new style on the formulation of policy. As the authors of a National Security Council (NSC) staff study recognized in the spring of 1952, "it is doubtful whether the U.S. or the U.K., or both together, could maintain and defend Western interests in the area in the 19th century fashion."* Policies of aid, assistance, and Development satisfied the requirements of the time.

From the mid-1940s to the late 1950s, by which time Development programs were firmly fixed on the foreign policy agenda, the essential ingredients in the redefinition of that policy and the place of assistance projects within it were repeatedly discussed. Stimulating economic growth at home, promising economic expansion abroad, guaranteeing access to raw materials, and controlling the feared effects of sociopolitical

* See National Security Council 129/1 (April 24, 1952), an NSC staff study entitled "United States Objectives and Policies with Respect to the Arab States and Israel." Recently declassified, this and other references to NSC documents that appear in the following pages have been made available on microfilm in the important collection of archival materials presented by University Publications of America.

change in non-Western states were among the major reasons cited in connection with the support for such programs. Tabled under the general category of securing the "national interest" in the face of Soviet threats, Development policies were increasingly perceived as an arm of foreign policy that benefited the position of the United States in the global arena. This connection was spelled out in the recommendations of the NSC in the winter of 1950 (see NSC 68/4, "A Report to the President by the NSC on United States Objectives and Programs for National Security," December 14, 1950). According to that text, there was no ambiguity about either the purposes of aid programs or the manner in which they ought to be disbursed: The "objective in providing economic aid outside the NATO area is to create situations of political and economic strength in the free world especially in critical areas whose present weakness may invite Soviet thrusts." Given the limited resources available, such aid was restricted to three general purposes: "(1) investment to increase the production and facilitate the distribution of critical materials directly needed for defense; (2) aid to strengthen the defense effort of our allies; and (3) aid to enable governments which are or can be expected to become friendly members of the free world to win the confidence and support of their own peoples as a solid foundation for political stability and national independence."

Three years later, in another report to the NSC, the current view of "the uncommitted areas of the world" offered the rationale of Development policies in the context of foreign policy.

Despite the Soviet threat, many nations and societies outside the Soviet bloc, mostly in the underdeveloped areas, are so unsure of their national interests, or so preoccupied with other pressing problems, that they are presently unwilling to align themselves with the United States and its allies. Although largely underdeveloped, their vast manpower, their essential raw materials and their potential for growth are such that their absorption within the Soviet system would greatly, perhaps decisively, alter the world balance of power to our detriment. Conversely, their orderly development into more stable and responsible nations, able and willing to participate in defense of the free world, can increasingly add to its strength.[1]

In a later passage, the authors noted that "the United States should furnish limited military aid, and limited technical and economic assistance, to other free nations, according to the calculated advantage of such aid to the U.S. world position." Such aid did not preclude "its being used as a quid pro quo in achieving military objectives," as a later high-level discussion of policy with respect to the Middle East indicated.[2] In short, the innovation in political style represented by Development programs satisfied interpretations of national interest as these were defined by postwar administrations, while meeting the requirements of the new diplomatic order in which the United States and its European allies found themselves.

Before the language of Development became commonplace in discussions of policy, deliberations on postwar economic policy pointed to the rationale for programs of economic aid in conjunction with political and military assistance. In December 1943, the Special Committee on the Relaxation of Trade Barriers declared that "a great expansion in the volume of international trade after the war will be essential to the attainment of a full and effective employment in the United States and elsewhere, to the preservation of free enterprise, and the success of an international security system to prevent future wars."[3] Dean Acheson, as assistant secretary of state, put the matter bluntly when he spoke before a congressional subcommittee on Postwar Economic Policy and Planning in the fall of 1944: "We cannot go through another 10 years like the 10 years at the end of the twenties and the beginning of the thirties, without having the most far-reaching consequences upon our economic and social system."[4] In Acheson's opinion, the problem was one of markets. Its long-range solution involved, among other things, support for foreign investment facilitated by the International Bank for Reconstruction and Development.[5] The solution met with approval from the Council of Economic Advisors.[6]

The thrust of Acheson's warning was that unless strong measures were adopted, there was the dangerous possibility that the postwar crises following World War I would be repeated. Others made the same point. Adolf Berle, economist and presidential advisor, repeated it in 1946 when he argued for a more aggressive economic policy. Its advantages were thought to be self-evident. The use of agricultural surpluses, for instance, had both domestic and international implications. They might play an effective role in the competition with the Soviet Union and in the domestic effort to control the "cycles of boom and bust which disfigured our pre-war economy."[7] The prospects loomed menacingly in the aftermath of the great war. Unemployment and a lagging economy revived vivid memories of World War I and the Depression. And then, as in the aftermath of World War II, its results would not be restricted to a single country. The anticipation of what such results might produce on the economic as well as political levels figures in the U.S. response to conditions in Europe and, notably, in the eastern Mediterranean.

In the latter region, the imminent withdrawal of British forces was interpreted by the Truman administration as a threat to national security. Viewed in conjunction with the political changes occurring in Western Europe, particularly in France and Italy, the call for intervention was justified in terms that linked the political outcome of the struggle in Greece with events in Western Europe and, ultimately, in the United States. It was Dean Acheson in another audience with congressional leaders who warned of the future if the United States and the West did not move to contain events in the Eastern Mediterranean. With one fell swoop, the political future of Greece was related to the outcome of political transformations throughout the Middle East, Europe, and the United States. Acheson warned that "like apples in a barrel infected one by rotten one, the corruption of Greece would infect Iran and all to the east. It would also carry infection to Africa through Asia Minor and Egypt, and to Europe through Italy and France, already threatened by the strongest domestic Communist parties in Western Europe."[8] It was Assistant Secretary of State Will Clayton who described the prospects of such development in direr terms still, referring to the possibility of "economic anarchy" if such "key areas" as Greece fell out of friendly hands of control.[9]

The Truman Doctrine, which was formally presented to Congress in March of 1947,[10] underlined the linkages just suggested. Moreover, it emphasized the urgency of national action for international ends that were construed as essential to the national welfare. None, according to the arguments offered by supporters of the doctrine, could turn away from events in Greece or the Eastern Mediterranean. None could ignore the demands for economic, political, and military aid. The effect was not to be restricted to Greece. Assistance programs directly related to the Truman Doctrine included such seemingly diverse projects as "the European Recovery Program, Greek Turkish aid, Interim Aid to Austria, France and Italy, the Mutual Defense Assistance Program, Chinese and Korean aid."[11] Two years later the second major postwar economic aid program was launched, this time in Western Europe. The Marshall Plan, heralded for its humanitarian motives, was a response to postwar conditions. It was a response not only to the devastation caused by war but also to the fear lest social dislocation promote radical movements that, in turn, would change the character of governing coalitions.

From the perspective of Development programs, however, it was another postwar project that was of particular relevance. The Point IV program, officially introduced in President Truman's Inaugural Address of 1949, recommended a "bold new program for making the benefits of our scientific advances and industrial progress available for the improvement and growth of underdeveloped areas."[12] Such a program, in principle, addressed the aspirations of newly independent states toward political independence and socioeconomic reform. But the interpretation given these aspirations and the concern to channel their expression indicated the preoccupation with the prospects of an emergent nationalism.[13] Studies commissioned in the period between 1950 and 1954 confirmed the growing importance attributed to the relationship of domestic economic growth with foreign economic policy and the securing of essential raw materials as well as markets. In this context, assistance projects played an important role, not only in making "scientific advances and industrial progress available" but also in ensuring the political as well as economic benefits of such assistance.

The specialized reports associated with such advisors as Gray (1950), Rockefeller (1951), Paley (1952), Bell (1953), and Randall (1954) focused on various aspects of the economy, including the existing and projected patterns of trade and investment. They dealt with the matter of promoting incentives for private as well as public investment abroad, and with the question of guaranteeing access as well as stimulating production of essential raw materials. In the light of the Korean War, the reassessment of such projections took on an urgent character. The value of assistance projects was similarly heightened. The Gray report was among those that considered the support for Development in both political and economic terms, employing a language and an approach that was amplified in subsequent academic analyses.[14] But it was not an isolated case. That Development projects were increasingly being integrated into foreign policy was indicated at the highest levels of policymaking. In the recommendations of the National Security Council (NSC 129/1, April 24, 1952), problems of socioeconomic change were addressed in the context of the Middle East.* But the nature of the problems and their analyses were of more general relevance. In contrast to the specialized studies cited earlier that dealt with particular aspects of the economy, the NSC statement dealt with the political implications of Third World change for U.S. policy.

Problems of social and economic change were identified in the NSC report as important to the United States "because of the political developments to which they may lead. There is growing danger that the process of internal political change going on in these countries may lead to disorder and to a

---

* The discussion that follows is taken from the NSC staff study entitled "United States Objectives and Policies with Respect to the Arab States and Israel," which is part of the NSC 129/1 report.

situation in which regimes subject to the influence or control of the Soviet Union could come to power." Change was not to be prevented so much as channeled in such a way as to "offer the least threat to Western interests and the maximum assurance of independent regimes friendly to the West." Starting from this premise, certain policy recommendations followed. According to the authors of the report,

> We should seek to use the social and economic tools available to us in ways that will reduce the explosive power of forces pressing for revolutionary change to the point where necessary changes can be accomplished without uncontrollable instability. This may often mean that we should work with and through the present ruling groups and, while bolstering their hold on power, use our influence to induce them to accommodate themselves as necessary to the new forces that are emerging. As new leadership groups emerge, we should also work to associate their interests with our own and, if and when they gain power, cooperate with them in working out programs that will assist them to attain constructive objectives—a course of development which will tend to give a measure of moderation and stability to their regimes.

The authors went on to specify the advantages of supporting agricultural as opposed to industrial development, the value of short-term as opposed to long-term projects, and the contradictions inherent in supporting programs that might well undermine the very ruling groups endorsed. In summary style they spelled out what was to become the principal agenda of Political Development studies within less than a decade: the impact of change on various strata within society and its effect on the leadership and the military. Objectives were unambiguously stated: "In their work in these countries the U.S. missions should bear these considerations in mind, and it should be our objective to use our assistance programs to shape and guide social and economic developments in these countries in ways which will help us to attain our political goals."

Two years later, in another statement that had official endorsement, the "interim report of the Princeton Conference" was issued. Drafted by two analysts who were to play important roles in the academic study of Development, W. W. Rostow and Max Millikan, it addressed some of the same questions as those posed in the NSC report mentioned earlier. The objective of the "global development project" initiated under the Eisenhower administration was defined in terms of U.S. foreign economic policy:[15] "It is the immediate purpose of the foreign economic policy of the

United States to participate in a partnership with the nations and peoples of the free world designed to promote the health and growth of the free world economy. By economic growth we mean a sustained increase in production per head, which gives or promises to give a higher real income to every free world citizen. . . ,"[16] This, the authors claimed, had particular significance in the light of the cold war. To illustrate their point, they referred to the importance of "free world success in seeing the underdeveloped countries through their difficult transition to self-sustaining growth [that] would deny to Moscow and Peking the dangerous mystique that only Communism can transform underdeveloped countries."[17]

Development and Domestic Economic Growth

By the end of the 1950s, the assumption that Economic Development was essential to the implementation of foreign policy interests was matched by the conviction that economic growth was itself attainable "only in a world which was capable of both buying from the United States and selling to it."[18] That argument was vigorously pursued through support of economic assistance programs. Persuading congressional representatives of the worthiness of such programs, however, was another matter. Some were offended by what they perceived as overly liberal internationalist attitudes prominent in foundations that were viewed as interfering in the foreign policy process. Conservatives pointed with dismay at the positions of the Ford Foundation, the Carnegie Endowment, and the Rockefeller Foundation as promoting an undesirable orientation in foreign affairs. Arguments offered in the Report of the Special Committee to Investigate Tax Exempt Foundations and Comparable Organizations (1954) revealed the nature of dissent on the subject of economic aid, assistance, and Third World politics.[19]

There were other voices, however, that endorsed economic assistance programs as directly beneficial to American business.[20] Far from opposing aid to Third World states, these programs, given the increased productivity associated with them, were understood to be a boon to American business. The Committee on Foreign Relations of the 83rd Congress heard such views in defense of Development. The record cited by its advocates demonstrated that aid and assistance programs, by supporting the increased economic productivity of Third World states, opened the door to increased exports and to the possibility of importing needed goods. Prefaced by moral pronouncements, such official statements as those offered by Paul Hoffman, the U.S. representative to the United Nations General Assembly in 1957, underscored this position.[21] Referring to a 1954 assessment of investment in Latin America by the U.S. Department of Commerce, Hoffman noted that "as much as one-tenth of the value of goods and services produced in the area may be accounted for by United States owned enterprises."[22] In the case of mining or petroleum, the ratio would be higher, roughly 15 percent. Moreover, "some 25 percent of total exports to the United States by foreign countries is produced by United States direct investment companies abroad which have developed and made possible this large trade with the United States."[23] That argument was in support of the role of private investment for the American economy as a whole. Looking at the period between 1945 and 1957, Hoffman found that the United States provided over $8 billion for reconstruction and development to "less developed countries." But this figure told only part of the story.

In the fall of 1957, Vice-President Nixon spoke before a conference on International Industrial Development. He called for an increase of private investment by American business in "the developing nations of the world."[24] Reviewing the goals of such policy, he noted that in 1956 new investment had totaled nearly $4 billion. He added, "This amount seems large, but if the United States were investing abroad the same proportions of our national income that Great Britain invested abroad in 1910, we would be investing not $4 billion a year but nearly $30 billion."[25]

Some months earlier, the assistant secretary for International Organization Affairs, Francis O. Wilcox, reaffirmed the importance of investing abroad for American business. He noted that "American aid is no one-way street. The United States needs its allies just as much as they need us. They provide us with bases essential to the effective employment of our strategic air power. They maintain their own military forces for the joint defense of the free world. Without them, many thousands of American soldiers would have to be stationed overseas—and at an annual cost to us of from 7 to 35 times what it requires to maintain a foreign soldier."[26] He reminded his audience—the American Association of University Women—that without the aid that stimulates the production of strategic goods, tin, rubber, industrial diamonds, manganese, and more, "our economy would hobble along in low gear. . . ."[27]

Such explanations did not preclude different rationales for support of Development policies. Secretary of State Dulles, in the same year, argued in terms of the cold war. He maintained that "international communism is waging against us what is sometimes called a 'cold war'" and that long-term Development assistance, in association with military aid, constituted an invaluable weapon.[28] The linkage of economic assistance to mutual security arrangements was to be a prominent feature of Development programs under successive administrations. Although this merger was a source of discomfort to some supporters of Development, policy-oriented social scientists found favor in it.

But for the authors of the report entitled "Foreign Economic Policy for the Twentieth Century" issued by the Rockefeller Brothers Fund in 1958, it was not the cold war but economic considerations that dictated support for Development. The sense of urgency conveyed by the authors of the report was explained in terms of the need to "explore all means for averting economic collapse in many areas of the free world."[29] Such a collapse would have dire consequences for the United States as well as for Third World states. In contrast to those who warned that the Soviet Union was winning in the economic competition with the United States and the West, the authors of this report argued otherwise. They reminded their audience that "trade competition from the Soviet bloc has not had, and for many years to come probably cannot generate, the capacity to supply a substantial portion of import needs and export outlets of the less developed countries. The competition which it offers is essentially political."[30] In 1956 the sum of American private investment and economic aid—excluding military aid— came to more than $6.6 billion. In contrast, Soviet loans totaled about $200 million, or about "3 percent of the United States figure."[31]

Why then the urgency? The critical issue, according to this account, was not the fear of competition. It was the relationship between domestic needs and the purchasing power of the Third World. In short, the problem lay in the nature of trade relations and the vulnerability of Third World economies. "Between 9 and 10 percent of all desirable goods produced in the United States is sold abroad. Significantly enough, these sales provide the margin between profit and loss for a large segment of American industries."[32] As an illustration the authors noted that "about 4.5 million workers, or 7 percent of the entire United States labor force are directly dependent upon foreign trade for their livelihoods. Foreign trade provides more direct employment in the United States than the automobile, steel, chemical and textile industries combined."[33] The argument favored a liberalization of trade policies and the support for expanded capital investment programs abroad. Hence the relevance of economic assistance programs and the rationale for Development policies.

The predicament to which the Rockefeller report pointed was inherent in the dependent nature of Third World economies. Many of the states concerned relied on exports of primary products, raw materials, and agricultural goods to fuel their own development projects. In the presence of severe price fluctuations affecting such goods, both the plans and in some instances the stability of governments were jeopardized. Along with the fall in food prices in 1957, there was a fall in the price of coffee, tin, copper, and crude rubber. The problem was widely recognized. Wilcox, for example, argued that the United States imported all of its "natural rubber and tin, 85% of our bauxite and manganese, and 64% of our tungsten. In fact we have to obtain 10% of all the raw materials we use from overseas sources. Many of them come from underdeveloped countries."[34] In an effort to exercise a measure of control on the situation, the Rockefeller Brothers Fund report recommended policies designed to increase investment abroad by the promotion of tax incentives, protective measures for businesses interested in such investment, and the increase in accessibility of loans and credits to Third World states. Liberalization of trade policies was advanced as a measure that would increase the opportunity and profit of American business while at the same time benefiting the economies of the Third World states. As the authors of the Rockefeller report observed, "The immediate problem is to start the more than a billion people now living in the less developed areas up the road toward rising production and consumption while maintaining the growth of the industrialized areas. As we have pointed out, the two problems are intimately related."[35]

In another assessment published some years later, the foreign assets of U.S. corporations in the period 1950–1961 were reported to have risen "from $11,800 to $34,700 million, an increase of $22,900 million. During the same period, net direct investment outflow totalled $13,700 million and direct investment income came to $23,200. . . . During this period American corporations were able to take in as income $9,500 million more than they sent out as capital, while at the same time expanding their foreign holdings to the tune of $22.900."[36] For those concerned with the anticipated effect of expanding investment abroad in the context of such programs as those supported by the Rockefeller Brothers Fund, the benefits were readily apparent.

From Economic Development to Development

The same period that witnessed an accelerated interest in support for economic assistance projects was one in which there was an increased emphasis on the broader aspects of Development programs. Again, without reviewing the history of postwar foreign policy in the Third World, in which such programs figured, it is useful to consider their official rationalization as a basis of comparison with the language and approach of policy-oriented social scientists.

The authors of the Rockefeller Brothers Fund report emphasized the cause and effect relationship between economic change and certain social and political conditions. Their interpretation led to an expanded view of Development that took into consideration such questions as health and education as well as political and economic issues. Moreover, in the attempt to give the subject a measure of depth, they pointed to the historic roots of some aspects of Development in the practice of colonial powers who had "brought with them doctrines of administration and popular participation in government which in time proved inconsistent with their own continued rule."[37] For the most part, it was not history but contemporary interests that dictated the approach to Development. These interests involved advertising this approach in moral tones and not merely with respect to pragmatic considerations. Development programs became symbolic of support for more general economic, social, and political reforms, whose justification was in terms of American values.

In the spring of 1959, Under Secretary of State Dillon spoke before the House Foreign Affairs Committee. He explained President Eisenhower's commitment to Development programs and his concern that they be presented to the public in a manner that would offer "an affirmative, positive image of the United States to the world, an image of the great tradition of enterprise and idealism that has motivated the American people since our earliest beginnings."[38] Dillon later elaborated on the position. On yet another occasion he emphasized that Development programs rested not only on economic interest but also on support for the "development of free political institutions, of respect for law, of regard for human decency."[39]

Similar themes were heard during the Kennedy administration. Notwithstanding the support for counterinsurgency warfare in which Development programs played a significant part, administration officials insisted on the moral obligations that inspired American interest in Development. These obligations were indicative of support for "economic equality between as well as within nations."[40] It was the historic mission of the United States to promote "orderly political growth" as part of the positive social change that would be strengthened by such programs.[41] In his inaugural address of January 20, 1961, Kennedy identified U.S. policy with support for the world's poor. These people were to be recipients of Development aid not simply because of a Soviet threat, but, in Kennedy's language, because of the inherent justice of their cause: "If a free society cannot help the many who are poor, it cannot save the few who are rich." Administration spokesmen dramatized support for Third World Development in similar terms.

At the United Nations, U.S. representatives spoke about Development as an aspect of the special relationship between peoples and states committed to a new diplomatic order. Adlai Stevenson, addressing the subject in the summer of 1961, remarked that the United States was seeking "greater equality between nations as well as within nations. . . ."[42] The decade of the 1960s, he noted, would be a "decade of development not only for ourselves but, we hope, for our fellow men everywhere." In the spring of the same year Kennedy declared existing Development projects to be inadequate. He called for the separation of economic and social programs from those pertaining to military aid. In the new and expanded view of Development, land reform as well as educational and social measures were to be considered. Congress was asked to allocate $2.4 billion for such projects in a foreign aid bill brought before Congress in the late spring. Such pronouncements yielded no information on the increasing militarization of aid and assistance programs in Southeast Asia or on the extent to which their role in counterinsurgency was becoming part of the accepted doctrine of Development.

Members of the Kennedy administration who effectively stressed the humanitarian aspects of these programs, such as Chester Bowles, were useful spokesmen in emphasizing the moral character of the American commitment. Before a Methodist National Convocation on Christian Social Concerns in the spring of 1961, Bowles asked whether Development was a form of charity, a response to the fear of Soviet competition. "The real basis of the world revolution is not Marxism but our own American revolution, with its promise for national freedom and personal dignity."[43] What was needed, according to Bowles, was an affirmation of this commitment by the American public. "We need to help new nations to build their political and social institutions, to develop skills in government and administration, to achieve minimal requirements in education, and to acquire the basic skills of industry, agriculture and business." Above all, insisted Bowles, there has to be a human dimension in the Development process. Otherwise the objectives sought would be sabotaged. In their place would occur that "political explosion which we are most anxious to avoid."[44] In yet another passage within this talk, Bowles redefined Development in terms of the need "to help developing nations to achieve orderly political growth. . . ."[45] In Bowles's political vision this meant something more than elite control of change.

The proposition that Development included all aspects of social and economic change, that it had political repercussions, that it led to democratic government, was implicit in a good many official pronouncements. The passage of Title IX, the amendment to the Foreign Assistance Act of 1961 that received Congressional endorsement in 1966, sanctioned this broad approach. Under the Nixon administration, Rudolph Peterson's report on foreign assistance claimed that Development programs involved "more than economic growth. Popular participation and the dispersion of the benefits of development among all groups in society are essential to the building of dynamic and healthy nations. U.S. development policies should contribute to this end."[46] Although the Peterson report underlined the danger of assuming that economic growth meant democratic political change, it also maintained that "political stability is unlikely to occur without sound economic development."[47]

The Military Connection

At the very time that spokesmen of postwar administrations offered eloquent support for Development in terms of its historic relationship to social and political change, the integration of such programs into mutual security arrangements was taking place. Not all economic assistance programs were affected, but the connection was implicit in many such programs from their inception.

Under the Kennedy administration, when the emphasis on Development in terms of economic equality and social justice was at its peak, Development programs were integrated into specifically designed counterrevolutionary policies. Counterinsurgency, an issue in which Kennedy took great interest, was advocated by some military specialists persuaded of the need to develop more effective planning.[48] Military critics of the defense establishment were convinced of the need to enhance the "capability to react across the entire spectrum of possible change, for coping with anything from general atomic war to infiltrations and aggressions such as now threaten Laos and Berlin. . . ."[49] In response, the administration increased the budgetary allocation for the Defense Department, augmented the size of the army, and initiated programs of internal security in the Third World.[50]

Counterinsurgency was viewed in such quarters as an appropriate response to the pervasive malaise of Third World states, of which instability was the most dangerous symptom. The definition offered by the *Dictionary of United States Military Terms for Joint Usage* struck a somewhat different tone. There, insurgency was defined as referring to movements, revolts, or insurrections "against a constituted government which falls short of civil war";[51] in the same passage, counter-insurgency was defined as the "military, paramilitary, political, economic, psychological, and civic actions taken by a government to defeat subversive insurgency." Modeled on the counterrevolutionary experiences of France in Algeria and Indochina, and Britain in Malaya, the Kennedy administration applied the approach to events in Central America and Southeast Asia.[52] The alert was signaled by events in Cuba and Vietnam.

By 1962 counterinsurgency courses were on the curriculum for political and military personnel as well as diplomats and aid administrators with assignments in the Third World.[53] Development programs in such courses were described as leading to an improvement of the "U.S. capability for guiding underdeveloped countries through the modernization barrier and for countering subversive insurgency."[54] The description of the transition process as constituting a barrier evoked images of sociopolitical change as an obstacle course. In other contexts, the same movement was viewed as something approaching illness, particularly when it gave rise to radical movements. In this light, counterinsurgency was interpreted as a form of "preventive therapeutic and regenerative medicine."[55] That its application resulted in widespread human suffering and social dislocation was not relevant to such accounts or policies.[56]

Development and the New Diplomatic Order

Within a decade, then, the language of Development was not only firmly placed on the foreign policy agenda, but its political and military aspects were recognized as integral elements of policy. From an emphasis on economic aid and assistance to the more general emphasis on social and political change, Development was finally affixed to counterinsurgency policies. To note that these policies subverted the formal intentions of Development programs as defined in official discourse is an extreme example of understatement.

The trajectory of Development, as understood and rationalized in official sources, was apparent in a group of reports specially prepared for the Senate Foreign Relations Committee in 1957–1960. Their interest lies, in part, in their authorship. The specialists from MIT, Harvard, and Syracuse Universities included many who were subsequently to be recognized as leading experts on Development studies. Although Development programs were still interpreted largely in an economic context, such reports increasingly indicated the attention given to their noneconomic dimensions.

Some analysts went further. They recommended support for Development in terms of its relationship with the "evolution of mature democratic societies whose fundamental interests in the world will be compatible with our own."[57] Such was the view expressed by the authors of the report entitled "Objectives of the United States Economic Assistance Programs," prepared in 1957 by the MIT Center for International Studies. The goal of economic assistance programs, in such interpretations, included the creation and/or support for regimes described as more or less "mature political democracies."[58] From the perspective of U.S. foreign policy, the achievement of economic growth and "social maturity within a democratic framework" were twin goals of considerable importance, particularly for nations in Asia and Africa.[59]

Other academic consultants emphasized different kinds of considerations with respect to economic aid programs. They endorsed the official view of Development with its concern for instability, access to Third World markets, and the guarantee of strategic interests. Increasingly in such accounts, the legitimacy of intervention in the internal affairs of Third World states, explained in terms of foreign policy and the requirements of assistance programs, was approved. Discussed in considerable detail as a feature of foreign policy necessitated by the conditions of postwar Third World development, the question of intervention was addressed under different guises. According to one source, no country had an "internal 'power structure'" that policy makers could afford to ignore.[60] On the other hand, intervention was more specifically linked to the pursuit of certain foreign policy objectives by Third World regimes. While some counseled a moderate attitude toward those adopting neutralist policies,[61] others did not. The latter group regarded such policies as an expression of pro-Soviet support. In the opinion of one of the authors of the Syracuse University report, entitled "Operational Aspects of United States Foreign Policy" (1959), the critical issue was the extent to which Third World leaders supported the West in the cold war.[62] In this context, support for progressive political institutions was as irrelevant as the question of intervention per se.[63]

By far the most elaborate and noteworthy discussion of the meaning of Development appeared in the report prepared by the MIT Center for International Studies, "Economic, Social and Political Change in the Underdeveloped Countries and Its Implications for United States Policy" (1960). In terms of its analysis of the nature of Development as a historic process and the strategy to be used to implement it as a contemporary policy, the MIT report provided a model to be replicated in subsequent academic analyses of Development. In part, its influence in this environment was a result of those who participated in its deliberations. The MIT Center housed some of the more active contributors to policy-oriented Development studies, a position recognized at the highest levels.

The importance of the MIT Center was apparent in its role in the Senate hearings of 1957–1960. It was supported in citations of the NSC with respect to U.S. economic policy planning. According to NSC 5719/1 (March 21, 1958), the MIT Center was involved in the preparation of "a long-range study, with respect both to the independent and the emerging colonial areas, out of which the economic section will develop possibilities for international arrangements which could contribute to beneficial inter-dependence between Europe and Africa, and will discuss the US role in promoting economic growth in Africa."[64] This material, the NSC noted, was scheduled for completion by the beginning of May 1958.

Two years later, the MIT Center presented the Senate with its report on the economic, social, and political dimensions of Development and their impact on U.S. policy. Containing a detailed interpretation of the Development process, its recommendations with respect to intervention merit attention. These constituted an apology for intervention in political and historic terms, shaped to suit the current interests of policy.

The development process, the authors of the report argued, was a comprehensive, interrelated one. It involved changes described as leading from agricultural- to urban-based industrial economies. In some circumstances such changes were accompanied by political transformations, such as the emergence of democratic political systems, a possible though not necessary historical eventuality. Qualifying their remarks on the subject, the authors noted that Modernization was not to be interpreted as "a sufficient condition for democratic politics, for clearly it is not. But it is more than just a necessary condition; in some ways it can help to promote democratic politics. Something of the same may be said of the relation between modernization and private enterprise."[65] The same connection was emphasized in another reminder that European capitalist development was the historic model on which current Development programs were based, although it was not capable of being reproduced. Interjecting the familiar though erroneous contrast between the evolutionary development of Western states and the disorderly, revolutionary-prone process of transition in Third World countries, the authors claimed that the latter represented a major concern for U.S. policymakers.[66] And, they added, the United

States had special leverage in this domain, since "the principal instruments available to the United States for influencing the transition are economic instruments."[67]

Intervention was not broached as a forbidden, clandestine theme. On the contrary, the question of intervention was introduced as necessitated by the particular historical circumstances in which Third World Development occurred. These circumstances, the authors explained, were the result of the conditions of Development, the uneven cultural and technological relations of advanced, industrialized countries, and the less advanced conditions of Third World states. "The fact must explicitly be recognized that the relationships between states in today's world, particularly between the technologically advanced and the lesser developed countries, are qualitatively on a different order than those which prevailed until recently."[68] For policymakers, the implications were candidly stated. The internal policies of Third World states, as indicated in the same passage, were of paramount concern. Under the circumstances, "the foreign policy of the United States will no longer be concerned solely with the external relations of states; the evolution of their domestic life has become a direct and legitimate concern."

Arguing from this position, the authors of the MIT report readily concluded that it was time for a reevaluation of the premises of U.S. diplomacy.[69] Existing conventions of diplomacy, according to this argument, assumed a set of relationships between more or less equally developed states. Since relations between Third World and Western states did not satisfy this condition, customary diplomatic practice was urgently in need of modification. "Can the basic principle of nonintervention be maintained when a primary international activity must be the transferring of talents and skills, including those of administration and policymaking? And when there is a gross difference in levels of technology, can the obligations of alliances be shared equally?"[70] The questions were rheteorical. In their new guide to diplomacy, or more accurately, their guide to the new diplomacy, the authors argued that the United States needed to accommodate the new conditions imposed by the international politics of uneven, dependent relations. Using a different terminology, the report counseled policymakers to shape their "diplomatic practices to meet the present need to create a new system of international relations which can provide an acceptable basis for relationships between societies at radically different stages of development."[71] What followed was a review of Development programs as instruments of aid and intervention, a position that the MIT report was not alone in advocating.

Development programs were introduced in this context as enabling instruments meant to further the movement of Third World regimes toward "responsible government and to play a useful cooperative role in the international community."[72] But more was involved. Diplomatic officers assigned to aid programs were advised to "enter deeply into the substantive objectives and problems of specific programs" in order to ensure their progress.[73] In practice, this meant taking advantage of non-diplomatic personnel as well. Thus, the authors of the report entitled "Operational Aspects of United States Foreign Policy" indicated that Americans traveling abroad in the Third World would make useful sources of information and intelligence. Of an estimated 1,590,000 Americans presumed to be abroad, those "businessmen, missionaries, teachers, students, relief workers, journalists, and even the hundreds of semi-private enterprises (consulting firms, universities and others) that subsist on Government contracts abroad" were invited to join in the effort.[74] Some years later the committee headed by Senator Church, in its assessment of the practices of the Intelligence community, argued a different perspective on precisely this kind of auxiliary support.

At least as instructive from the point of view of how the implementation of Development programs was perceived, and how it would be rationalized in academic analyses, was the attention paid to the role of the military. An expanded role for the military of Third World regimes, as well as for the U.S. military forces, was strongly endorsed by the authors of the MIT report. Explanations of such policies centered on the evident fragility of political institutions throughout the Third World. Military intervention was therefore offered as an "alternative to the prevailing chaos."[75] According to the MIT report, the role of the U.S. military was to protect Third World regimes and states from foreign intervention and from "subversion by an armed minority supported by an outside power."[76] Examples were drawn from the Philippines, Burma, South Vietnam, and Malaya. What such examples demonstrated was the masking of Development programs in the analogy of social change with stress and illness (a frequent refrain in later Development studies) and the justification of intervention in terms of cold war considerations. Protecting Third World societies "from a Communist conquest during their most vulnerable stage, they may well find their feet, consolidate their nationhood, and begin to move toward modernization."[77] The military, in a noncombat role, could facilitate this transition process, according to the report.[78] No reference was made to the experience of counterinsurgency programs that adopted a similar rationale.

The rationalization of military intervention, however, was made in additional ways that found merit in academic interpretations of Development. Conceptually describing the army as a school for modernity, the authors of the MIT report explained that it had the added advantage of inculcating "such basic attitudes as the respect for authority and organization which are essential to modern life. The army can be a highly significant training ground for large numbers of men, preparing them for new roles in society."[79] And approaching the reasoning common to advocates of counterinsurgency, the authors argued that by integrating the military into Development programs, the traditional alienation expressed by civilians for the army might be counterbalanced.[80] Such a role was particularly to be emphasized, they noted, in the light of the "internal wars" and insurrections that were considered an inescapable part of Third World change. "In many areas the most likely form of war is internal insurrection aided from abroad and conducted along guerrilla lines. The outcome of guerrilla operations often hinges on the sympathy and support of the peasantry, who have it in their power to deny information and supplies to either side. The use of the military establishment in constructive enterprises at the village level can create close working links between the soldiers and the peasants."[81]

Development, Counterinsurgency, and a Typology of Intervention

What the reports to the Senate Foreign Relations Committee advised with respect to Development, and particularly in connection with Development and counterinsurgency, other policy analyses elaborated in greater detail. The same bifurcated view of Development as historic process and Development as instrument of foreign policy was evident. And the same assumptions with regard to the conditions of Third World states were operative. Development programs in such analyses emerged as pretexts for intervention as well as processes justifying intervention.

Douglas Blaufarb, in *The Counterinsurgency Era: U.S. Doctrine and Performance* (1977), took note of the fact that the Center for International Studies at MIT played an important role in training courses on counterinsurgency, providing one of the more popular lecturers on the subject.[82] But it was another member of the MIT team, W. W. Rostow, whose policymaking role was more influential and whose views on Development and counterinsurgency were unambiguous. As an advisor on national security affairs under President Kennedy, and as assistant and coordinator of foreign policy under President Johnson, Rostow was credited with formulating the "comprehensive 'strategic concept' for counterinsurgency" along with

Roger Hilsman, director of the State Department's Bureau of Intelligence and Research in the Kennedy administration. Given his position in the policymaking hierarchy and his subsequent influence on policy-oriented students of Development, Rostow's views merit consideration.

Clearly the merger of Development programs with counterinsurgency policies represented no conflict for Rostow. He perceived both as furthering common interests in the United States' Third World policies. In his address to the graduating class of the U.S. Army Special Warfare School at Fort Bragg in June 1961, Rostow described the importance of guerrilla warfare in terms of events in Cuba, the Congo, Laos, and Vietnam. These regions, he declared, symbolized "the efforts of the international Communist movement to exploit the inherent instability of the underdeveloped areas of the non-Communist world, and each had a guerrilla warfare component."[83] These "scavengers of the modernization process," according to Rostow, might be routed by the policy of counterinsurgency, which was advertised as protecting the "independence of the revolutionary process now going forward" in the Third World. From this vantage point there was nothing incompatible about supporting the Special Forces that, according to Rostow, were being sent out to "help fashion independent, modern societies out of the revolutionary process now going forward" and the subversion of revolutionary and independence movements to which such forces contributed. Others in the Kennedy administration upheld similar views.[84]

Twenty years later, support for counterinsurgency was presented in similar terms. This "much misunderstood and maligned doctrine," which was "selectively applied in over 30 countries during the '60s and '70s," according to the former staff director of the Special Group on Counterinsurgency, represented programs of assistance "aimed at protecting the development process during its vulnerable stages from the forces of political violence whether from the right or the left."[85] Such a doctrine, according to the same former official, was not meant to be a "blank check to worthless oligarchies, much less to dictator-lackeys posing as 'friends,'" a claim that practice did not sustain. If such was the policy, the same author argued, then counterinsurgency programs would serve "to keep the most brutal regimes in power."

In the same year in which W. W. Rostow addressed the graduating class at the Special Warfare School, another consultant to government who was to become an expert on the academic study of political change, S. P. Huntington, prepared a report for Project Vulcan that was commissioned by the Special Studies Group of the Institute for Defense Analyses. "Instability at the Non-Strategic Level of Conflict" (1961) was a primer on intervention in which the changing environment of Third World states and bipolar competition were the major elements. Huntington's approach to the analysis of socioeconomic change and its relationship to intervention was similar to that found in the Senate Committee reports discussed earlier. Where Huntington's essay differed was in its delayed taxonomy of intervention and in its attention to the timing and political impact that such intervention might be expected to have.

Huntington recommended a strategy for maximizing the advantages of rapid intervention in the Third World—an intervention that he argued would almost inevitably be brought about as a result of the process of socioeconomic change occurring throughout Third World states. The interpretation rested on the assumption of "bipolar strategic stability; infrequent interstate wars and a high degree of boundary stability; intensive competition between the Soviet Union and the United States in world politics; [and] rapid social, economic and political changes in the developing countries."[86] From the point of view of U.S. policy perspectives, two questions were paramount in the consideration of Third World politics: commitment and stability. Commitment, Huntington observed, was easy enough to discern. Whether or not a state pursued policies that were pro-Soviet as opposed to pro-American was not difficult to determine. Stability, in his estimate, was a far more difficult question. "Indeed, a government can only be said to be definitely stable if it survives."[87] Obviously, coups, insurrections, revolutions, and civil wars were indications of instability. Linked to commitment, such developments were signs of changes on the level of government policy.

The interrelationship of commitment and stability to internal politics, and to international responses to such politics, is what Huntington's essay dealt with in considerable detail. Less concerned with stability, per se, than with its underlying conditions, Huntington observed that "long-run political stability depends upon the broadening of the scope of politics. From the domestic viewpoint a stable government is one which cannot be overthrown in a coup d'etat. From the international viewpoint, however, a brief coup d'etat is much less unstabilizing than a prolonged revolutionary war or civil war." His conclusion, in the same passage, is of particular interest to the work of Development theorists, given their preoccupation with the question of participation and Development. According to Huntington, "The broadening of participation in politics which contributes to long-run domestic stability may also contribute to short-run international instability."[88] If policy assumed a priority of interests such that international instability was among the less desirable options, and this argument was followed, then participation was not within the parameters of domestic politics to be supported.

Whether or not intervention was advocated, according to this typology, was determined by the importance of the particular country to U.S. interests.[89] As Huntington noted, "The need for direct military intervention by American forces increases as the likelihood of victory for the groups we are allied with decreases."[90] Given the fact that many of the groups with which the United States was allied were those that repressed social change, the United States was confronted with a particularly severe dilemma if it wished to minimize the opportunities for long-run civil wars and revolutions. The solution: preventive intervention. "What is required is a strategy of pre-military intervention, indirect intervention, and positive action to shape the course of politics and to strengthen the groups committed to our side or most likely to enhance stability, before the situation gets grave enough to raise the issue of direct military intervention."[91] Negative examples were provided by the regimes of Franco, Salazar, Trujillo, Somoza, Chiang, and, "potentially Diem," all of which were described as increasing the possibilities of domestic violence and international (or U.S.) intervention.[92] By contrast, the regimes of South Korea and Turkey were advanced as supporting the policy recommendations implicit in Huntington's formula. In these cases, stability was presumably grounded in governments that were capable of implementing some reforms and effectively repressing the demands for other changes without giving rise to massive, organized discontent.

In comparing U.S. and Soviet policies, Huntington found the latter more pragmatic with respect to the Third World. The USSR, he noted, was willing to ally itself with "'bourgeois' nationalist groups, so long as they were non-Western oriented." On the other hand, the United States, according to Huntington, "has been reluctant to back groups which did not have clear pro-Western commitments. It has tended to divide groups into the 'good guys' and the 'bad guys' and to back the former irrespective of the effects which this may have on our long-term goal of stability. In this area, the Soviets have been pragmatic, and we have been the victims of our own dogma."[93]

Domestically, Huntington argued, the United States faced a special problem. Public opinion tended to oppose intervention whereas the needs of foreign policy supported relations with "superficially 'stable' dicta-torships," which often required the kinds of intervention cited earlier. As demonstrated by the material that follows, considerable attention was paid by official and academic specialists to the matter of justifying intervention in the name of Development and its importance to foreign policy.

4

Transparent Boundaries: From Policies to Studies of Political Development

Forging a Foreign Policy Consensus

What is the relationship of the official discourse on Development to the academic field of Political Development studies? What of the relationship between interpretations of Development designed by policy-oriented social scientists and the interpretations that prevailed in academic circles? Are such relationships incidental or formative in the history of Political Development studies? The questions are as obvious as they are vital to the understanding of the production of Political Development studies as a political and intellectual exercise.

In what follows, something of the movement of ideas about Development between the official and academic environments is traced. Some of those responsible for conveying the official interpretation to the academy are identified. But more important than singling out individuals or institutions important to this process is recognizing the support for achieving a foreign policy consensus that Development studies have promoted. In this connection, policy-oriented social scientists have played a paramount role, one that was far out of proportion to their number in the larger community of Development scholars. They provided interpretations of Development, as a historic and contemporary process, that conforms to what became the common view of the subject in academic circles.

As demonstrated in the discussion that follows, however, the search for consensus in foreign policy antedated the formal study of Development. It was not a feature unique to contemporary policymakers. Doubtless a response of any government concerned with public opinion, it was a subject about which some social scientists expressed concern much earlier. That they were also individuals who belonged to the extended intellectual family of Development scholars suggests the connection, recommended earlier, between social scientists interested in policy (i.e., policy scientists) and those concerned with policy consensus from the official government angle. H. D.

Lasswell was one such social scientist who exercised a formidable influence on the political scientists of his generation and, incidentally, on some who became specialists of Development. Characteristically blunt, Lasswell had some perceptive and particularly appropriate comments to make in an article that appeared in 1942. The "end of ideological policy," as Lasswell understood it, was fairly close to what a significant group of Development theorists were committed to, namely, the formation of favorable attitudes toward government policy. With Daniel Lerner, another key figure in the study of Modernization and Development, Lasswell launched the "policy sciences" approach, an approach that conveyed the objectives of the "end of ideological policy." There were other political scientists, such as Gabriel Almond, who shared similar interests and who emerged as critical figures in Development studies. Almond wrote on foreign policy in the late 1940s, commenting on U.S. policy in Western Europe. Some time later he turned to the question of domestic public opinion and foreign policy, in interpretations that have had a direct bearing on his better known contributions to Political Development.

Social scientists and foreign policy were the subjects of an extended investigation by the House of Representatives in the 1960s. Its inquiry into the "Behavioral Sciences and the National Security," among other things, disclosed the vast resources allocated by government agencies to Development-related research. One of the projects lavishly funded was Project Camelot, better known for its failures than for its content. What Camelot was intended to accomplish in Latin America was basically what policy-oriented theorists of Political Development considered to be their own purpose in studying Third World change. The business of identifying social forces committed to change and predicting their actions so as to contain them was what Camelot was intended to achieve. Its failures, as supporters of the project repeatedly pointed out, were only temporary.

To judge by their own proclamations of purpose, students of Development not previously associated with Camelot had similar ambitions. These were amplified in their deliberations on the role of the military in Development policies. No subject in the writings of policy-oriented theorists of Development so mimicked the official view while exaggerating its justifications. Policy-oriented students of Development who wrote on the question of the military, and who gave public lectures on the subject, were adamant in their support of the greater involvement of the military in Third World Development.

Elaborating a rationale rich in psychology and history, these exponents of the military role in social reform were prepared to argue that they were not advocates of the militarization of politics. Yet, in fact, they propagated myths of Development that simultaneously supported the view of the military as models of democratic, nonauthoritarian training while arguing that the militarization of politics was an undesirable feature of Third World politics.

More important in the overall discussion of the transparent boundaries between government and the academy with respect to the study of Political Development was the map of Development produced by academic consultants at MIT. The MIT report entitled "Economic, Social and Political Change in the Underdeveloped Countries and Its Implications for United States Policy" (1960) was a landmark work from this perspective. Composed by well-known specialists, many of them to become recognized theorists of Political Development, it provided a historical and strategic approach to the question of Third World change that largely dominated the academic study of the question. The report elaborated on the work of such figures as Daniel Lerner, Lucian Pye, Everett Hagen, Edward A. Shils (not a member of the MIT team), Richard Eckhaus, Ithiel de Sola Pool, and Walt W. Rostow, in addition to its director, Max Millikan. It constituted a synthesis of existing interpretations of the subject and an influence on their subsequent formulation. In short, the report contributed to a definition of the political language of Political Development studies, indicating proper themes and their approach. It also identified one of the major problems in Development policies and theories—namely, the relationship of social to political change and, more specifically, the relationship of Development to democracy and participation.

Some years later, the issue was again raised in a context that brought together Development scholars from MIT and government officials associated with various aspects of policy. The conference to discuss the passage of Title IX of the Foreign Assistance Act of 1961 was instructive. It demonstrated the common views on a question of central significance to the implementation of Development programs.

Events such as the MIT report and its dissemination among scholars of Development, the analyses of the role of the military in Development, the interpretations of participation in the context of policy, are among the indicators of the degree of conformity and collaboration that marked the views of policymakers and Development specialists. The question remains: How representative were the views of those who were primarily policy oriented in their approach? Many who became committed to the study of Political Development did not see themselves as conformists or consultants. The active policy-oriented specialists on Political Development were, as suggested earlier, few in number. Yet what Millikan said in his cover letter to the MIT report of 1960 applied to the literature of the field in a more general way; in short, it offered a "broad rationale for U.S. policy."[1]

If there were active dissenters, either from policy or its expression in accepted interpretations of Development, they were on the margins of the field. Or, to borrow a metaphor popularized by Albert Hirschman in *Exit, Voice and Loyalty* (1970), those who did not like the results had the option of voting with their feet. For the rest, the activity of a prolific group of policy-oriented scholars was differently interpreted, if at all. In retrospect, however, their importance cannot be ignored. Pivotally situated between the capital and the academic market place, these scholars were in a unique situation. Well placed in terms of access to policymakers and their aides, funding sources, and students and scholars eager to work on Development issues, their situation gave them uncommon advantages. They understood policy needs as well as academic conditions and could respond to both. Without taking measures in any way coercive, they found a receptive audience and helped shape its orientation to problems of Development. That they were capable of doing so was a measure of the extent to which they articulated a set of common assumptions about the nature of social and political change.

The "End of Ideological Policy"

"Psychological warfare—*the planned use by a nation of propaganda and activities other than combat which communicate ideas and information intended to influence the opinions, attitudes, emotions and behavior of foreign groups in ways that will support the achievement of national aims.*"

"Propaganda—*any organized effort or movement to disseminate information or a particular doctrine by means of news, special arguments or appeals designed to influence the thoughts and actions of any given group.*"[2]

In 1942 H. D. Lasswell, prominent and eclectic political scientist and specialist on propaganda and communications, psychology, and politics, wrote of the importance of forming "favorable attitudes" toward government.[3] With the emergence of liberal democratic states, Lasswell argued, "ideological policy" changed. Whereas in "pre-liberal, pre-democratic states" the aims of such a policy were straightforward, "to detect sedition at home and conspiracy abroad and to encourage the reverent acceptance of state, friendly religions,"[4] in liberal democratic states the purpose was different, yet it failed. What occurred was a "bifurcation of market and government" such that the preoccupation with markets subordinated democratic interests.[5] Struck by the conflict, Lasswell noted that "in the liberal, democratic state men spoke of 'prosperity,' not of 'power'; yet prosperity was not their ostensible goal. The cardinal value was the dignity of man, but prosperity was not translated in terms of human dignity."[6]

Lasswell's solution was prophetic in terms of its managerial approach to social problems, an approach implicit in the academic analysis of Development. In Lasswell's view, communication methods and propaganda held the keys to resolution of the problem. It was a matter of identifying the "key symbols and symbol elaborations" of the state,[7] in an effort to improve "zones of poor democratic performance and determine the factors that contribute to their continuation."[8] This was where ideological policy fit. According to Lasswell, "each public policy calls for two types of intelligence: ideological and technical. By ideological intelligence is meant facts about the thoughts, feelings, and conduct of human beings. Other facts are technical."[9] In his writings Lasswell dealt with both. He analyzed "key symbols" of state power, and he investigated the means of making use of "ideological intelligence." Others joined in these efforts, as the expanding field of communication studies was to demonstrate.

Daniel Lerner argued the same points in his work on psychological warfare in World War II, *Sykewar* (1949). There he claimed that U.S. strategy "with its emphasis on economic and strategic superiority might one day have to recognize the need for 'the intelligence specialist (the social scientist) and the communication specialist (the propagandist)—rather than, or in addition to, the diplomat, the economist, and the soldier.'"[10] Two years later, in their joint work on *The Policy Sciences* (1951), Lasswell and Lerner appealed to scholars to become effective as scientists and to be relevant as policymakers.[11] Lerner, in his contribution to the text, described the self-image of the American scholar in terms appropriate to the sciences. The emphasis was on the desire of the scholar to be recognized for his contribution to policy, and for his ability to make such a contribution in the same manner as did the scientist. "Policy scientists," according to this interpretation, combined the aims of what Lasswell had described as "ideological and technical intelligence." In practice, the term "policy scientist" became something of an embarrassment to policy-oriented students. Its evident conformism was unacceptable.[12]

Lasswell and Lerner collaborated on other ventures, such as the series of studies that issued out of their work on revolutions. In addition to

The World Revolution of Our Time: A Framework for Basic Policy Research
(1951) were works such as the slim volume that Lerner and his colleagues
co-authored, *The Nazi Elited*.[13] For the most part uneven in quality, these
works were oriented toward cold war ideology. In the same period, Lerner
himself contributed a number of essays with a similar ideological bent. His
statement on European neutralism, published in "International Coalitions
and Communications Content: The Case of Neutralism,"[14] took a pseudopsychological approach. Neutralism, according to Lerner, was a form of
deviation, an indication of instability and disloyalty. It signified poor communication as well as faulty personality and political adjustment. With
some modifications, the same approach was to appear in his work entitled
The Passing of Traditional Society (1958).[15]

By contrast, Gabriel Almond's writings on U.S. foreign policy in the
late 1940s were strikingly sober. In a series of essays written for the Yale
Institute of International Studies, Almond considered developments in
postwar France, Italy, and Germany in relation to U.S. policy.[16] That policy,
in his evaluation, was "the primary force behind the preservation of the
political stability and the historic values of the Western world."[17] Stability
and Western values, however, were threatened by political developments
in Europe, according to Almond. What Almond described were social
and political movements of left and right. Those of the left, particularly in
France and Italy, appeared more dangerous in his accounts. The situation in
postwar Germany was obviously different, yet some of the same reasoning
was applied. The emergence of left-wing parties threatened the effectiveness of a "third force," a moderate political coalition designed to contain
the forces of left and right, according to Almond. The theme echoed
discussions of European politics in the postwar period on the official level,
in which precisely the same concerns and far more extensive recommendations of policy were made.

The conformity with policy was evident in *The Struggle for Democracy in
Germany* (1949), a work that Almond edited and to which he contributed.[18]
There, he advocated a hastening of the de-Nazification policies and an
increased emphasis on the role of German anti-Nazi resistance groups
during the war. The approach supported the views of those who favored
the rapid reintegration of Germany into a staunchly anti-Soviet and anticommunist Europe.

It was in his work entitled *The American People and Foreign Policy* (1950),
however, that Almond elaborated on the importance of the domestic
consensus in support of foreign policy. Accepting the legitimacy of the
cold war view of international politics, Almond defined those who rejected

it as deviants and underlined the importance of reinforcing the outlook of its advocates. Therein lay the role of social scientists. Their function was to translate the meaning of foreign policy into domestic terms and to augment its acceptance. "The believing Christian, the trade unionist, the democratic Socialist, the liberal, the conservative—all save a small sector of the population—experience the Russian and Communist pressure as a grave threat to fundamental values. This is what gives the problem of foreign policy its special poignancy."[19] Resisting such pressure required an all-out effort on several levels, the "economic, diplomatic, propaganda, and if necessary, military means" as well as establishment of "a peaceful and legal international order in which American material and security interests would be protected."[20]

Were such means and objectives approved by the public at large? In an attempt to answer this question, Almond reviewed the position of such collectives as trade unions, business organizations, women's groups, religious associations, and others. Those found not to be in accord with the underlying premises of domestic and foreign policy were classified as "radical appeasers" or as "reactionaries."[21] Criteria for qualification in either classification depended on attitudes toward the relative importance of domestic, welfare legislation as opposed to national defense. Internationalists and pacifists were among those included in the first category. Their opposition was regarded as a form of deviance incompatible with the need for national consensus.

How to forge such a consensus and maintain it were responsibilities that Almond assigned to social scientists. In the first place, the need for a "coherent theory of society and politics" was stressed. "The aim of such a theory would be to clarify the value premises and conflicts of the politically significant cultures and social groupings of our time."[22] Those best placed to perform this function were the social scientists. Their contribution was identified as important both for policymakers and the public at large. "Developments in the social sciences in this direction would make it increasingly difficult for the policy and opinion elites to produce those magnificent inconsistencies, non sequiturs, and frequent elisions of logical analysis which confuse and obscure the public debate of important policy questions."[23]

By 1952, as indicated earlier, official interest in promoting a nationwide effort in this direction was given support in administration circles. Although such a campaign did not begin with the Eisenhower administration, it *was* under Eisenhower that the International Information Activities Committee was formed in 1952 to coordinate the intellectual and political campaign against the expansion of Soviet power. Classified as part of an overall psychological warfare program, it furthered the collaboration of both governmental and nongovernmental agencies such as the "representatives of the State Department, C.I.A., National Committee for a Free Europe (Radio Free Europe), the Psychological Strategy Board, and members of MIT's Center for International Studies (CENIS), a CIA think tank created by Truman. . . ."[24]

Social Science Research and the National Security

"Behavioral Sciences and the National Security," which constituted Part IX of the congressional hearings on "Winning the Cold War: The U.S. Ideological Offensive," was issued in 1966 by the House of Representatives.[25] By the time of its issuance, the identification of the social science contribution with the "national security" was far more elaborate than anything anticipated in the Eisenhower years. Both the evolution of the so-called behavioral sciences and the amount of money channeled into the "ideological offensive" had reached awesome proportions. What Lasswell had termed "ideological and technical intelligence" had reached an unprecedented scale of organization and funding. Its focal point in this report, and an increasingly significant issue during this period, was the relationship of social science research to U.S. policy in the Third World.

For a period of three years prior to the issuance of the report, the Subcommittee on International Organizations and Movements of the House Committee on Foreign Affairs had been investigating the social science connection with foreign policy. What the "behavioral sciences" could contribute was a subject of consuming interest in this group: "What they tell us about human attitudes and motivations, and how this knowledge can be applied to governmental undertakings designed to carry out the foreign policy of the United States—has been of keen interest to our subcommittee."[26] That interest was further piqued, however, by the scandal that surrounded the demise of one of the more expensive Defense Department projects, Camelot, which spoke directly to the problems associated with Development and Third World change. The scandal, occasioned by adverse publicity, made the social science connection a subject of public scrutiny.

The revelations of the subcommittee report were not all that surprising: expensive research projects that yielded trivial findings; the acceptance of counterinsurgency as a legitimate arm of foreign policy; and the occasionally mocking response of a skeptical member of Congress to the role of the army in the making of foreign policy. On the approach to the Third World and its problems there was more rather than less agreement. That this widely different region would determine the course of U.S.-Soviet relations was unquestioningly assumed. Few disputed the proposition that social and political change could bring about an increase of communist and Soviet influence. Against this background, the collaboration of the various government agencies and the private sector in the form of social science researchers was strongly endorsed even when its results were challenged. This highly regarded collaboration was seen as a weapon, "one of the vital tools in the arsenal of the free societies."[27]

One after the other, various members of the Defense Department presented the case for support of social science research in the interests of counterinsurgency and unconventional war. According to the chief of research and development in the Department of the Army, Lt. Gen. W. W. Dick, Jr., the research division in his program sought an "improved performance in counterinsurgency, military assistance, unconventional types of warfare and psychological operations through social and behavioral science studies of methods for predicting the reactions of indigenous troops and populations in foreign areas; and other studies as may be needed for direct support of stability operations." In another passage General Dick informed the subcommittee that $8.2 million in 1965, and $8.3 million for 1966, had been allotted and/or planned.[28]

Under Secretary of the Air Force Brockway McMillan agreed that such research would contribute to an understanding of "intercultural communication and interaction with foreign populations" in situations of "cold, limited or total war."[29] Seymour J. Deitchman, special assistant for counterinsurgency, Office of the Director of Defense Research and Engineering of the Department of Defense, held that social science could play an important role in the military effort. For this reason, he explained, the Department of Defense had called on "anthropologists, psychologists, sociologists, political scientists, economists—whose professional orientation to human behavior would enable them to make useful contributions in this area."[30]

Against the array of high-level Defense Department, Agency for International Development (AID), and State Department figures, occasional voices of dissent were heard questioning the military involvement in the conduct of foreign policy. Congressman Fraser questioned Secretary of State Dean Rusk about another aspect of the hearings, the nature of the research itself. In his opinion the subject of "political development" was central to the problem, but it was apparently being ignored. "I don't see any agency that has responsibility for that. But it seems to me that much of these behavioral and social science studies relate to the question of political development. What we want are stable democratic societies, but we ignore political development and skirt around it."[31] Others disagreed, particularly those in charge of the research programs. Their conception of political development was not ignored so much as managed through the agency of counterinsurgency warfare.

Among other things, the hearings revealed the enormity of the bureaucracy handling social science research. Planning was in the hands of agencies such as AID, the United States Information Agency (USIA), and the Department of State. Information concerning budgetary allocations made in this period suggest the scale of such involvement.

As earlier indicated, the Department of the Army allocated $8.2 million in 1965, with an increase for the following year. Not all was to be used for the social sciences. Those plans that applied to social science research were carried out by the Human Resources Office, the U.S. Army Personnel Research Office, and the Special Operations Research Office (SORO). The Human Resources Office worked under contract with the army and with George Washington University as of 1951. It conducted research "in support of training motivation, morale, and leadership."[32] In conjunction with the American University, SORO worked on research "in support of counterinsurgency, military assistance in developing nations, unconventional warfare, psychological operations, and civil actions and stability operations."[33] It was associated with the Department of Defense Counter Insurgency Information Analysis Center. The Department of the Navy had a program that was funded at $3,609,000 in 1965, although it claimed that only a fraction of this amount went directly to foreign areas study.[34] The Agency for International Development spent a total of $5.7 million on some twenty projects in the period from 1962–1965.[35] The Department of Defense concluded that its expenses for research and related programs had increased from $10 million in 1960 to nearly $160 million in 1966, with 97 percent of this going for equipment and weapons for the military side of counterinsurgency warfare.

In 1964, the Foreign Area Research Coordination Group assumed the task of coordinating this research empire. Two years later, as a result of the publicity surrounding Project Camelot, there was further reorganization. SORO became the Center for Research in Social Systems (CRESS), which included the data-gathering agency specializing in counterinsurgency, the Counter Insurgency Information Analysis Center, and the Social Science Research Institute—the latter responsible for studies on "unconventional warfare, psychological operations, military assistance programs and other studies and evaluations of foreign cultures."[36] For this effort, CRESS received nearly $2 billion in 1968.

Counterrevolution in the Revolution

Development Studies on the Agenda

Policy-oriented social scientists specializing in Political Development were generally blunt about the purpose of their studies. They made clear their thinking on Development as a process of historic proportions that was beyond the capacity of most Third World statesmen to control, let alone to implement. Such a position carried implications about Third World states and societies, U.S. policy, and the role of social scientists in relation to both. Evident in debates over such issues as Title IX[37] and the testimony of various academic consultants before congressional committees deliberating on foreign aid, these implications were also clear from the pronouncements of social scientists on the subject of Third World change and the challenge it presented.

Writing about Chinese studies, one scholar described the search for "an alternative to Communist theory" that had been a fact of academic life since the mid-1940s.[38] An involved scholar-diplomat noted that it was imperative to offer Asians explanations with which to counter Marxist interpretations of imperialism, nationalism, and economic growth.[39] Lucian Pye, in a study entitled *Guerrilla Communism in Malaya* (1956), claimed that the purpose of "checking Communism in Asia is one of finding some other auspices under which the transition from the traditional form of social relationships can be effected."[40] According to Pye, social scientists had a role to play in this process particularly given that, in the opinion of the author, Third World statesmen and intellectuals were inexperienced. They labored under the psychological traumas of colonialism and decolonization. They were incapable, according to this view, of simultaneously providing a "creative, predictable, and accommodating political process in societies comprised of people in various stages of transition."[41]

By no means all policy-oriented social scientists were persuaded of the ability of their colleagues to provide models of social and political change. The MIT report to the Senate Foreign Relations Committee of 1960, "Economic, Social and Political Change in the Underdeveloped Countries and Its Implications for United States Policy," disclosed a certain skepticism on the subject. Pye was part of the team that produced the report. There was no disagreement in the view of Development as a revolutionary process that had to be stemmed. A process of state formation in which the transition from an agricultural to an industrial urban economy occurred, Development was described by the authors of this report as having a holistic and destabilizing quality. "In a real sense our subject is revolution, for the entire fabric of these societies with which we are concerned is being torn apart, the old and time-honored being replaced by totally new economic, political, and social forms."[42] What experience was there in guiding such processes? asked the authors. Very little, they claimed. "Social scientists have not yet learned how best to analyze processes which combine all these factors, and efforts to do so can at this stage only be first approximations."[43] The social sciences were described as overly specialized, narrow, and unfit to deal with the processes involved in Development. "The transitional process, of its nature, involves interaction among political, social, economic, psychological, and cultural elements. No social science discipline is yet very skilled in dealing with these processes of complex interaction as they proceed through time."[44] The authors noted that governments needed to act, however. Under the circumstances, social scientists who agreed to link "their perceptions to the concrete choices governments confront" were perceived as part of the solution to problems connected with sociopolitical change.[45]

In very different language another author expressed the view that it was imperative to identify signs of social and political dislocation, lest their effect be destabilizing. Hence the importance of "identifying in advance probable future instances of dissynchronization between value structures and patterns of environmental adaptation—that is, conditions requiring either politically sanctioned change or revolutionary change."[46]

Identification of relevant social forces whose impact on political order could be damaging was a major concern of policy-oriented studies as well as of those more theoretically inclined quantitative analyses of violence and revolution. Strong on numbers and often weak on explanation, these abstract declarations substantiated the prevailing view of Development. By the 1960s, in fact, the study of revolution and Development had become something like a growth industry on the American campus. Character-ized by a consensus on "appropriate techniques, questions and conceptual apparatus,"[47] its rise to prominence was "related to a parallel extension on the part of American power abroad and to a sudden natural interest on the part of American policy makers in the problems of 'modernizing' societies."[48]

Project Camelot illustrated the concern with revolution and the cor-responding approach. It involved large-scale government funding and academic participation. One of the best-financed and most ambitious of social science schemes initiated by the Special Operations Research Office, it was launched as a joint venture with numerous U.S. and foreign scholar participants.[49] Camelot was scheduled to take three and a half years to complete, at a cost of no less than an estimated $44 million. From the point of view of the Department of the Army and its contractor, SORO, Camelot justified the expense, on the condition that the project be implemented.

What Project Camelot promised was not only an *explanation* of anticipated changes in certain Third World states but a guide to controlling them as well. Camelot was the promise of a counterrevolutionary model, a guide to strategies that would offset the losses represented by Greece, Cuba, the Philippines, the Dominican Republic, and Vietnam. These failures, according to congressional hearings, were attributed to an inability to deal with problems "intimately related to the social structure, culture, and behavioral patterns in the countries involved."[50] Camelot was to undo such failures by providing tools for intellectual understanding and political strategies.

> On the one hand, Project Camelot was intended to assist in identifying the forerunners of social breakdown and the resultant opportunity for Communist penetration and possible takeover; on the other hand, it was also expected to produce basic information which would furnish some guidelines with respect to actions that might be taken by or with the indigenous governments to foster constructive change within a framework of relative order and stability.[51]

In spite of the public scandal that eventually surrounded the project, the director of SORO repeatedly stressed the army's interest in Camelot's objectives. "Anticipating social breakdown"[52] was one such objective; finding an alternative policy was another.[53] In testimony before the subcommittee that investigated "Behavioral Sciences and the National Security," Dr. Vallance, the director of SORO, offered a description of what Camelot was to accomplish.

> Two of these things may be included in the idea of developing a model of society; that is, a symbolic description of how a society operates and how it changes, how things happen within it.
> This development of a symbolic picture, somewhat generalized, of how a society operates, was the basic objective of the project, as a feasibility study, as I said before, of how far can we go in modern behavioral

science toward a fairly explicit and fairly precise, and yet generalizable description of how a society operates, grows, fails in various ways.

Now, within that, then, [when] these two objectives follow as important aspects of the life of any society, what kinds of developments within it cause some people to become unhappy and lead them into actions which might tend to upset established order in such a way as to slow down the development of a society]?] Change is good. This is part of the modern way of looking at all kinds of life, growth, development, improvement, betterment, and so on. However—

Mr Rosenthal: Mr Fraser suggested, for example, the Alliance for Progress fosters change.

Dr Vallance: Indeed. However, change may become so rapid in some parts of a society that other people become disaffected, feel they are being discriminated against, and thus a potential may develop for an effort to change things in a violent way or to change the political structures of a society, so that there is a net loss over, say, a period of 15 or 20 years rather than a net gain.

If you have a violent revolution, the gains that may be fostered by other programs might be lost.[54]

Vallance's statement paralleled the premises of Development ideology: Change breeds instability; instability is dangerous; change may spark revolution. The commonality of outlook on problems of societies in transition may have been a factor in attracting academic researchers interested in Development. The roster of participating scholars, after all, contained the names of a number of Development scholars.[55] Once the project was exposed as something other than a disinterested research plan, Camelot generated an intense debate among policymakers and scholars, including those not involved in it. Among its vocal critics was Senator Fulbright, who pointed to the transformation of the universities in the wake of counterinsurgency research. Such campuses, he remarked, "are inhabited by proliferating institutes and centers with awe-inspiring names that use vast government and contract funds to produce ponderous studies of 'insurgency' and 'counterinsurgency'—studies which, behind their opaque language, look very much like efforts to develop 'scientific' techniques for the anticipation and prevention of revolution, without regard for the possibility that some revolutions may be justified or even desirable."[56]

Officially, the U.S. government dissociated itself from Camelot. In the aftermath of its demise, new guidelines for research on international affairs were issued.[57] But as Lt. Gen. W. W. Dick told members of the House subcommittee investigating these matters, "It was Project Camelot which was cancelled. This does not mean that we have backed off in any way from the objectives that Project Camelot was designed to meet."[58] General Dick's contention was borne out by the kinds of research projects funded by the Departments of State and Defense in the years from 1965 to 1968. These included studies on the role of the military in social and political change; the role of values and group psychology in social and cultural dimensions of change; and problems of stability and counterinsurgency.[59]

Considering the Means: Myths of the Military as Modernizer

Not all policy-oriented social scientists worked on projects such as Camelot. Not all specialists on Political Development worked on Camelot. But there was nothing in the statement of purpose of Project Camelot that contradicted the objectives of Development as defined by policy-oriented social scientists. One area in which their conformity was evident was their concern with controlling political change; another was their concern with exploiting the role of the military in accomplishing that goal.

It is the mystification of this role that emerges in the writings of some Political Development specialists. Whereas policymakers appeared content to identify the reasons for endorsing greater involvement of the U.S. military and its local counterpart in Development programs, policy scientists and those who regarded themselves as allied theoreticians of Development rationalized the role in romantic terms. Their language was one of psychology and state building. It was not considerations of power or politics that seemed uppermost, but psychological maturity and cost efficiency. Unlike congressional representatives who challenged the role of the military in the making of foreign policy, as did some in testimony before the House committee considering "Behavioral Sciences and the National Security,"[60] policy scientists who espoused this role of the military turned on their critics, whom they thought to be naive and uninformed.

Throughout the early 1960s, the role of the military in the politics of Third World countries was a popular theme. It was elaborated in conferences and publications on Development and Third World change and in inquiries concerning "internal wars" and counterinsurgency. There were differences among academic specialists on the subject.[61] Where some described, others recommended. John Johnson's *The Role of the Military in Underdeveloped Countries* (1962) is particularly interesting in this regard.[62] It features contributions by some of those who were to become prominent theorists of Political Development, such as Edward A. Shils, and the work of others already well known in policy circles, such as Lucian Pye. Their interpretations provide an indication of the approach to the subject that was adopted by others as well. Pye had presented his views on the subject of "Armies in the Process of Political Modernization" at a conference sponsored by the Rand Corporation in 1959. The same text was subsequently published in the Johnson volume. In it Pye argued that the military in Third World countries represented a unique group. Unspoiled by corruption and inefficiency, they were skilled and free of crippling psychological disabilities attributed to the response to colonization common in Third World states. "Military leaders are often far less suspicious of the West than civilian leaders because they themselves are more emotionally mature. This sense of security makes it possible for army leaders to look more realistically at their countries."[63] According to the same argument, such a "sense of security" enabled Third World military leaders to accept the weakness of their countries in relation to the West "without becoming unduly emotionally disturbed or hostile toward the West."[64]

In his address on "Southeast Asia and American Policy," delivered before the National War College in 1959, Pye elaborated on the same themes. On that occasion he argued in terms of power politics as well as the particular virtues of a compliant military. The fragility of Asian and Southeast Asian state structures, Pye noted, rendered them vulnerable to the possibility of Chinese communist expansion. Against this background it was imperative for the United States to make use of the military forces of Third World states in addition to its own. The justification for this position was in the terms suggested earlier—namely, the special character of the military and their particularly warm rapport with American soldiers. Pye claimed that "on the basis of the professionalism of the classical military tradition and a warm personable approach, [American soldiers] have been able to achieve a degree of intimacy which has eluded our diplomats and our technicians of economic aid."[65] Skeptics were decried as naive and uninformed.[66] In an apparent effort to validate his argument in more persuasive terms, Pye pointed to the noncombat role that had been played by the military in U.S. history. The same rationale was offered by the Joint Chiefs of Staff in 1962.

Edward A. Shils was a candidate far less likely to use this kind of rationalization than was Pye, who wrote more frequently on the subject of the military and counterinsurgency. But Shils, a prominent sociologist who was actively involved in organizing conferences on Third World problems for the Congress for Cultural Freedom during the 1950s, joined in the campaign on the edification of the military. His pronouncements on "The Military in the Political Development of the New States" were similar to those of Pye, albeit written in a different style. Like Pye, Shils argued that the military was a caste apart. It was outside of the "circle of traditionality. Military organization has little to do with the structure of traditional society, from which it is set off by its technology, most of its ethos, its organization, and its training—all of which are either imported or follow foreign models."[67] From this, according to Shils, it followed that members of the military were not constrained by the pressures of such societies. They had the advantage of being active participants in communities moved by nationalist fervor but not bowed by outmoded traditions. They were, according to this account, secular in what were still largely religious societies. They were molded by military discipline, accepting of hierarchy and order, and therefore far more effective as organizers and political movers than many who held office and most who did not.

More concrete in its approach to the military role in foreign policy was the report of the MIT Center for International Studies on Third World change (1960). In it the coercive and manipulative aspects of the politicization of the military were readily conceded. Emphasis was on strategic considerations, the advantages of alliances between the military and the "'secular intelligentsia'—the economists and engineers and agronomists, the lawyers and administrators, the doctors and public health officers, the deans and professors, the 'communicators' who manage the flow of public news and views that no modernizing polity can do without."[68] The role of the military was thought to be indispensable, insofar as the ability of the civilian political elements to dispense with it was given little credence. As the authors of the report claimed, "Ultimately, if they are to make more than a short splash, the secular intelligentsia ally themselves with the military sector."[69] Arguing, in the same passage, on the basis of *realpolitik*, the planners endorsed the alliance on the ground that the military offered the "coercive power needed to maintain stability; the secular intelligentsia have the knowledge needed to effect change."

The value of such an alliance was discussed in another context some years later. In 1962 Princeton University held a conference on "internal wars" at which Pye, among others, gave a paper. Although attention was paid to the historical precedent for such wars, emphasis was on their contemporary implications—notably in the form of counterinsurgency warfare. The politicization of the military in programs of social and political change was less the theme of such analyses than the "art of controlling rebels who would destroy the prospects of democratic development and establish the rule of tyrants," as Pye declared.[70]

In book form, the MIT report to the Senate Foreign Relations Committee that appeared in 1962 under the title *The Emerging Nations* basically developed the same argument at greater length. The possibility of "internal wars" throughout the Third World was taken for granted. Their significance was unquestioned. Reflecting the stakes in the transformations of Third World societies in which the assumptions of instability and radicalization were anticipated developments, Millikan and Blackmer, editors of this text, underlined the importance of furthering sympathetic relations between the military and the peasantry. "The outcome of guerrilla operations often hinges on the sympathy and support of the peasantry, who have it in their power to deny information and supplies to either side." And describing what became the rationale for the Vietnam policy of "village hamlets," the authors noted that "the use of the military establishment in constructive enterprises at the village level can create close working links between the soldiers and the peasants."[71] Greater U.S. military aid and involvement were urged. Such aid was described as a means of combating "internal subversion by an armed minority supported by an outside power."[72] Intervention preserved independence and the stability of states, according to such interpretations.

In 1964 the Center for Research in Social Sciences became the channel for funding government resources into the study of the military in Third World change. The University of Chicago's Center for Social Organization Studies received the largest subcontract for a series of studies on military sociology.[73] Under the direction of Professor M. Janowitz, scholars produced an array of studies dealing with the role of the military in Latin America, Africa, the Middle East, and China.

Arising from the midst of the enthusiasm for this subject were dissenting voices among Political Development scholars, who offered different descriptions of the military. Hence, in a work by no means considered to be policy oriented (*Bureaucracy and Political Development*), the editor, J. LaPalombara, expressed a more skeptical tone. "It is fairly obvious, for example, that the specialists in destruction, the military, often enjoy a position of superior power precisely because they are technologically the most 'modern' element in the developing areas. To be sure, their power is often also owing to their control of troops and weapons, but they remain, nevertheless, among those groups more readily willing to accept change."[74]

Without viewing the military as "specialists in destruction," policy-oriented social scientists who wrote on the subject were eager not to appear to endorse militarism, even when they advocated the militarization of politics in the context of Development policies or when they justified military intervention. This position accounts for their occasional shifts in analysis or emphasis. Thus, a work such as *The Emerging Nations*, while virtually identical to the text presented by the same authors to the Senate Foreign Relations Committee in 1960, presented intervention in a different light in its book form.

In the text presented to the Senate hearings, the authors situated political and military intervention in the context of the new diplomatic order. How was it possible not to intervene, they asked, given the realities of different stages of development between advanced and Third World countries? In *The Emerging Nations*, the emphasis was on a different mode of explanation. Abstention from intervention was presented as a form of indifference. Although the new diplomatic order was still interpreted as the basis for redefining relations between states at different stages of technological development, the question regarding intervention was posed in moral terms: "Can the presumption of unconcern about internal developments in other nations be maintained?" the authors asked.[75] There was, they argued, a "new system of international affairs which can provide an acceptable basis for relationships among societies at radically different stages of development."[76] These relationships included an expanded role for the military—both of American origin and from the various Third World countries that were trained by U.S. forces.

Several years later the subject was raised in a somewhat altered form. Scholars questioned the effects of militarism and, more generally, "the whole process of the militarization of society as a result of increased activities by the armed forces in the political sector."[77] In the same passage, I. L. Horowitz challenged the proposition that the "civilianization of the military [was] a result of the interpenetration of military and civic activities." That position, advocated by Morris Janowitz, was part of an argument in which the author contrasted the absence of militarism in the United States and the West with its presence in "many 'societies' throughout the world seeking to become modern nation states."

One cannot ask too frequently why the military officers of the Western nation states and the United States in the nineteenth century did not decisively dominate their societies, as has been typical of many "societies" throughout the world seeking to become modern nation states. The history of the West is the history not only of the early emergence of the industrial forms of production and modern military institutions but also of the specialized civilian control of military institutions.[78]

One can argue, however, that support for the militarization of foreign policy and for the militarization of Development policies did little to encourage civilian control of the military in Third World states. This is not to place the blame for the ascendance of the military in various Third World states on such considerations alone; but where they have been politically significant, to ignore them appears disingenuous.

For a student of this period, that is, the 1950s and 1960s, the increased support for conventional and unconventional forces, such as internal security forces, must be taken into consideration. Under the Kennedy administration, as indicated earlier, counterinsurgency assumed a more important role in the context of military programs in the Third World.[79] Particularly true for Southeast Asia, it reached its apogee in the course of the Vietnam War. With the Nixon doctrine, the approach was generalized. Military aid increased "from an average of $2.4 billion per year during the Kennedy and Johnson administrations to approximately $4 billion annually during the Nixon era."[80] In accordance with the Nixon doctrine, such aid was designed to increase the forces available to surrogate states in regions of particular importance to U.S. policy. The political effects of such aid, both internally and regionally, were neither disguised nor denied.

On the academic front, in certain works about political change written by policy-oriented analysts, the militarization of politics was decried as an unfortunate characteristic of Third World regimes at the same time that the effect of U.S. military aid and intervention was deemed to be of no consequence. In a work such as *Political Order in Changing Societies* (1968), both themes were evident. The militarization of Third World regimes was identified as a sign of the "decline in political order, an undermining of authority, effectiveness, and legitimacy of government."[81] This dismal condition was attributed to mismanagement and, more emphatically, to the politicization of all aspects of national life—a trait of so-called praetorian regimes. Military intervention in politics was described as

> only one specific manifestation of a broader phenomenon in under-developed societies: the general politicization of social forces and institutions. In such societies, politics lacks autonomy, complexity, coherence, and adaptability. All sorts of social forces and groups become directly engaged in general politics. Countries which have political armies also have political clergies, political universities, political bureaucracies, political labor unions, and political corporations. Society as a whole is out of joint, not just the military.[82]

In such interpretations, increased military aid, training, and intervention in politics to which the U.S. policy contributed was viewed as being of marginal importance. There was no "convincing evidence," according to Huntington, "of a correlation between the American military aid and military involvement in politics."[83] Such aid, far from being considered essential or relevant to such results, was set aside as being "politically sterile." It was said to "neither encourage nor reduce the tendencies of military officers to play a political role." The same position was advocated in a later work on postwar U.S. foreign policy, in which the extension of U.S. power was compared to the absence of its extension of sovereignty.[84] Vietnam was the notable exception, according to this account. Otherwise, "the bulk of U.S. government interventions—the military, economic, and political—in the domestic politics of Third World states after World War II have been relatively discreet, ad hoc efforts to maintain or to restore previously existing access conditions for U.S.-based transnational organizations. . . ."[85]

The contrast between Huntington's apology and official statements of policy is instructive. It suggests the need for a subtle understanding of the transmission process to which policy scientists contributed in their rationalization of policy. Reference to a single case illustrates the point, although it in no way provides the extensive evidence available to document this contrast. "A Report to the National Security Council by the National Security Council Planning Board on United States Policy Toward Iran" (NSC 175, issued on December 21, 1953) presented a different rationale for military aid to Iran. Far from undermining its political importance, the authors explicitly defended such aid for political reasons. As they further argued, "military aid to Iran has great political importance apart from its military impact. Over the long term, the most effective instrument for maintaining Iran's orientation toward the West is the monarch, which in turn has the Army as its only real source of power. U.S. military aid serves to improve Army morale, cement Army loyalty to the shah, and thus consolidate the present regime and provide some assurance that Iran's current orientation toward the West will be perpetuated."

The Map of Third World Change: Politics and the Transition Process

At the root of discussions about military intervention and Development was a map of Third World states in transition and an assessment of the policy implications of such movement. By the early 1960s the elements of such a map existed. Among the cartographers were policy scientists associated with the Center for International Studies at MIT who helped to shape the official and academic discourse on Development.

According to their major report on the economic, social, and political dimensions of Third World change, which was presented at the Senate Foreign Relations Committee hearings on foreign assistance (1960), an interpretation of Third World Development emerged that reflected the views of participant specialists as well as those of policymakers. Modernization was defined as "the basic shift to urban and industrial life."[86] Such transformation was viewed as a function of political elites, the presence of entrepreneurs and the appropriate psychological climate. Those societies defined as "traditional" were described as virtually condemned to a "kind of long-run fatalism."[87] In such instances, change would be the product of external pressure, "physical intrusion, economic example, and the communication of skills and ideas. . . ."[88] Resistance to change would have to be overcome in "human attitudes, politics, economic, social structure."[89]

Three categories of states were identified in this process, albeit at different stages and with different problems. There were " 'traditionalist oligarchies,' 'modernizing oligarchies,' and 'potentially democratic societies.'"[90] In the first category, transformation of a rural-based, agricultural society was linked to land reform as well as agricultural development. In the second, "the basic issue is the adaptation of institutions of Western origin to local conditions."[91] Or, more accurately, the absence of adaptation was explained in terms of the inadequacy of existing political institutions and the fragility of state structures. Conditions such as these were important to the consideration of a subject paramount in discussions of Development among academic specialists: the question of participation. Moreover, in this second category of societies, according to the authors of this review, "there are potentially dangerous trends toward disintegration. If they are to be halted, and gradual process begun toward stabilization and the establishment of effective democratic procedures, certain crucial problems will have to be tackled with skill and energy."[92] These included problems associated with state formation, the establishment of bureaucratic structures, political institutions and the identification of legitimate channels of participation.[93] Thus, "the rationale and purpose of local welfare and improvement programs should not only be to bring the urban elite and rural masses into meaningful political relationship but also to give citizens some sense of the role of their own initiative and individual participation in promoting the development of the nation as a whole."[94]

Although more advanced, societies classified in the third category raised the greatest concern. They illustrated the primary fear of policy analysts, the nature of their political character and course. Here, it was alleged, was the choice between communism and democracy, "more sharply posed in these societies than in societies in a more traditional stage of politics. Traditional values and institutions have already been deeply eroded, and the success of the modern sector is therefore even more crucial to stability."[95] Safe passage from one stage to another was the dangerous phase. And in a departure from the analyses of Political Development scholars who seldom attended to economic issues, the authors of this text identified the key to political change as "the relationship between economic progress and political change. Modernization of the economic is likely to have consequences for politics as well."[96] Among the objectives that "modernization of the economic" accomplished was the broadening of the popular base directly implicated in pressures for increased political participation. Herein lay a clue to the danger, according to such interpretations. The rate of change was linked to its destabilizing effects. And pressure for rapid change was viewed as one of the characteristics of Third World states impatient to achieve political as well as economic reforms. "In this desire for rapid progress lies the danger that the effect of mass media will be to increase popular desires and demands faster than they can be satisfied by economic and social growth."[97] Such was among the risks "posed by the very nature of democracy."[98]

In part description and prescription, the MIT report offered a digest of the views of Development specialists in keeping with broad policy formulations of Development programs. It identified the direction and instruments and dangers of change in a manner that reproduced the interpretations of specialists and then proceeded to disseminate them in policy-oriented as well as academic circles. Political Development and Modernization as state building, the role of political elites, the emphasis on entrepreneurs and their role in capitalist development, and the dangers of popular participation subsequently dominated the academic literature much as it did policy analyses of Third World change. An example of the deliberations to which some of these interpretations led was disclosed some years later in another event in which some of the same participants were involved.

In 1968, Max Millikan and Lucian Pye served respectively as chairman and cochairman of a "Conference on the Implementation of Title IX of the Foreign Assistance Act of 1961." The passage of this legislation in 1966 was considered a high point in congressional support for a liberal interpretation of Development. Popular participation in promoting social and economic change was given major endorsement.[99] There was a call for increased public participation "in the task of economic development on the part of the people in the developing countries through the encouragement of democratic private and governmental institutions."[100] Two years later, there was a general discussion of the implications of such a move. Participants included representatives of the State Department, the Agency for International Development, the Rand Corporation, the Brookings Institution, and a number of academic specialists on Development, under the direction of Chairmen Millikan and Pye. The reason for the conference was to consider congressional complaints to the effect that the lack of participation in economic aid programs acted as a "brake on economic growth," and did "little to cure the basic causes of social and political instability which pose a constant threat to the gains being achieved on economic fronts."[101]

There was no formal disagreement with the tone of such remarks. According to conference proceedings, "the United States can afford to see greatly widened political and social participation stimulated, in part, by American participation in the process."[102] There was a commitment to "democratic social and political trends in recipient countries."[103] Evoking the "American dream of the good society," conference participants praised its defense of the common people as opposed to governing elites. In this vision, described as "more populist than elitist," it was the people who made "decisions concerning their fate, rather than, as in the Platonic vision, relying on the decisions of a wise elite. That basic faith, always endemic in Americans, has been revitalized in recent years as Americans have sought to reshape their own society."[104]

Just how such a vision was interpreted became clear in the course of conference discussion. Support for participation in the context of Third World Development was a product of calculations based on strategic and economic interest. The explanation offered, however, was given in other terms. Support for democratic participation, for example, was described as a valuable goal but by no means one held by peoples or governments the world over. To insist on it was viewed as a form of ethnocentrism. The argument was repeated in a volume published in the same year by Pye entitled *Aspects of Political Development* (1966), in which the connection between democracy and Development was explored. To avoid the charge of ethnocentrism, conference participants argued that economic assistance was not to be linked with democratic change. There was no reason to assume "that people in all cultures are equally anxious to participate in public decision making and the choice of those who rule them."[105]

The self-serving aspect of the argument was apparent in the discussion of participation and foreign policy.

Our general interests will usually be served if other political societies are more open, if there is more freedom of movement and economic activity and cultural and intellectual exchange across frontiers. But we should recognize that increased political "participation" may subject regimes to domestic political pressures which lead them to adopt policies counter to long-run US interests. More democratic practices may facilitate the rise to power of groups which feel US foreign policy or private economic activity abroad is opposed to their own best interests.[106]

Where the United States was believed to have important strategic interests, there was the advantage of possibly exercising influence in the direction of democratic change. But there was the corresponding reluctance to apply such pressures lest they undermine the interests involved. In such situations, the conferees maintained, U.S. influence "is often limited by US economic interests which will not want us to 'rock the boat,' unless State/AID and these interests come to a consensus regarding the long-run implications to these interests if politico-social conditions remain the same."[107]

Another kind of argument was marshaled to support the same position. This time, the relationship of economic growth to uneven development was cited as a feature with desirable characteristics.[108] "The point here is that the increased inequality of income is often a necessary concomitant of development (or at least of a stage of development) and therefore desirable. To prevent it would inhibit development. The short-run Title IX interest should not, perhaps, be weighed as equal to the long-run growth interest."[109] Governments might consider other means of dealing with the social effects of change, including the creation of more employment opportunities, according to conference discussants. In other words, increased popular participation, although applauded as a characteristic of democratic societies, was viewed as endangering the politics and policies of Third World states. Further, although the relationship of participation to economic change was readily conceded, the conditions making for participatory demands were assessed as integral elements of economic growth whose social and political consequences were open to different forms of treatment.

To shield the audience from the implications of such an outlook, the argument was clothed in such a way as to be deceptive. Tolerance for nondemocratic states, for nonrecognition of participation, was supported in terms of a liberal appreciation for pluralist systems. "Emphasis on economic development tends to stress certain presumed universal criteria and permits less capacity for accommodating to local conditions."[110] Accommodating such conditions meant that "senior officials in AID, State and the Congress must be prepared to accept the idea that among the underdeveloped nations there will be a multitude of patterns of development and that we cannot expect to urge upon them any single model for their course of political development."[111] The Jeffersonian model was not relevant to all states, the discussants maintained.[112] Instead, an argument for what was considered a more "relativistic view of the goals of development" was espoused. Respecting the integrity of states meant not imposing "certain abstract economic criteria that seem to come from our ethnocentric views about economics."[113] In the same manner, there was to be no imposition of views about the social or political aspects of Development, according to the conference delegates. As a result of such abstention, whatever congressional support for democratic support existed, would be contained.

Discussions such as those that transpired among participants in the conference on Title IX indicated how far the interpretation of Development had come from earlier official pronouncements on the subject. An apologetic for nonsupport of participation at those times when its implementation carried policy risks, the view of Development implicit in deliberations on Title IX formally associated it both with support for democratic political change in Third World states and with the pursuit of economic and strategic interests by the United States. As policy scientists and academic specialists of Political Development interpreted the policy and process, however, its contours changed. Those concerned primarily with the political aspects of overall societal transformation sidestepped its programmatic connection with economic change. The explanatory bias in such discussions applied to interpretations produced by the more theoretically inclined scholars as well as by those committed to empirical studies of political change.

5

Defining the Parameters of Discourse

Disenchantment and the Roots of Domestic Consensus

How can one explain the selective memory about Development that emerged in the writings of scholars more attentive to its historical than its programmatic origins? How can one make sense of the amnesia that seemed to grip those who waxed eloquent about the benefits of "modernity" but were unprepared to confront its socioeconomic roots? The art of this kind of forgetting was carefully tended. The product neither of foreign policy interests nor Development policies alone, its sources lie elsewhere. The bias that affected the interpretation of Political Development, apparent in the discussion of some policy scientists (as the previous chapter has shown), was more than an expression of specialized interest on the part of those concerned with Political as opposed to Economic Development. It conveyed a view of politics and society that constituted another intermediary step in the definition of conventional interpretations of Development. According to this view, the socioeconomic origins of Development were subordinated to its political dimensions. And these were expressed largely in cold war terms.

This time, it was not policy scientists who took the lead. Those who crafted the language in which Political Development studies were to be discussed were the cold war intellectuals. Their concerns, however, were not primarily about the Third World but about the First. Their interest was not in matters of Development but in questions of cold war politics. Their formative experiences were set in recent European and U.S. history. It was Naziism and Stalinism, and the conservative interpretation of their social and political origins, that were at the root of their view of the danger of radical politics. Seizing on the long and bleak period of Europe's postwar crises and committed to the maintenance of U.S. hegemony, the cold war intellectuals championed the ideology of the "end of ideology."

Unlike policy scientists who addressed congressional committees dealing with foreign assistance, or who wrote on questions of intervention and counterinsurgency, the militant intellectuals took their stand before a different public. They published their views in journals not restricted to academic or policymaking circles. Implicit in their views was a polemical defense of the existing order as well as an intellectual strategy designed to reproduce it. Both were evident in the debates on McCarthyism, in the mobilization of intellectuals associated with the Congress for Cultural Freedom, and in the wide-ranging discussions on mass culture and society, in which many of the cold war intellectuals participated.

Out of this defense and strategizing came the political language that influenced the analysis of social change common to Development studies. To a large extent the general ambience in which Development studies emerged encouraged this transfer. But the process was aided by intellectuals who played significant roles in both circles, ideologues of the cold war as well as founders of Political Development. The place of E. A. Shils, for example, was paramount in this connection. He was involved in the analysis of McCarthyism, in the organization of Congress for Cultural Freedom conferences, and in the great debate on mass culture and society. At first glance, none of these events appears to have any relevance to the discourse on Third World Development. In practice, however, they served as vehicles that shaped the course of Political Development studies and its prevailing views of politics and change.

Popular myth has it that the domestic climate of the 1950s was one of contentment with the nation and its place in the world. According to exponents of this view, the expansive phase of American capitalism offered proof of the "exceptionalism" of American experience. Those who held this position argued that the American case demonstrated the possibility of achieving economic growth through capitalism without conflict or class war. Some writers related the so-called decade of contentment to the "open-ended prosperity and the return to the homilies of family, education, and Eisenhower."[1] For others, "the middle and late 1950s were predominantly years of complacency. After the bitter divisions over McCarthyism and the Korean War in the early 1950s, Eisenhower achieved in actuality what he said he wanted to achieve: 'an atmosphere of greater serenity and mutual confidence. . . .' The prevailing atmosphere was one of contentment and satisfaction."[2]

Not everyone agreed. A contemporary recalled the decade as one of disillusionment and cynicism.[3] And a recent study of the Eisenhower years has overturned conventional interpretations of this "long and trivialized" era.[4] Why and how such interpretations were perpetuated are questions that go beyond the subject of this study. But part of what Blanche Cook considered to be the "divided legacy" of the Eisenhower years is relevant to the interpretations of Political Development that surfaced in the same period. The conviction that the United States stood at the crossroads, its future to be determined by competition with the Soviet Union in the Third World, had a direct impact on the analysis of Development. And, as earlier discussion has suggested, there was a substantial difference between the attitude toward Economic Development supported by those who argued in terms of domestic as well as foreign economic needs and that of those opposed to its rationalization in cold war terms. Both were evident in the discussions of Development policies.

Between the end of World War II and the decade of the 1950s, a succession of events intensified the fear of communist and Soviet expansion. Interpretation of these events in this light took on alarming implications. To cite some of these: In 1946, the Canadian spy ring was exposed. Two years later Elizabeth Bentley and Whittaker Chambers launched a number of public exposes of alleged communist espionage. Challenged, the accusations nevertheless spread fear. Alger Hiss was indicted for perjury. The Rosenbergs were tried and executed as traitors. Abroad, other developments heightened the fear of Soviet and communist power. In 1948 there was the blockade of Berlin. Toward the end of the same year communists seized power in Czechoslovakia, and following events in Poland and Hungary, the area became a zone of Soviet control. In 1949 China "fell." In the same year the Soviet Union exploded an atomic device. And in 1950 there was war in Korea. Cumulatively, these events were interpreted as warning signals and as confirmations of the continuing struggle between East and West. At home, a fervent anticommunist climate had its own repercussions. Between 1951 and 1954 the inquisitorial atmosphere generated by McCarthy and his supporters left a trail of bitterness and destruction.[5] In 1951, the Senate Internal Subcommittee chaired by Senator McCarran rivaled the activities of the House Un-American Activities Committee.

Intellectuals were not spared in this process. They proved to be as vulnerable as others, though working in what some considered to be the safe havens of university life. In practice, the extent of collaboration, the intensity of intimidation, and the penalty of resistance affected intellectuals as much as it did others.[6] Left-wing intellectuals were viewed as suspect by liberals who condemned McCarthyism. Their support for radical movements was denounced as symptomatic of a more serious political naivete. The approach was exported to intellectuals outside of the United States, as in the discussions organized by the Congress for Cultural Freedom, at which the intellectuals were exhorted to mobilize against the communist satan.

Out of this period came a reaffirmation of the politics of the "vital center" and an interpretation of the responsibility of intellectuals in conformist terms. The former notion, with its tendency to assimilate extremes of left and right, was not an innovation of the McCarthy period. Earlier, such leading thinkers as John Dewey, Arthur Bentley, and Sidney Hook, among others, upheld similar views.[7] After World War II the position surfaced once more. In *The Vital Center*, Arthur Schlesinger, Jr., argued that left-wing intellectuals were politically naive, unrepentant in their attitude toward communism, the Soviet Union, and other expressions of radical politics. Although parties of the right had been exposed in the course of World War II, Schlesinger argued, the same had not been true of left parties. Only the crisis that followed the death of Stalin exposed the nature of Soviet politics and the bankruptcy of left-wing parties supporting it, he claimed. Contemporary politics, in consequence, needed a new orientation. With the demystification of the left now complete, the emergence of a sober "vital center" was long overdue. Schlesinger found considerable support for his position among liberal intellectuals, particularly those who believed that the time had come to do away with "Utopian illusions and heady expectations."[8]

Wide-ranging interviews with intellectuals on the nature of American culture and society, published in *Partisan Review* in the early 1950s, supported the same outlook.[9] Although some questioned the proposition that the United States was tolerant of dissident intellectuals,[10] others agreed that intellectuals were politically simple-minded. They had not come to grips with the realities of the cold war, according to James Burnham.[11] C. W. Mills, representing a minority point of view, asked the editors to explain the apparent shift they were describing in American society. Why, he asked, "don't you want to ask from what and to what the shift has occurred? From a political and critical orientation toward life and letters to a shrinking deference to the status quo; often to a soft and anxious compliance, and always a synthetic, feeble search to justify this intellectual conduct, without searching for alternatives, and sometimes without even political good sense."[12] Philip Rahv, another participant in and editor of *Partisan Review*, pointed to the disenchantment of the intellectuals who had abandoned their political commitment and, with it, their passions and hopes. Against this background, he warned, a neophilistine type would emerge, the product of the "defensive reaction to Communism, which, if unchecked by the revival of the critical spirit, threatens to submerge the tradition of dissent in American writing."[13]

Neither the critical questioning of a C. W. Mills nor the warning of a Rahv was typical of the intellectual climate that prevailed in this circle. And, parenthetically, neither one spoke the political language that was to be so readily accepted by students of Political Development. In this milieu it was the outlook of a James Burnham that was more representative. Consumed by cold war rhetoric, Burnham provided a disparaging view of European intellectuals critical of what they termed the "Coca Cola civilization." Admittedly, Burnham explained, "culturally we remain what we have been: a 'semi-barbarian superstate of the periphery,' dependent still on the older spiritual soil in spite of new roots, with Rome and not Athens the potential form of the future."[14] This concession led not to self-criticism but to a call for a greater "realism" among intellectuals. In Burnham's terms this meant facing the realities of U.S. hegemony and rallying to its support at all costs.

One year earlier, Burnham made the same appeal to an audience of Indian intellectuals under the sponsorship of a local affiliate of the Congress for Cultural Freedom. The event was of more than passing interest from the perspective of Development studies. It was in such meetings held throughout the Third World as well as in Europe that the mobilization of anticommunist intellectuals was pursued. In the Third World such conferences provided occasions to consider the relative importance of intellectuals and their political roles. It also provided the organizers of such conferences with the opportunity to reflect on the challenge represented by Third World societies in change. The results of the conferences directly affected the conventional interpretation of Third World Development.

G. Almond and E. A. Shils on Some Lessons of the 1950s

Among those who attacked the issues debated by cold war intellectuals were two figures of particular importance in the study of Political Development. Both Gabriel Almond and Edward A. Shils, in very different works, drew similar conclusions about the lessons of the interwar years, the demise of Stalin, and the American experience with McCarthyism. Elements of both works affected their subsequent interpretations of political change, in the American context and, later, in that of the Third World. In the spectrum of contemporary intellectuals, Almond and Shils emerged both as adamant anticommunists and liberal critics of McCarthy. Suspicious of radical intellectuals, they were in agreement on their naivete and their alienation from the mainstream of American political life. But beyond these dimensions of their work, the two men differed in their approach.

The Appeals of Communism (1954), by Gabriel Almond, belongs to the literature on consensus and foreign policy discussed earlier. It is an interpretation of the subjective meaning of radical politics set in a canvas broader than that of individual experience. Almond was concerned to discover why individuals joined communist parties. Reviewing the conditions to be found in Europe and the United States, he concluded that social, cultural, and historical as well as political conditions affected the matter of political choice. Where communist parties were legal, their membership had a different caste than in the case of clandestine or even marginal parties. The contrast applied to Europe and the United States, in which regions, Almond argued, these conditions affected the nature of party membership. In the American context, to become a member of such a party was to place oneself outside the mainstream. Under such circumstances, Almond asked, why would people be drawn to party membership?

On the basis of files contributed by psychoanalysts, Almond elaborated an answer that drew heavily on psychological explanations. Party membership emerged as a form of personal and political deviance. Those who became members were viewed as misfits. Middle-class radicals were presented as maladjusted, prone to intellectualization of emotional problems, and given to an excessively moralistic view of politics. As Almond argued, those who "are under pressure to justify the expression of resentment in moral terms are more likely to be susceptible than those who cope with these problems through simpler forms of direct action such as the direct expression of resentment, or through physiological narcoses such as alcoholism and sexual promiscuity."[15] Others, in short, indulged in violence, sex, drink and sports—not mentioned here—as alternative expressions of discontent.

In another aspect of Almond's study, of particular interest to Development theories, the author linked radical political action with the stress of recent emigration. According to this argument, emigrants were generally adversely affected by the stresses of trying to adapt to new societies. As a result, they often misread the signs of their new social and political environment, falling back on responses that originated in their previous homelands. In this connection, Almond described them as resorting to the radical politics of their previous homes.

The question of emigration, or immigration, was relevant to studies of Third World change, as later discussion indicates. So was the question of stress identified with such moves. Social scientists drew varying conclusions from these experiences. Lerner (1958) considered the ability to imagine oneself in a dramatically different place a characteristic of those capable of becoming "modern." Deutsch (1961) regarded such phenomena in historical perspective and warned of the possibilities of "social mobilization." Pye (1962) made stress the center of his interpretation of the Burmese predicament in which the difficulties of transition were alleged to produce a kind of political immobilism.

Almond's conclusions pertained to the United States. It was here, he argued, that recent emigres, dislocated by their move and their inexperience with U.S. politics, were drawn to radical politics as an atavistic reaction. For his data he relied on documentation compiled by the attorney general for the Immigration and Naturalization Subcommittee of the Committee on the Judiciary of the U.S. Senate, in 1947. According to this material, "91.4 percent of the American party militants were either foreign born, first generation native born, or married to foreign stock. . . . Only 9 percent of the militants were native born or native stock, and married to native stock."[16]

In *The Torment of Secrecy,* Shils provided a different explanation of McCarthyism and the nature of intellectual participation in politics. Left-wing intellectuals were subject to bitter criticism, but neither the arguments of emotional stress nor indications of maladaptation were singled out as relevant.

There was no ambiguity as to where Shils stood on the question of McCarthyism. He considered it dangerous to "civil society." Pointing to the spurious legality of public hearings conducted by the Senate committee under McCarthy's direction, Shils denounced the mock loyalty and security programs that were approved as signs of congressional abdication of its responsibilities.[17] Neither communists nor fellow travelers, both of whom were roundly criticized, were described as threatening to American society. On the other hand, Shils did not refrain from scathing attacks on right-wing populism and its illegal tactics. The anticommunism of the 1950s, Shils maintained, was a revival of a nativist tradition that was xenophobic, isolationist, and populist in character. Americans who were suspicious of foreigners, Shils argued, were moved by a myriad of complex sentiments.[18] Those who were themselves of foreign extraction often exhibited contradictory sentiments about their own past.

Shils noted that there was a hierarchy of immigrant groups formed on the basis of the status of the country from which they came. That hierarchy was a reflection of a deeply rooted bias to be found in different sectors of American life. Working-class as well as middle-class Americans reflected its effects, according to Shils. It was obvious in their preference for things English as opposed to products coming from further east. Labor and immigration laws revealed the very same tendencies, Shils pointed out.

Although xenophobia was a factor relevant to Shils's portrait of American life, it was not the principal focus of his attack on McCarthyism and the intellectuals of the left. This latter group he found to be especially deserving of blame. The cold war had changed the international climate, Shils maintained, and it was time to recognize that the Soviet Union was the major threat to global peace. Intellectuals who had been members or supporters of left-wing parties were viewed by Shils as naive, ignorant, and, in some respects, a burden to their society. Evidence of their naivete and ignorance was found in the persistence of their mistaken views. The Depression, the Spanish Civil War, Naziism, Stalinism, should have educated the intellectuals, Shils argued. But in fact they were accused of misreading the nature of Soviet intentions as well as the nature of American political life. It was this last factor that made them a burden, in Shils' view. In search of legitimacy in a none-too-receptive environment, American intellectuals sought power without propriety.[19] They contributed to their own demise, Shils claimed, by allowing "themselves to be drawn into an alliance with communist extremism."[20] As a result, they contributed to the imposition of that alliance of conservative politicians and businessmen "with a band of moral desperadoes" that the United States was made to suffer under McCarthyism.[21]

The lesson of these years was one that Shils felt American intellectuals had not yet taken to heart. The dividing line in politics today was not between left and right, but "between pluralistic moderation and monomaniac extremism," he claimed.[22] In the context of Shils's analysis of McCarthyism, this statement was a call against the dangers of fundamentalist politics. It was a warning to those who supported the nativism that Shils saw endangering the fabric of American politics and society. The commitment to "pluralist moderation" in a different context, such as the Milan meeting of the Congress for Cultural Freedom where Shils had further elaborated its purpose, revealed other aspects of the term. In that light, it was not associated with tolerance and diversity so much as with political conformism.

The Congress for Cultural Freedom: Mission to the Third World

The Congress for Cultural Freedom was part of the international campaign to discredit left-wing politics among intellectuals. What has been ignored, however, was the impact of this campaign on the interpretation of Third World politics that gained credence among American intellectuals and social scientists in the 1950s and beyond. Yet Congress conferences proved of paramount importance in this regard. They provided the opportunity to discuss issues relevant to Third World change and, more pointedly, to elaborate a strategy through which to interpret them. In the process, the lessons of the 1950s, as understood by liberal anticommunists, were exported to Europe and the Third World where politically compatible intellectuals were invited to collaborate in a common effort. Among those active in this campaign were intellectuals and social scientists who later emerged in the front ranks of Development scholars, where the message was the same even though the medium differed.

As an organization, the Congress was based on the 1949 Association of Americans for Intellectual Freedom. Supported, it was later learned, by funding from the CIA, its membership was made up of a coalition of former radicals and liberals, most of whom were staunchly anticommunist.[23] The attempt to mobilize a response to left-wing intellectuals was not confined to the United States. Between 1950 and 1955 branches and affiliates were established in a number of countries, such as England, France, Germany, Italy, India, Japan, and Australia. Committees were set up in the Scandinavian countries and in Latin America; moreover, according to one source, there was to have been an Israeli branch as well.[24]

From its inception in Berlin in 1950, the ideological character of the Congress was unambiguous. Addresses delivered at the opening session by such participants as Raymond Aron, Arthur Koestler, Sidney Hook, Franz Borkenau, and James Burnham left little doubt as to the militantly anticommunist cast of the meetings. Not all Congress activities were overtly political, however. What began in 1950 as a fairly limited operation eventually grew to include activities of a social and cultural as well as a political kind. Moreover, as these activities expanded, the membership and the number of those who participated in its meetings on an ad hoc basis also expanded. The range of opinions, albeit within a predictable spectrum, increased, and with it, the dissatisfaction of some elements who felt that the purpose of the Congress was compromised by this kind of expansion and dissolution of militancy.

James Burnham was one of the discontented. He made his own views known in one of the early ventures of the Congress into the Third World, the conference held in India in 1951. Organized by an outspoken critic of Prime Minister Nehru, M. R. Masani, the Indian affiliate of the Congress ran into difficulty from the outset. The government barred its meeting in New Delhi, with the result that the session opened in Bombay.[25] There, according to a Paris publication of the Congress, seventy-eight delegates and sixty-two observers attended. Describing the conference as an opportunity "for confronting Eastern and Western points of view," the same text went on to note that although there was much criticism of the West, "there was no divergence in condemning unanimously all racial segregation, or in opposing the concentration camp system as a tragic violation of the dignity of man and a menace to the social foundation of all cultural freedom."[26]

Something less than an advocate of Indian independence prior to 1947, Burnham took a didactic approach to the Indian intellectuals in 1951.[27] He lectured them, along with their statesmen, on the threats posed by neutralism and communism, both of which, he argued, led to totalitarianism. Communism, according to Burnham, represented "the worst form of totalitarianism. . . . Not only is it the worst. Today, as the past six years have daily proved, communism is also the most powerful and immediate totalitarian threat, the present danger."[28] Left-wing intellectuals were accused of being weak on the subject, prone to accept the claims of those whom Burnham regarded as corrupt and evil.

Some years later, in the winter of 1955, M. R. Masani appeared as a member of the Executive Committee of the Congress giving the welcoming address at the Burma meeting in Rangoon. Under the theme of cultural freedom in Asia, the role of intellectuals, their relationship to communism, and "totalitarian threats to cultural freedom" were discussed.[29] Attention was also paid to noncultural matters, such as economic planning and its implications for democratic government. What Philip Hauser, one of the participants, stressed was the inimical relationship of planning to democracy—a formulation that was to be repeated in other Congress sessions, and notably in Milan, in the same year. As Hauser put it in Rangoon, "the challenge that confronts the free nations of Asia is that of demonstrating whether the freedoms can indeed be preserved, while economic planning is pursued in the interests of the welfare state."[30] Economic planning, from this point of view, precluded the preservation of freedom. So important did Congress members regard the question that it was included in the agenda of the forthcoming Milan meeting. As Masani announced, "the future of freedom" would be discussed on that occasion. In addition to serving as a "forum for the expression of diverse views in economics, sociology, and political philosophy," the Milan meetings, as Masani reminded his audience, would hold the vital matter of "economic progress in the underdeveloped countries" as a high priority.[31]

Milan is of special interest in terms of the relevance of Congress conferences to Third World politics. It was in Milan that the cultural cold war was aimed not only at European intellectuals but at Third World politicians and intellectuals as well. It was at Milan that some of the most active Congress organizers, such as Shils, articulated the concern with the political future of Third World movements and the imperative of dealing with them. As he wrote in his *Encounter* magazine summary of the Milan meetings, the objective was to get ahead "with the task of formulating more realistic and more inclusive ideas on the conditions of the free society."[32] Such ideas were expressed in terms that reappeared in *The Torment of Secrecy*. The new "realism" was based, according to Shils, on the assumption that the "once clear distinction between 'left' and 'right'" had all but disappeared.[33] Like Schlesinger in *The Vital Center*, Shils argued that the experience of the preceding thirty years demonstrated the essential similarity of left- and right-wing extremism. What then was to be done? And how was the political future to be conceived?

Raymond Aron dealt with the same issues, affirming a common position to the effect that "the underpinnings of the great ideological conflicts of the first part of this century had largely been pulled out."[34] Milan, from this perspective, was a celebration of the "end of ideological enthusiasm." It was, in Shils's terms, the time to take stock of a long-delayed political maturity that would, at last, replace the political naivete of earlier days. To that end, a number of papers dealing with "doctrinairism, fanaticism and ideological possession" were read.[35] Yet this celebration gave cause for worry. So successful had the defeat of "ideological enthusiasm" been, according to Shils, that the "atmosphere of a post-victory ball" dulled the sense of danger that Milan was meant to stimulate. The widespread feeling that "Communism had lost the battle of ideas with the West"[36] produced a lessening of tension, a diminution of "anxiety about Communist infiltration," that was regarded as inappropriate.[37]

What complacency existed did not survive the confrontation between participants on questions of Third World change and its relationship to economic growth and political freedom. Expectations were rudely altered, as Michael Polanyi observed upon reflecting on his own reactions.

I took it for granted at the time that the decisive problems of our age were those raised in Europe by Europeans. That we had only to resist victoriously and finally to overcome the explosive force of Moscow's Leninism, to regain the peaceful leadership of the world which had temporarily slipped from our hands. But the intervention made at this meeting by Asiatic, African, and South American delegates have [sic] made me realize that this perspective was altogether distorted.[38]

The intervention, according to Polanyi, was occasioned by the forced confrontation of the delegates with the "poverty of the areas held by the new Asiatic and African nations, and the instability of their public life."[39] Shils saw it somewhat differently. He pointed to the "economism of the Africans and Asians" as the crux of the problem. What Shils described as "economism" was the insistence on the part of some Third World delegates that economic change was a prerequisite to political development and that the West owed Third World, formerly colonized states, compensation. Neither position was acceptable. Both offended the ideological and political sensibilities of Congress organizers, provoking accusations of radicalism and irresponsibility.

Speakers addressing the subject of economic growth and political change, such as Eric da Costa, Arthur Lewis, and Bertrand de Jouvenel, emphasized different aspects of the problem. Lewis was "insistent on the need for strong measures which he thought fully compatible with political liberty and representative institutions in the newly sovereign states of Asia and Africa."[40] De Jouvenel took the position that "there was no short cut for the economically underdeveloped countries. They would have to go through an industrial revolution which, for the severity of life it inflicted on the people as consumers, would not be less painful than the industrial revolution in the West or the development of Soviet industry."[41] De Jouvenel's presentation disclosed one of the "subsidiary intentions of the Congress," namely, to persuade Third World intellectuals "that they should not think that, by renouncing the ample political liberties which they now enjoy, they will be able to make more rapid and better economic progress."[42]

The enjoyment of "ample political liberties" was by no means a universal condition in Third World states. But the conviction that economic planning would eliminate such liberties as existed was widely accepted among Congress partisans. And while none advocated the renunciation of political liberties, there were indeed some Third World delegates who championed the prospect of rapid and more effective economic progress. The reaction to this latter stance was transparent. Shils regarded the linkage of economic to political change as insupportable, rejecting the view that rich nations were in any way obligated "to provide economic aid to the poor countries."[43] Those present at Milan, Shils claimed, had "disavowed any sympathy for the idea that liberty rests on an economic basis. Not only were they anti-Marxist but they were opposed to the same line of thought when it emanated from the extreme liberals, who insisted that political liberty depended on a free market economy."[44] The proposition made a mockery of Development programs, admittedly not on the agenda at Milan. It also served to explain, however, the approach of those cold war intellectuals whose reading of Political Development divorced it from considerations of economic change.

Not everyone present at Milan agreed that relations between Western and Third World delegates had been well handled. Dwight Macdonald considered the meetings at Milan to have been a failure from this perspective. Third World delegates, he recalled, had not come to be lectured at. They had come to "find out what 'freedom' really meant to people with white skins—and to present to these cultural representatives of their present or former masters a list of complaints and grievances."[45] They wanted, Macdonald observed, to learn whether there existed a "minimum code of conduct in the West." They wanted to learn what Western democracy stood for.

Although his own description of Third World participants belied a certain europocentrism, in comparison to some of the other delegates, Macdonald seemed to be less out of tune with the meaning of the confrontation. For some of the organizers, at least, the following formula applied. "The imperatives of action specified the causes that were not acceptable, and they selected the causes that were. The most obvious of the possible causes of poverty that had to be excluded was the economic system."[46] Shils, for one, concluded that there was an obvious deficiency of political understanding among those who clashed, and particularly among Third World participants. "Problems of liberty"—these problems Shils believed were imperative to discuss.[47] "Our theories of liberty, of the relations between religion and progress, tradition and intellectual independence, must be thought out and formulated in such a way that they will do justice to the situations of the new countries of Asia and Africa and South America."[48] The bias implicit in Shils's proposal was the one that was to be reproduced in organizations of Third World conferences under Congress sponsorship. With few exceptions, these conferences emphasized culture and political institutions, as both obstacles and prerequisites to change.

Between 1957 and 1959, a succession of conferences was held that focused on diverse aspects of Third World Development. The first, a conference on economic growth that took place in Tokyo, was designed to "strengthen the democratic approach to economic growth and to have these by-products: 1. it will be widely publicized in Tokyo and have considerable importance in Japanese academic life where the need is large for an anti-Marxist thinking; and 2. it will contribute . . . to the strengthening of communication between Western and Eastern scholars."[49]

At Rhodes in the fall of 1958, and in Ibadan in the spring of 1959, political change was the primary focus. Shils was the moving force behind these meetings. He was "chairman of the seminar for most of its meetings" at Rhodes, where the decision was made to "have a series of discussions about representative government on political democracy in the new states of Asia and Africa."[50] At Ibadan, Shils played the same role. There, he was described as "one of the brain-trusters of the Congress for Cultural Freedom arranging the present series of international seminars on the general theme of 'Tradition and Change—Problems of Progress.'"[51] According to the associate professor of the Institute of African Studies at the University of Ghana, K. A. B. Jones-Quartey, Shils was instrumental in preparing many of the "subject outlines to which participants at these seminars direct their research and eventually the presentation of their papers."[52] Forty intellectuals attended the Rhodes meeting, according to a published review of the proceedings. Some of those present came from Latin America and Asia to "ponder the problems of 'Representative Government and Public Liberties' in the new states of Asia and Africa."[53] Participants included De Jouvenel, Gaitskell, Mehta, and Shils, the last two acting as secretaries of the proceedings. There were a number of departures from the emphasis on political institutions and cultural traditions. Attention was paid to problems of the transition from preindustrial to industrialized societies. And, on occasion, radical critics attacked Congress orthodoxy with respect to questions of social change. The director of the Gokhale Institute of Politics and Economics at Poona, India, for instance, emphasized the social consequences of economic change in urban areas where there was a "concentration of wealth and power . . . and proletarian mass society grows apace in number."[54] In such circumstances, as D. R. Gadgil remarked, the need was for urgent social programs that the powerful opposed. The call for "economic liberty" in support of private enterprise and free initiative often masked opposition to social change, according to Gadgil.[55] Reversing the line of argument expounded by Shils at Milan, Gadgil concluded his address with the reminder

that democratic forms have meaning only when there exists in society a basic minimum national level in education and when conditions of economic security and living are such that men do not have to worry about their survival. If this is agreed to, urgent implementation of the so-called "egalitarianism" programme in the new States is no more than an essential condition for the functioning of democracy and the preservation of public liberties.[56]

Shils, at Rhodes, acknowledged that "liberal democracy and economic progress seem to be sufficiently worthy objects of commitment, and there is no need to justify them before a competition whose claims command no respect."[57] But the accepted interpretation of "liberal democracy and economic progress" tolerated no relationship between the two issues, equally worthy of emphasis, save to confront the other kind of competition that hovered in the background of Congress discussions. At once pleased and apprehensive about how little attention was paid to the danger of communism, Shils turned to another range of questions. The authority and legitimacy of the state interested him. The question of "whether a civil sense had developed which united the population into a nation" preoccupied him.[58] And there was reference to the so-called paradox of Rhodes, namely, the relationship between reform and stability—a theme that haunted some of the speakers and dominated discussions of Development programs and their academic translation.[59]

The meeting in Ibadan, according to Jones-Quartey, "afforded the first opportunity for a direct confrontation between French-speaking and English-speaking African intellectuals, academics, politicians, journalists, lawyers and others actively involved with the new problems, the strenuous commitments, of their respective countries."[60] The array of participants and observers ranged from political personalities, such as Patrice Lumumba,[61] to academic specialists who were to pioneer Development studies, such as David Apter and S. N. Eisenstadt, among others. That there should have been dissent on this occasion is hardly surprising.[62] Although Apter spoke about "the role of the political opposition in new nations,"[63] Eisenstadt lectured, in Parsonian terms, on "Patterns of Political Leadership and Support." What, Eisenstadt inquired, "are the elements in this process that can help in the development of autonomous social groupings and independent centres of prestige and power within the society, centres that are either organized according to modern criteria of universalism, specificity, and achievement, or have interests and points of view which can be mediated by proper elites?"[64] What a political figure such as Lumumba would have thought of the discussion of "proper elites" and "independent centres of prestige and power" has not been recorded in the proceedings of the conference. Others, however, raised objections to the condescending tone of some of the lecturers.

In fact, Shils's presentation prompted such objections. Focusing on West African intellectuals, their role in nation building, and the construction of a "political society" as one that incorporated a sense of "civic responsibility,"[65] Shils's approach evoked opposition. As one listener observed, the assumption underlying a presentation of this nature was that no such community of intellectuals existed, that guidance was needed to bring it into being.[66] Shils's comments on the nature of modernity, described in terms of a secular rationality, left little doubt about the prevailing interpretation of African political community, which did not conform to the social, economic, or political organization that was implied under the rubric of technological rationality.[67] And the concern with the excessive politicization of intellectuals—a recurring theme in contemporary analyses of political change—masked the criticism of dissident intellectuals. The gap, at Ibadan and Rhodes and other Third World conference sites, was not between foreigners and natives but between those holding radically different conceptions of politics and the legitimacy of political change.

If Congress meetings in and about the Third World were designed to instruct the natives in the art of government, Congress organizers themselves drew their own lessons from the experience. Although little, if any, attention has been paid to the relationship between conferences of the Congress for Cultural Freedom and the parallel organization of Political Development studies in the United States, the connection deserves consideration.

Different as they were, the environments of the Congress conferences and the more academic settings in which Development studies were launched reflected a similar approach to questions of Third World politics. Certain individuals, among them Shils, played a prominent role in both. Certain themes dominated the two centers of discussion: the emphasis on state and nation building, the role of political parties, pluralist associations, leadership and responsible oppositions, the dangers of excessive politicization, the fickle role that intellectuals could play in Third World societies, and the importance of culture as a determining factor in the transformative capacity of society. What emerged at Milan and in other Congress conferences, as in the meetings that were held in Chicago and Dobbs Ferry, New York, in the same period, was the possibility of applying the elitist interpretation of democratic theory to the analysis of Third World politics. Given that some of the principal figures interested in Development studies were also contributors to what critics referred to as the revisionist interpretation of democratic theory, there was little coincidence in the results.

During the same year in which the Congress conferences were held in Rhodes and Ibadan, there was an upsurge of interest in organizing Third World studies on university campuses and research centers in the United States. In 1958–1959, Shils and a number of his colleagues, including Apter, conceived the idea of establishing a Committee for the Comparative

Study of New Nations at the University of Chicago. In 1959, the Social Science Research Council Committee on Comparative Politics, under the chairmanship of Gabriel Almond, called an important meeting at Dobbs Ferry, New York. There, the approach to Political Development studies was hammered out. By 1959, according to Almond, the committee had become increasingly interested in "the theory and public policy aspects of processes of modernization."[68] For Dobbs Ferry, Shils prepared a working agenda composed on the basis of his paper entitled "Political Development in the New States." This he presented at the same meeting at which David Apter presented his own paper, "The Role of Traditionalism in the Political Modernization of Ghana and Uganda." Still others contributed papers that, in retrospect, turned out to be important stepping stones in the analysis of Development ("Key Texts" in Chapter 6 of this volume).

Meanwhile, at the University of Chicago, Shils and Apter, respectively, became the chairman and executive secretary of the Committee for the Comparative Study of New Nations. In 1960 the committee sponsored the publication of *Old Societies and New States*—coincidentally, the title of Shils's paper at Rhodes. Apter's description of the purpose of the committee built on the same themes as those described earlier—namely, the emphasis on nation building, the identification of relevant political and bureaucratic institutions, the importance of leadership and elites, and the fear of politicization among intellectuals and masses. Such politicization, linked to the movement of change itself, was viewed as that aspect of Third World Modernization uniquely responsible for widespread instability. As Apter wrote in *Old Societies and New States*, the "new nations" are involved in social and political transformations that have the effect of politicizing all aspects of life. "In this the new nations are different from most older and established nations. They are characterized by a singular urgency to get on with their tasks. The rapidity of such changes creates an element of social stress that poses questions related to more general social phenomena. Discontinuities appear in tradition, culture, social organization, and material standards and are being met by new cultural and political forms."[69]

The statement reflected not only certain interpretations heard in Congress sessions but also those that came to dominate the discourse on Political Development. The belief that Third World nations presented social scientists with a unique set of conditions was probably accurate. But these conditions were met with an approach to political change that was not at all novel. The association of change with stress, the rapidity of change with instability, and profound social change with discontinuities that rendered individuals "available" for unpredictable political actions echoed interpretations of mass society and the conservative statement of democratic theory. Thus, Apter's conclusion to the text cited earlier needs some modification. In his words, "The new nations present fresh political mechanisms, political beliefs, and social attitudes that are not only grist for the Third World social scientists' mill, but also deeply affect the future of us all."

That such developments would affect the future was a cardinal assumption of those who became theorists of Political Development. As for the "fresh political mechanisms" presented by Third World societies in transition, they were interpreted at Congress conferences in the same manner as in academic centers—that is, according to the conservative premises of the debate on mass society and democracy.

The Mass Society Debate and Its Implications for the Interpretation of Third World Politics

Throughout discussions at Berlin, Milan, and Dobbs Ferry, in exchanges between social scientists and political theorists on the meaning of democracy, the dangers of political change, and the risks of Third World development, a persistent theme kept reappearing: the question of mass society. On the surface it seemed unrelated to the activities of future theorists of Development. Their interests were focused on the complexities of analyzing Third World politics, though admittedly in a conservative framework that bore a good deal in common with prevailing interpretations of mass society and democracy. The connection, once identified, is apparent. Although it was based on a particular reading of European and American experience, the conservative interpretation of mass society influenced prevailing views of political change. The themes associated with Congress conferences, with the deliberations of Development theorists in the United States, reflected the currents of the mass society debate. And that debate affected the revisions introduced into the analysis of democratic theory, which further affected the formulation of theories of Political Development (as discussed in detail in the next section of this text).

In Milan, some of the major exponents of the conservative view of the mass society question presented papers. Shils applauded most of them. Indeed, he had a good deal to say on the question himself, as one of the more militant advocates of mass culture and society visa-vis its critics. To review some of the principal arguments in the debate on mass society, then, is hardly a detour to an irrelevant subject, from the point of view of the conventional interpretation of Third World change. To neglect these arguments, in fact, is to lose sight of the origins of positions advocated with respect to Third World politics that derived from the analysis of First World societies.

Although references to mass society generated intense controversy, there was little agreement about the meaning of the term. Was it a theory, a notion, an idea, a descriptive term, a fiction?[70] Daniel Bell thought the existence of a theory of mass society improbable.[71] Others obviously disagreed. But most of those involved in the debate seemed to know what it was they were defending and what it was they were against. From the outset, there was a deceptive air about the debate. Partisans of mass culture were the conservative critics of the critics of mass society. The former thus emerged as its erstwhile defenders. The critics, on the other hand, appeared to be intolerant with respect to some of its manifestations, whether in politics or the arts. When the debate on mass society was transferred to the analysis of Third World politics, the former defenders of mass society appeared to be its most adamant critics. In the context of the Third World, their arguments took a different turn.

Among the First World defenders of mass culture were such partisans as Shils, Bell, and Talcott Parsons, to name a few.[72] Among its critics were sociologists such as Seymour M. Lipset and William Kornhauser, with whom the former were in agreement on the question. Other critics, with whom both of the aforementioned groups were in discord, included intellectuals such as Theodor W. Adorno, Max Horkheimer, Herbert Marcuse, Leo Lowenthal, and Dwight Macdonald.[73] And then there were those considered to be the aristocratic critics of mass society, such as T. S. Eliot and Ortega y Gasset, clearly an oddly assorted collection of critics, if indiscreetly combined with the former. To construct such lists is sufficient to demonstrate the difficulty in generalizing about its members. Nonetheless, there were broad and significant differences that made sense of the groupings. These differences are not clarified by reference to mass society alone. The debate was not about a single or simple question. Rather, it concerned the nature of advanced industrialized capitalist societies, their social and political composition, their relationship with fascism. Those who were critics of mass society did not necessarily approach these questions from the same perspective, as the above names suggest. Where they differed was on the relationship of mass society to democracy.

Shils was a persistent advocate of the view that mass culture, a product of mass society, was an advertisement for the benefits of democracy and widespread literacy. He claimed that its critics were elitists in disguise.

Critics of mass culture, on the other hand, were convinced of its limits, although they explained these variously. For left-wing critics, culture was a social product, and mass culture was therefore an expression of mass society. Neither the producers nor the consumers of culture were free of the effects of market society values,[74] although doubt remained as to precisely how such values affected the arts, and critics differed among themselves on the question. The position the critics shared was that culture was a social product, incapable of being divorced from its surroundings.

For critics of the critics, it was not the position of the aristocratic writers and poets that counted but that of the left-wing intellectuals. The selection of those critics worthy of response was instructive. It demonstrated the extent to which the debate centered on the defense of capitalism and on a particular reading of its evolution.

In a series of polemical essays, Shils argued the case for mass society and against its critics in a manner that substantiated this position. He made it clear that he considered the Frankfurt School Marxists to be maladjusted Europeans who had not come to terms with life in the United States. Although committed, in principle, to the democratization of politics and culture, they were, according to Shils, unable to accept the realities of popular, democratic culture in the United States. "Whereas in Europe an educated person of the higher classes could, and even now still can, avoid awareness of the life of the majority of the population, this is impossible in the United States. What is a vague disdain in Europe must become an elaborate loathing in America."[75] The criticism of the critics veered into a general accusation of anti-Americanism. By contrast, what Shils offered appeared to be a eulogy of mass culture and society:

> The enhanced dignity of the mass—the belief that, in one way or another, vox populi, vox dei—is the source of the mass society. Both elites and the masses have received this into their judgment of themselves and the world; and, although they believe in much else and believe in this quite unequally, the maxim which locates the sacred in the mass of the population is the shaping force of the most recent developments in society.[76]

Those unable to appreciate this position were accused of harboring negative views, perverted hopes, "disappointed political prejudices, vague aspirations for an unrealizable ideal, resentment against American society, and at bottom, romanticism dressed up in the language of sociology, psychoanalysis, and existentialism."[77] The roots of such an ill-conceived romanticism were located in the writings of nineteenth-century social theorists. The cast was not minor: Tonnies, Durkheim, Weber, Sombart, Hegel, and Marx were among those identified. Critics who accepted their interpretations were viewed as modern malcontents, blind and alienated, and given to imposing their private ills on the social order. Some years earlier, in a contribution to a text cited in the previous chapter, Shils had indicated the kind of critique of modern society that he found acceptable. The contrast is revealing.

In a contribution to *The Policy Sciences* (1951), edited by Lasswell and Lerner, Shils talked of Elton Mayo and his positive analysis of capitalism. The regret, according to Shils, was that so few American sociologists saw things the same way. Mayo undermined the pessimistic critics of mass society by denying the historical transformations to which capitalist development had given rise, in Shils's reading. According to Mayo, there was no need for either class conflict or alienation. Both could be successfully managed in an intelligent and rational organization of labor. In this connection, Shils wrote, Mayo offered an alternative. He confronted the "anomic state of industrial relations within the factory and . . . the alienated primary group as a component element of modern anomie, without losing faith in the system.[78] In the same passage Shils noted that Mayo had developed a "theory of modern society which contrasts the 'traditional' with the 'adaptive society,'" in a manner that was reminiscent of Tonnies but without his pessimism. Workers could be taught to cooperate, to create noncoercive communism, to live free of conflict yet produce according to demand. The key, in this approach, was the correct management of workers. The approach found favor among industrial supporters of Taylorism who were less concerned with debating critics of mass society than in managing industrial production in a manner that threatened neither their profits nor their political vision.

Mayo's work confirmed Shils's view that capitalism need not result in alienation or anomie, that its adverse social consequences might be contained if not curtailed. In this light, the argument that late capitalism and the conditions leading to political movements such as fascism and Naziism were not unrelated met with scant approval. Shils rejected the proposition in its entirety. Critics falsely claimed, he maintained, that alienation and uprootedness contributed to the acceptance of Naziism.[79] But this, he continued, was as irresponsible an accusation as that mass society was responsible for cultural trivia.[80] Shils's answer was that fascism had triumphed, as in Germany, Italy, and Spain, where the masses had not yet entered the cultural mainstream.[81] In a less polemical mood some years later, Shils speculated that "Hitler was important to American sociology because National Socialism gave to sociologists a model of total society different from any conceived of previously—namely, the 'mass society.'"[82] The remark suggested a dramatically different view of the subject. But there was no reason to assume that it reflected a different interpretation of capitalism and its social consequences.

At Milan, in 1955, there were other presentations on the subject that Shils welcomed.[83] They included papers on the "end of ideology" and on the alleged authoritarianism of the working class. Like Shils, Daniel Bell agreed that "ambient ideas from European sociology" did not apply to the American case.[84] The application of the stock of "conventional class and mass theories, neo-Marxist in inspiration," did not fit the situation developing in the United States, according to Bell.[85] As he argued in the introduction to *The End of Ideology,* "politics today is not a reflex of any internal class divisions but is shaped by international events."[86] And these events, Bell maintained, had, in effect, "reworked the map of American society."[87] That society had to be evaluated in terms of the challenge "posed to Western—and now world—society over the last two hundred years: how, within the framework of freedom, to increase the living standards of the majority of people and at the same time maintain or raise cultural levels."[88] Unlike Shils, Bell did not categorically reject the social critique implicit in the works of mass society critics. He later recalled that what he had rejected was the claim that such a critique represented social reality. But in *The End of Ideology,* Bell took issue with the view that "mass society, because it cannot provide the individual's real participation in effective social groups, is particularly vulnerable to Communist penetration, and that the mass organization, because it is so unwieldy, is particularly susceptible to Communist penetration and manipulation."[89] How these views departed from the orthodoxy of Development theorists is discussed further on. Suffice it to note here that attention to the social roots of discontent undermined the tendency, common to conventional interpretations of Political Development, to make precisely the kinds of connections that Bell regarded as invalid.

On other occasions, Bell identified mass society with the end of traditional society, an interpretation closer to the interests of Development theorists. He noted that mass society had become a euphemism for the "shattering of the traditional primary group ties of family and local community. . . ."[90] In such circumstances, mass society came to symbolize the isolation of the individual. And Bell acknowledged that mass society and alienation came to refer to themes that were central to "critical judgments of the quality of life in modern society."[91] After World War II, the term was associated with "mass politics, the fear of passionate politics, a fear of what happened when the world is so disordered that there are no norms or rules."[92] Naziism was one source for this association; another, Bell remarked, was Stalinism, which was another particularly meaningful source for this association, for the Old Left.[93]

Among theorists of Political Development, it was the association of mass society with "mass politics," the fear of radical mass-based movements and their destabilization of the existing political order, that took priority. In this light, Shils's defense of capitalist development, with its eulogy of mass society, was ideologically compatible but intellectually irrelevant to the arguments pursued. The issue not of the benefits of mass society but of its dangers is what animated discussions of Third World politics. Nor were Bell's comments on the relevance of the mass society critique to "critical judgments of the quality of life in modern society" any more acceptable. To the extent that they sympathized with the critique of American society, they fell, once again, beyond the parameters of orthodox interpretations of political change. The argument in defense of the "end of ideology," on the other hand, found a ready and sympathetic audience among exponents of Political Development—and among the larger professional milieu of which they were a part. It was a thesis central to the arguments presented at Milan, where the obsolescence of ideological politics was heavily underscored. It was of capital importance in the views associated with arguments stemming from Schlesinger's interpretation of U.S. politics entitled *The Vital Center*, published some years earlier.

Interpretations of mass society that resonated with particular clarity in conventional analyses of Political Development were those that claimed to document the danger to democracy represented by popular participation. Works by Seymour Lipset (1960)[94] and William Kornhauser (1959) were frequently cited in this respect. Of the two, it was Kornhauser's *The Politics of Mass Society* that spoke directly to social and political transformations relevant to orthodox analyses of political change. It offered a psychological profile of actors in mass society, a graphic description of the nature and consequences of their political involvement, and a sociological sketch of the underlying conditions prompting such behavior. It takes little effort to make the transition from the application of these ideas to Western experience to their export in interpretations of Third World politics, according to the maxims of Development theorists, as demonstrated in the discussions that follow.

In distinguishing between so-called mass tendencies and pluralist tendencies—the former dangerous, the latter compatible with liberal democracy—Kornhauser proceeded to explain the conditions leading to the emergence of mass societies.[95] These were described as a function of "discontinuities," which were responsible for "long-run mass tendencies" as well as "short-run mass tendencies."[96] The resulting conditions accelerated social dislocation and political instability inimical to democracy.

Mass society, in this usage, was a process, a condition, and a political tendency. It was both a cause and an effect of social change. It was generated as a result of changes in which the relations between "elites and non-elites" were dramatically altered. Thus, when "elites are readily accessible to influence by non-elites and non-elites are readily accessible for mobilization by elites,"[97] the stability of political order explodes. Implicit in this position was the view that when "non-elites" gained power, they would dismantle or greatly weaken the mediating role of pluralist institutions, interest groups, and parties, such that the protection acquired by individuals in the context of liberal democratic states would be emasculated.

In a further expansion of the term, mass society was linked with signs of "mass behavior," and applied to the involvement of individuals in political movements who expressed concern with objects regarded as "remote from personal experience and daily life."[98] The emphasis was on the involvement in politics, more than on the concern for "remote" objects, which, as Kornhauser indicated, could include such things as national and international events as well as "abstract symbols, and whatever else is known only through the mass media."[99]

What applied to individuals was magnified in the case of mass-based movements. These movements, too, were criticized for their "remote and extreme" goals and for their predisposition toward activism.[100] Mass movements allegedly inspired "mass politics." The phrase summarized the dangers that were associated with mass behavior and mass movements: increased politicization and participation in politics, which were not confined to existing channels or institutions. In explaining his position, Kornhauser indicated that he had concentrated on conditions in the West that supported the emergence of mass politics, defining this as something that occurred "when large numbers of people engage in political activity outside of the procedures and rules instituted by a society to govern political action. Mass politics in democratic society therefore is anti-democratic, since it contravenes the constitutional order. The extreme case of mass politics is the totalitarian movement, notably communism and fascism. Less extreme examples of mass politics are McCarthyism and Poujadism."[101]

Kornhauser went on to explain that contemporary democratic systems were especially vulnerable to this form of politics since they encouraged participation. He also made it clear that he sought to identify the safeguards for the maintenance of the liberal democratic system in the face of such potential dangers. His approach, he argued, was an attempt to synthesize the various interpretations of mass society, not to support the view "that a theory of mass society necessarily is antagonistic to liberal democratic values, or that it is a prophecy of doom."[102] But in the hands of certain readers, the interpretation that defined political activism outside the established channels as inherently anticonstitutional and antidemocratic was capable of being used for precisely such an argument. The formula left little room for meaningful opposition. Adopting the legitimacy of existing regimes and systems as its starting point, it proscribed organized dissent and did so on the individual as well as the social and political levels.

Why should such interpretations have found favor among theorists of Political Development? Arguing from the same premises but directing their interpretations at Third World societies, where the phenomenon of mass society appeared to be more widespread, these theorists transposed aspects of the mass society debate that were compatible with their own conservative view of political change. Discussions that focused attention on the traumas of social change, while offering typologies of political behavior that identified dissent with deviance, served to discredit the individuals and movements involved. Such interpretations provided a rationale for the defense of elites and the existing order.

From this perspective, Shils's earlier defense of mass society against its critics appears to be at odds with his attack on the dangers of mass society in the Third World. Superficially it is, save that the object of Shils's defense was entirely compatible with the world view of conventional Development theorists. His remarks on Mayo attest to this. The fear of mass society was at bottom a fear of increased political participation. Mayo, in Shils's estimate, had found a solution to some of the problems generated by the same form of development that gave rise to the contemporary explosion of participation. Translated into political terms, the managerial approach to political change was precisely that which theorists of Development favored.

6

The Academic Translation:
Liberal Democratic Theory and
Interpretations of Political Development

Changes in Postwar American Political Science

The great debate on mass society, the fear it aroused, and the conviction it inspired that mass society endangered democracy affected interpretations of democratic theory in the decade of the 1950s and after. Controversies generated by the debate supported the move to reinterpret democracy in terms of a new "realism" and a new "political maturity." The results were apparent in public debates, such as those that occurred in conferences of the Congress for Cultural Freedom. They were apparent in other domains of intellectual activity as well. They emerged, for example, in the specialized language of political science, which directly affected the discourse on Political Development.

Theories of Political Development and, more generally, interpretations of Third World political change were based on contemporary theories of liberal democracy. They expressed the pessimistic mood about the relationship of mass society and democracy that dominated mainstream political theory. Critics of conventional theories of Political Development were aware of the implications of such an approach for the analysis of Third World societies.[1] Critics of mainstream political theory were aware of its impact on the analysis of American society.[2] Although there was active communication between some engaged in these critical inquiries, the task of documenting the evolution of Political Development studies within postwar political science fell to those conservative exponents of the genre. And those who functioned as the informal historians of Political Development, such as Almond (1956), Almond and Powell (1966, 1978), Almond and Verba (1963, 1980), and Pye (1966), as well as Huntington (1971) and Huntington and Dominguez (1975), were, with exceptions, largely indifferent and/or hostile to critical assessments of normative political theory.[3]

What changed in postwar political science in the United States? What effect did such change have on the evolution of Political Development? Without attempting anything more than an itemization of some of these developments, this chapter attempts to disclose their impact on the interpretation of political change.

As far back as World War I, there was a sense of discontent with the state of the discipline that moved some political scientists to act. According to critics of the field, political science had become exceedingly legalistic. Regarded as irrelevant to the practice of politics, it was considered to be out of touch with the very experience it was designed to explicate. Charles Merriam was one of those who expressed such views. That he influenced a number of scholars who, in turn, became influential within the milieu of Development theorists makes his response of particular interest. What Merriam advocated was an opening to other disciplines and a more empirical orientation. At work teaching in the University of Chicago, he was also involved in local politics. *New Aspects of Politics* (1925) reflected his thinking on the subject.[4] It set forth his recommendations for a political science that would integrate the complementary approaches of psychology, social psychology, and medicine. H. D. Lasswell was one of Merriam's students and collaborators who took the master's suggestions to heart. And there were others at the university and elsewhere in the country who were moved by the desire to experiment and broaden their perspective on the approach to political theory.

With the coming of World War II, the emigration of European social theorists and sociologists familiar with new modes of research affected American social science.[5] From the point of view of Political Development studies, it was the impact of behaviorism that was to be dominant and controversial. The field was defended as a comprehensive approach to the study of politics,[6] but its results proved otherwise. Behaviorism as an approach to political analysis masked the interpretation of the social roots of political action. Although political scientists in the vanguard of Political Development studies were among its most ardent advocates, they eventually came to question its effects.[7] But the questioning came too late to alter the approach to politics that the behavioral persuasion promoted. Moreover, that approach was encouraged by those who dominated the profession and who were in sensitive positions to influence research in the field.

Research foundations that altered the course of postwar American social science contributed to this as well as to other trends.[8] They were great movers on the academic scene, sensitive to the national interest in social science research and prepared to sponsor those believed to represent its most promising trends. By 1952, the Rockefeller Foundation and the Carnegie Corporation had contributed several million dollars to the creation of international studies centers throughout the country. As early as 1948, one of the most influential of such institutions from the point of view of Development studies, the Social Science Research Council (SSRC), turned to area studies considered to be "vital to national interests and to intercultural understanding."[9]

Several years later, in a major report on comparative politics (1953), the SSRC echoed the criticisms directed at contemporary political science, describing it as ethnocentric and formalistic.[10] The changes it recommended were those that appeared to be dramatic innovations at the time, including the study of comparative politics and the application of the behavioral approach to political analysis. Parenthetically, it may be added that the authors of the 1953 report outlined themes of research. Some of these themes surfaced in the study of Political Development, such as the question of legitimacy and consensus and the problem of state formation. Less conservative in its description of what was to be done and what was to be avoided than subsequent interpretations of Political Development, the SSRC report pointed to ways in which "coercion, conformity, and the loss of political ultimacy to some superior groups or persons" are justified.[11] Legitimacy was not to be confused with the "conditions of obedience,"[12] the authors warned, in what proved to be a prophetic remark given the prevalent interpretations of politics that perpetuated precisely such a mix.

Thoughout the 1950s and into the early 1960s, works that reflected the new directions in political science appeared. They dealt with the renewed interest in group theory, pluralism, and political parties; the nature of public opinion and the electorate; and the question of political elites, decision-making, and leadership. The focal point of these works was the functioning of the democratic political systems, interpreted according to a revised and conservative formula. Taking their inspiration from works such as A. F. Bentley's *The Process of Government* (1908), an active and prolific group of scholars turned to the task of redefining democratic theory. They included D. Truman (1951), R. Dahl (1956, 1961), R. Lane (1959), E. E. Schaatschneider (1960), V. O. Key (1961), G. Almond and S. Verba (1963), and G. Almond and B. Powell (1966).[13]

One critic described the general thrust of this literature as constituting an inquiry into "one of the oldest and hardiest arguments in traditional political theory: how should the subject be guaranteed against the State?"[14] But the general thrust of such an inquiry could more accurately be described in terms of another question: How were the state and its leaders to be protected against those aspiring to political participation? Advocates of political "realism," the new theorists of democracy justified their approach as a corrective of existing, obsolete interpretations of democracy. In this they were supported by the grand theorist of the revisionist approach, Joseph Schumpeter, whose work, *Capitalism, Socialism and Democracy* (1942), exercised a considerable influence on subsequent interpretations of democratic theory.

Schumpeter called for a revision of democratic theory that would align it more effectively with the practice of politics in liberal democratic states. He claimed that what previous democratic theorists had assumed with respect to participation, the electorate, and its leaders, was unfounded. A more "realistic" perspective was needed. As a result, a significant shift in interpretation occurred. The focus was less on the objectives of democratic systems than on the processes involved in their implementation. Attention was paid to institutions, electoral processes, to the nature of leadership, its decision-making skills, and prerogatives. Schumpeter argued that "the role of the people is to produce a government, or else an intermediary body which in turn will produce a national executive or government."[15] His definition of the "democratic method" followed suit. It included "that institutional arrangement for arriving at political decisions in which individuals acquire the power to decide by means of a competitive struggle for the people's vote." There was no evidence, Schumpeter claimed, that "'the people' hold a definite and rational opinion about every individual question. . . ."

A generation of political scientists, and their descendants, followed in the wake of Schumpeter's thesis. Studies of voting and public opinion illustrated the revised theses on democracy. The well-known work by Berelson, Lazarsfeld, and McPhee (1954) appeared to some to vindicate the "new look." Not the nature but the frequency of voting patterns led the authors to conclude that nonvoting was a significant phenomenon deserving of careful consideration.[16] Its meaning was heatedly debated.[17] According to some readers of the literature, nonvoting was a sign of apathy. Others claimed that it represented a positive indifference, a support for the existing system and its incumbents that made the right to vote a privilege unnecessary to practice. One of the keys to the revisionist interpretations of democratic theory was to be found in the proposition that nonvoting was a contribution to the efficient functioning of the democratic process.

Works such as *The Civic Culture* (1963) supported the conservative interpretation of *Voting* (1954). Such works argued, with respect both to the redefinition of democratic theory *and* to the analysis of Political Development, that nonvoting was a sign of the flawed expectations of classical democratic theory. Citizens in democratic societies seldom lived up to what the authors described as the "rationality-activist model." "They are not well informed, not deeply involved, not particularly active; and the process by which they come to their voting decision is anything but a process of rational calculation."[18] Voter indifference, ignorance, and apathy were read as supporting the need for a revision of current theories of democracy. Yet they led to interpretations in which the same passivity was regarded as a form of benign neglect. Moreover, passivity was not considered to be incompatible with the efficient functioning of democratic government.

Not all political theorists persuaded of the imperative of revising democratic theories were susceptible to such interpretations. E. E. Schaat-schneider dissented from this view. In *The Semisovereign People* (1960), a work that seems to have left no discernible trace of influence on the interpretations that were incorporated into theories of Political Development, Schaatschneider parted company with his more conservative colleagues. Far from considering nonvoting a matter of indifference or something to be endorsed, he insisted that its meaning was significant so far as democracy was concerned.

Nonvoting, Schaatschneider claimed, was a sign of discontent reflecting the "suppression of the options and alternatives" that were meaningful to nonparticipants.[19] If they stayed away from the polls, it was because nothing significant had been offered to them. The act of nonvoting was therefore a symbol of the alienation of this segment of the electorate, not a sign of its passive approval. Excluded from a game whose rules they had no part in setting, they made their positions known by refusing to participate. Labeling such indicators as signs of ignorance or indifference, Schaatschneider noted, was the means by which "the exclusion of the lower classes from any political system" had always been justified.[20]

The Response to the Elitist, Pluralist, Equilibrium Model

Critics of the new look in democratic theory argued that such an exclusionary policy was far from incidental. From the 1960s on, political scientists and theorists dissatisfied with the claims of revisionist theories debated their meaning.[21] They questioned the extent to which such theories could be considered democratic. With justification, these critics commented on the normative bias implicit in the revisionist-elitist approach. They identified its conditional interpretation of democracy,[22] its commitment to "democratic elitism."[23] Some questioned the implications of an "empirical theory of democracy,"[24] while others argued that it was basically irrelevant to liberal democratic systems as they actually operated.[25] Still others argued that the justification of the new look in terms of the obsolescence of a "classical theory of democracy" was self-serving. None such had ever been agreed upon.[26]

In 1963, Lukes and Duncan attempted to explain the conditions that gave rise to the revised interpretations of democracy. They referred to arguments that had, in fact, already been aired in Milan at the Congress for Cultural Freedom meetings. "The now familiar dichotomies between totalitarianism and liberal democracy, between positive and negative liberty, between 'utopianism' and piecemeal pragmatism, have achieved something like a stranglehold over political theorizing. No middle way is conceded between the concentration camp and a cautious conservatism."[27] The latter, they pointed out, was interpreted in a way that legitimated the power of the ruling elite while depicting the masses as endangering democracy.

Peter Bachrach, approaching the question from a different perspective, supported similar findings. He described revisionist theories as reflecting the "disenchantment with the common man," who was the real target of such theories.[28] There had been a veritable "revolt from the masses" Bachrach noted, and it was less the extension of democratic rights than the preservation of existing political systems that was the order of the day in such interpretations. Maintaining the existing equilibrium of political forces was indeed to be high on the agenda of revisionist interpretations of political change. In the same passage, Bachrach observed that "the political passivity of the great majority of the people is not regarded as an element of democratic malfunctioning, but on the contrary, as a necessary condition for allowing the creative functioning of the elite."

Carole Pateman questioned the repeated references to the existence of a single "classical theory of democracy." There was no such theory on which students of the subject agreed, she noted. "Rousseau, the two Mills and Bentham, all of whom have a good claim to the title of 'classical' theorist of democracy," in fact disagreed on the meaning of one of its central elements, the question of popular political participation.[29] Pateman's criticism was acknowledged in the 1980 follow-up to *The Civic Culture*, but it had obviously not substantially affected the prevailing interpretation of the subject.[30]

In a different vein, critics turned to the historic origins of current liberal democratic theories and to their reliance on an analogy with the "equilibrium-market concept."[31] Such an analogy assumed that entrepreneurs and consumers, translated into political terms, operated in "conditions of free competition in which all energies and resources were brought to the market, with the result that the market produced the optimum distribution of labour and capital and consumer goods."[32] But the view of politicians and parties as entrepreneurs, and voters as consumers, while it corresponded to a language current in political thinking, did not serve to explain the functioning of the political system. The approach was unsatisfactory as a guide to contemporary liberal democratic systems.

Its application raised more questions than it answered. In whose interest did the market function? Who determined what the proper equilibrium of forces should be in the political system, and from what perspective? What of those who were disadvantaged and marginalized by the system? What of the nonvoters, excluded but would-be participants who had come to be regarded as the dangerous disrupters of democratic order? Who, in effect, defined the normative bases on which such interpretations rested?* The questions have lost none of their relevance to judge by the continuing debate among political scientists, even in establishment circles of the profession.

Development Theorists and the Elitist Interpretations of Democracy

Where did theorists of Political Development stand with respect to what became the normative interpretation of democratic theory? Among those who included the principal architects of Political Development theories, the approach won support. Far from being sympathetic to its critics, theorists of Political Development were themselves instrumental in contributing to and propagating the theses of the new democracy. Their export of revisionist interpretations of democratic theory to the analysis of Third World Development was, after all, an indication of their belief in the universal validity of this approach to politics.

Historians of the field were positive about the changes that political science had undergone.[33] There were differences among them, nevertheless. Huntington took issue with important aspects of the new look, but in practice his interpretations of political change conformed to the prevailing view. Others, who did not play the role of historian or chronicler of the field but who wrote about the impact of contemporary trends in political science, such as LaPalombara and Rustow, were also somewhat disenchanted. LaPalombara, however, remained within the circle and ambience of conventional theorists. Almond, by contrast, gave unconditional support

---

* Some critics of Development studies nonetheless remained committed to the market approach, such as W. Ilchman and N. T. Uphoff, *The Political Economy of Change* (1969).

to the new look. With the exception of the self-criticism expressed in the retrospective essay written in conjunction with Genco (1977), Almond was and remained a staunch advocate of the new directions in postwar political science. What the article with Genco revealed was a sense of the limits of behaviorism and the scientific temptation among students of politics.

In a work such as *Comparative Politics*, Almond and Powell made the connection between trends in the discipline, its emphasis on empirical research, the behavioral approach, comparative politics, and the study of non-Western areas. Such a relationship was seen as complementary. The authors claimed that the pioneering study of non-Western areas allowed the political theorist to carry on "research in his particular area on aspects of politics which have significance for the general theory of political systems."[34] In addition, the movement toward greater realism and precision was seen as an advance meriting the greatest support. It was an expression of the ambition of political scientists to become more scientific, which had implications for the study of the non-Western world, according to the authors. After all, they noted, there had been a significant "diffusion of scientific and technological attitude(s) in Western society" that positively affected the production of knowledge.[35] Comparative politics might stimulate a comparable contribution. No skepticism was expressed about the limits of the "naturalistic interpretation" of empirical theory.[36] Its advantages were regarded as compelling.

Almond returned on other occasions to these themes and to their bearing on the study of Political Development. At the 1966 meeting of the American Political Science Association, Almond discussed the breakthroughs in political science.[37] He emphasized the import of empirical research and the historic significance of systems theory. Several years later, in a retrospective essay, Almond dealt with the origins of the interdisciplinary character of postwar political science.[38] He described the influence exercised by current trends in sociology, psychology, social psychology, and anthropology. He cited the role of such major theorists as Tonnies, Weber, Malinowski, and Radcliffe-Brown. The same theme was underlined in a more recent address before the Joint Seminar on Political Development of Harvard and MIT (October 26, 1983), where Almond spoke on "Comparative Politics and Political Development, an Historical Perspective."[39] On that occasion he added some more names to the litany of sources for Development studies. Maine and Marx were identified as additional referents for comparative politics and Development theories. (Pye, on an earlier occasion [1966], had included much the same set of social theorists.)

There was little dissent regarding the proposition that contemporary political science, and notably comparative politics and Development studies, represented the synthesis of an eclectic heritage. Not all contributors to the study of political change were in agreement as to its merits, however. Huntington (1971), LaPalombara (1966, 1968), and Rustow (1968, 1973) were among those insiders who were less than enthusiastic about the new trends and their impact on political analysis. In his article entitled "Decline of Ideology: A Dissent and an Interpretation" (1966), LaPalombara took issue with the uncritical support for the behavioral "revolution." It may have declined, LaPalombara observed, "but it has left in its wake both obscurantist criticisms of empiricism, on the one hand, and, on the other hand, an unquestioning belief in 'science.' Quite often the latter belief is not merely anti-historical and anti-philosophical but also uncritical about the extent to which empirical observations can be colored by the very orientation to values that one seeks to control in rigorous empirical research."[40] In another article on "Macrotheories and Microapplications in Comparative Politics," published two years later, LaPalombara joined those who were disenchanted with the direction of comparative politics.[41] The attempt to formulate grand theories, he argued, was an error. The influence of systems theorists and structural functionalists was not beneficial to the study of politics. On the contrary, claimed LaPalombara, these tendencies compounded the apolitical character of contemporary political science.

The same position was taken by Rustow in an analysis entitled "Modernization and Comparative Politics," published in the same issue of *Comparative Politics* in which LaPalombara's essay had appeared.[42] The two joined in the critical assessment of comparative politics, its status quo bias, its indebtedness to equilibrium models of social and political change.* Rustow did not spare the behavioral approach and its adepts, such as Almond. He charged that its adoption in political analyses had done little to contribute to an improved understanding of political change. Systems theory, group analysis, and structural functionalist approaches to socio-

---

* By 1973, Rustow's disenchantment with current trends in political science found expression in his address to the Pennsylvania State Political Science Association meeting. On April 7, 1973, Rustow spoke on "Political Science Old and New: Professional vs Social Obligation." He denounced the facile attempt at rendering political science more "scientific," the fact fetish to which a false empiricism led, and the apologetic nature of what passed for neutral, objective social science research. Rustow concluded his address with the statement that what American political science needed was "political scholars of the passion, dedication, imagination, and ruthless rationality and honesty of a Max Weber. And an ideal profession of political science would be one where a Marx could debate a Tocqueville under the chairmanship of a Weber."

political change were all preoccupied with equilibrium. And equilibrium did not enhance the analysis of political change.[43]

Rustow pointed to the weaknesses of Almond's functional approach, an approach that colored the dominant interpretation of Political Development as represented by the work of the Committee on Comparative Politics of the Social Science Research Council. LaPalombara had done much the same thing, from the perspective of a regular participant in the committee's work. His contribution to *Items*, the SSRC bulletin, written while he was rapporteur of the Committee on Comparative Politics in 1961, revealed the same critical, if discreetly expressed, view.[44]

A decade later, S. P. Huntington, in an essay widely regarded as a major summing up of comparative politics and its approach to political change, joined the dissenters.[45] Huntington was clearly skeptical of the benefits of interdisciplinary studies and, notably, of their effect on the analysis of politics. The stimulation of interdisciplinary work had had the effect of undermining the study of politics, Huntington argued. As for the emphasis on popular research techniques, such as "survey data, interviewing, and participant observation," they contributed to denigrating history, Huntington warned.[46] In spite of these criticisms, Huntington viewed the emergence of comparative politics as an important step. Its heterogeneous origins had had the effect of putting political science into harmony with trends common to the other social sciences. Thus, the observation that structural functionalism and equilibrium models "tended to parallel, supplement, and reinforce from other methodological directions the message of the consensus school."[47]

By the late 1970s the criticism of comparative politics, the excesses of the behavioral approach, and the ambition of political science to be scientific had become commonplace. If political scientists appear to have lagged behind sociologists and anthropologists in self-criticism, they nonetheless came to agree that the assumptions of earlier years required moderation. Almond and Genco (1977) made the same point in their article entitled "Clouds, Clocks and the Study of Politics," in which they admitted that "in its eagerness to become scientific, political science has in recent decades tended to lose contact with its ontological base."[48] Behaviorism, on the other hand, reflected "epistemological and methodological assumptions which it has taken from the hard sciences. . . ."[49] These borrowings were judged to be inappropriate. Almond and Genco's criticisms appeared in the late 1970s, at which time the trends they skeptically described were widespread.

The Case of The Civic Culture

It is difficult to exaggerate the influence of Almond and Verba's *The Civic Culture* in affecting the political language and character of Political Development studies. The work integrated the basic elements of the new look in political science. It also articulated their expression in the new approach to democratic theory. In short, *The Civic Culture* was an ambitious undertaking. Based on a survey of some five thousand respondents in England, Germany, Italy, Mexico, and the United States, it was designed to produce "a scientific study, under university auspices, of problems of democracy and political participation."[50] What it offered was something more, an illustration of the conservative thrust of the elitist approach, the pitfalls of a conformist interpretation of political participation, and the limits of a psychological and sociopsychological interpretation of political action.

Several aspects of the work deserve particular consideration in the present context, as they demonstrate the consequences of such an approach for the interpretation of political change. The "civic culture," according to the authors, was "neither traditional nor modern but partaking of both; a pluralistic culture based on communication and persuasion, a culture of consensus and diversity, a culture that permitted change but moderated it."[51] Its most advanced and successful historical examples were Great Britain, followed by the United States. Little was said of the Third World in this context, although the discussion of Italy and Mexico had something in common with subsequent analyses of Political Development in which Third World politics was viewed as underdeveloped.

Yet the authors of *The Civic Culture* were not indifferent to Third World states. They shared the global outlook of those who believed that this disparate region held the key to the future of East-West relations. It was in that connection that the political future of Third World nations was evoked. Such states, according to Almond and Verba, faced a difficult choice. They could turn either to democratic or to totalitarian systems. The former "offers the ordinary man the opportunity to take part in the political decision making process as an influential citizen; the totalitarian offers him the role of the 'participant subject.' Both modes have an appeal to the new nations, and which will win out—if indeed some amalgam of the two does not emerge—cannot be foretold."[52] They continued with a description of "the open polity and the civic culture—man's discovery of a humane and conservative way to handle social change and participation," described as a Western phenomenon that might not so easily be transferred to non-Western regions.[53] And then it was not clear, they noted, as to whether or not Third World regimes were so interested in acquiring this "humane and conservative way" of handling change. Some years later, Almond and Powell (1978) expressed a somewhat different view of the matter, but the underlying premises remained unchanged.[54]

What characterized *The Civic Culture* was not its particular reservations about Third World politics but its interpretation and recommendations with respect to political practice in the West. Situating the study in the framework of contemporary trends in political science, the authors proceeded to demonstrate their application. They acknowledged their debt to social psychology and the "'culture personality' or psychocultural approach to the study of political phenomena."[55] The interpretations of political culture and socialization bore witness. They indicated further support for the behavioral approach, similarly evident in the attempt to "relate specific adult political attitudes and behavioral propensities to the manifest and latent political socialization experiences of childhood."[56] Exponents of the school of "realism," they argued that its application to democratic theory would enhance its interpretation. As for their own investigation, the authors described their objective as including the analysis of "the kind of partisanship that is consistent with an effectively functioning stable democracy."[57]

Democracy, in turn, was defined in accordance with the prevailing Schumpeterian mode. "Democracy is a political system in which ordinary citizens exercise control over elites; and such control is legitimate; that is, it is supported by norms that are accepted by elites and non-elites. In all societies, of course, the making of specific decisions is concentrated in the hands of a very few people. Neither the ordinary citizen nor 'public opinion' can make policy."[58] A far cry from the alternative choices described to prospective Third World leaders, this definition was closer to the current view of democratic theory. Policy, the authors pointed out, was the product of collective action in which pluralist associations—political parties and pressure groups—played a key role. The individual citizen exercised little influence. In the context of proper group action, on the other hand, such participation might effect change.

In an effort to identify the sociocultural background against which democratic systems emerged, Almond and Verba recommended the concept of political culture. "If a democratic political system is one in which the ordinary citizen participates in political decisions, a democratic political culture should consist of a set of beliefs, attitudes, norms, perceptions, and the like, which support participation."[59] A logical proposition, it was not supported in the ensuing interpretation of the conditions of participation, or what was discussed under the heading of civic competence. Instead, such discussion disclosed the elitist bias and reductionist tendencies in the collapse of political analysis.

The notion of competence was defined in terms of attitudes and behavior considered to be compatible with participation. There were different degrees of civic competence associated with different forms of participation. The critical combination was that which joined competence to a positive orientation toward the system. Its corollary was that negative attitudes toward the system were an indication of a lack of, or inadequate, civic competence. As the authors noted, self-confident citizens were those who were active and aware.[60] But there were other indicators of consequence, too. "Of greater significance in understanding political participation is the relationship between sense of ability to participate and the individual's allegiance to the system as reflected in his evaluation of the legitimacy and effectiveness of the system."[61] Such allegiance was linked to political stability on the one hand and to citizen satisfaction on the other. If it was true that satisfaction was derived from participation, then it followed that those who were involved—in the manner described earlier—were also judged to be "more attached to the system than . . . those who cannot participate."[62]

But it was not only positive attitudes toward the system that emerged as one of the criteria for civic competence; there was another portrait of the electorate that figured in this interpretation. It was one in which voter abstinence, positive indifference, and a belief in—rather than the practice of—political participation were underlined. Committed to the revision of what they described as the obsolete and irrelevant "rationality-activist model of citizenship,"[63] Almond and Verba argued that in reality participation in democratic systems was low. But this phenomenon was not to be condemned without reservation, they explained.

> The comparative infrequency of political participation, its relative lack of importance for the individual, and the objective weakness of the ordinary man allow governmental elites to act. The inactivity of the ordinary man and his inability to influence decisions help provide the power that governmental elites need if they are able to make decisions.[64]

The interpretation of voter apathy in which indifference accounted for abstinence, along with the "objective weakness of the ordinary man," stood in marked contrast to the characteristics associated with the dangers of participation, that is, intense interest in political issues. Yet, support of participation was perpetuated in descriptions of "subjective competence," in which self-confidence was said to be high.

> Compared with the citizen whose subjective competence is low, the self-confident citizen is likely to be the active citizen: to follow politics, to discuss politics, to be a more active partisan. He is also more likely to be satisfied with his role as a participant and, subject to certain exceptions discussed above, likely to be more favorably disposed toward the performance of his political system and to have a generally more positive orientation toward it.[65]

The tension between the two positions was not resolved, save in the sense that the authors introduced the idea of a participation myth. It was important, they argued, for the individual to believe in the possibility of participation.[66] In practice, the limits were self-evident. "Yet the very fact that citizens hold to this myth—that they see themselves as influential and as obligated to take an active role—creates a potentiality of citizen influence and activity."[67] Withheld participation, the anticipation of political activity, these were the compromises that reconciled the contrasting interpretations of participation.

Although conformist participation was endorsed, the absence of any participatory support was read as an indication of failure on the part of the individual and the political culture. In such situations, there was said to be a lack of competence and the existence of a sociopolitical environment that did not inspire trust. The analysis of the relationship between the individual and the political community revealed the authors' reliance on the behavioral approach—and its consequences. Absence of trust, they explained, a low score on the so-called faith in people scale, was a sign of difficulty.[68] Its effect was to diminish cooperation, and cooperation was essential to the formation of any social or political organization. In keeping with their interest in the attitudinal basis of political choice, the authors asked "how this combination of trust in people and willingness to cooperate with them in political activities is learned."[69] Political socialization was one answer to the question. And part of that had to do with "the orientations that people have to the political process. . . ."[70] Instead of analyzing the possible malfunctioning of the system, the authors took the individual and the community to task for their defective response.

The argument had a circular quality. Competence was linked to trust, trust to approval, approval to proper orientation, and orientation to competence. Or, in another order, competence was signified by approval,

approval assumed trust, trust assumed approval, and so on. The implications for the interpretation of politics and change were nevertheless clear. Civic competence emerged as an advanced level of political conformism, in which the educated belief in the myth of participation was a substitute for its usage. Where implemented, participation became cause for concern. Where entirely lacking, its attitudinal and social causes were ascribed to the absence of trust, which, in turn, was taken to be a poor omen for the possibility of political organization—and, specifically, of democratic organization.

Without formally abandoning the definition of democracy as involving equality and popular political participation, the reservations associated with its interpretation abridged its meaning. And with attention deflected from the interaction between the political system *and* its subjects, as opposed to the attitude of subjects toward the system, a significant shift in meaning occurred. Attention was concentrated on auditing the responses of individuals. Those whose behavior appeared to violate the participatory code were considered risks to the maintenance of equilibrium—hence, the emphasis on identifying civic competence with a positive orientation toward the system.

As the essays in *The Civic Culture Revisited* (1980) demonstrated, such an approach was appreciated in a variety of political systems.

Doctrine, Diversity and Problems of Explanation

Considered by contemporary political scientists to be a major work in the redefinition of democratic theory, *The Civic Culture* has a place in the evolution of Political Development studies that has gone largely unnoticed by critics of the field. Yet the vision of politics and society that *The Civic Culture* expressed was central to conventional interpretations of political change. That vision informed Political Development doctrine. Beyond the case studies that made up the literature of the subdiscipline of Political Development was a substratum of commonly held views. These rested on the conservative interpretation of democratic theory that signified adherence to the elitist, pluralist, equilibrium interpretation of political change. That interpretation was symptomatic of a particularly political outlook, and it was also an instrument for its reproduction.

The authors of *The Civic Culture* were well placed to advance their theses on democracy. Situated between political scientists on the one hand and specialists of Political Development on the other, they had privileged access to both. But it would be an error to suggest that they conveyed an unusual political outlook. In the overlapping circles of scholars with whom they shared a common outlook, the theses of *The Civic Culture* were readily accepted. They complemented a similar view of politics and society.

Translated into the study of Third World politics, the results were significant. No uniformity of expression characterized the literature of Political Development. None was imposed or, indeed, necessary. In its place, the adherence to the same doctrine of Development ensured a deep and broad compatibility of interpretation. Dangers of social change were magnified. The fear of political change intensified the concern with participation, while deepening the commitment to its affirmation. Political institutions, parties, bureaucracies, the machinery of government, and the state were implicitly compared to the pluralist institutions and functioning of elites in liberal democracies, as understood by revisionist theorists. And, inevitably, the former were found wanting. In this precarious situation, political and intellectual elites were welcomed, provided they were of the conformist type. The future participants were simultaneously viewed as objects and manipulators of change, depending on their political outlook.

As in interpretations of democratic theory according to the elitist mode, the commitment to democracy, equality, and participation was retained. Its centrality was not challenged—except by certain theorists of Political Development. But its interpretation was so conditional as to usurp the meaning of the three terms—democracy, equality, and participation.

The objective situation faced by Development theorists in attempting to transpose liberal democratic theories to the interpretation of Third World politics confronted them with the internal tensions and contradictions of these theories, which proved to be inescapable.

The Several Approaches to Political Development

Doctrinal adherence, then, "the recognition of the same truths and the acceptance of a certain rule—more or less flexible—of conformity with validated discourse,"[71] was characteristic of the diverse group of Political Development scholars. Yet Development theorists were well aware of the multiplicity of definitions and approaches to Development that characterized the field. In one of his commentaries on the subject, Almond acknowledged this fact. Nevertheless, he observed, "whether we call this set of trends a movement toward a 'world culture,' a 'development syndrome,' 'political modernization,' 'political development,' or 'political change,' it seems quite evident that all of us have been writing about movement in a certain direction."[72] The direction was to be more important than the approach, which, in spite of evident differences, remained within a similar overall framework.

What makes the process of identifying the different approaches to Political Development difficult is the permeability of boundaries between different orientations. At least three groupings have been identified as dominating the interpretation of Political Development: functionalists, supporters of the social-process approach, and institutionalists or neo-institutionalists. With exceptions among those who were rigorous in their interpretation, there was a good deal of boundary crossing and collaboration among scholars, in spite of their ostensibly different modes of studying the subject.

Functionalists, such as Gabriel Almond and the Committee on Comparative Politics of the Social Science Research Council, offered what one critic described as a "high degree of theoretical cohesion in the study of political modernization."[73] For many collaborators in the work of the SSRC committee, and they included more or less all of the dominant figures in the field at one time or another, adherence to the functionalist approach was largely nominal. What gave the project coherence was its organizational unity and the adherence of its members to the Development doctrine. The effect of the former is not to be underestimated. It accounted for the production of a considerable number of studies, the holding of conferences, and the establishment of an informal network of scholars able to communicate effectively on matters of related interest. Although the volumes that issued out of the SSRC committee bore the recognizable stamp of Almond's approach, many contributors merely acknowledged the merits of functionalist terminology in their respective introductions and conclusions and then proceeded with their own interpretations. Among the collaborators, some were faithful students of Parsons and a *more* rigorous interpretation of structural functionalism, from which Almond, in fact, sought to distance himself—hence, the interpretations of S. N. Eisenstadt, David Apter, and a far less frequent contributor to the literature, Marion Levy, Jr.

An example of the permeability of boundaries between different approaches to the subject was provided in the work in which Almond launched his own approach, *The Politics of the Developing Areas* (1960). While he outlined the meaning of functionalism for the analysis of political systems in his introduction, another major contributor to the literature, J. S. Coleman, expressed a very different view of the subject in his conclusion. The opening of the volume offered a functionalist interpretation; its closing was written in the style of those attuned to the social process approach.

Identified with the writings of sociologists as well as political scientists, such as Daniel Lerner and Karl Deutsch, respectively, the social process or sociodemographic approach concentrated less on the identification of political systems than on their interrelationship with socioeconomic factors. Associated with the effort to map a comprehensive interpretation of Development as an historic process, it found acceptance in the work of many scholars. Those writing within the framework of the SSRC committee, for instance, were as persuaded of the validity of the definition of Development in terms of a process or a "syndrome" as were others, such as Lerner, who more self-consciously underlined the integrated and systemic qualities of the Modernization process. But support of this approach involved no agreement as to the meaning of such integration or systemic unity. In fact, in many cases little more was offered than the identification of the constituent elements associated with modernity. Shils's "gaps," Lerner's declaration against "social determinism," Verba's admission of the failure to do more than itemize "crises and sequences,"[74] spoke to a significant shortcoming.

Some students of political change, such as S. P. Huntington, associated with the institutionalist or neo-institutionalist approach, objected to both the functionalist and the social process "schools." In "The Change to Change" (1971), Huntington made it clear that he considered both tendencies unsatisfactory. Functionalism was criticized for describing political change in terms of a pre-existing equilibrium. The social process approach "made politics dependent upon economic and social forces."[75] Although Huntington admitted that few actually adopted the "pure form" of this interpretation, he nonetheless argued against the excessive emphasis on "industrialization, urbanization, commercialization, literacy expansion, occupational mobility—which are presumed to be part of modernization and to have implications for political change."[76] Such descriptions, while they contained important elements, were deficient in the analysis of political change, according to Huntington. They left little "room for social structure and even less for political culture, political institutions, and political leadership."[77]

In their place, Huntington argued the need for more attention to the politics of political change, something he claimed was undermined by contemporary trends in political science. The alternative approach offered by Huntington was one in which the relationship between participation and institutionalization was heavily underscored. But this approach was not substantively at odds with that of other Development scholars. Their collective preoccupation with participation was precisely in terms of its effects on institutionalization, whether or not the effort to chart the historic changes in this relationship was actually made. Similarly, the emphasis on culture and political culture were trademarks of the field.

At bottom, Development theorists confirmed one of their own conclusions about politics, namely, that it could be reduced to a question of style. In the case of the different orientations that distinguished the production of Development studies, stylistic differences were significant but substantive differences were not.

Development Doctrine and the Problem of Explanation

The depoliticization of politics, a common characteristic of Development studies, to which Huntington took exception, was not resolved by shifting emphasis to political institutions and leadership. The problem was deeper. The ambition to explain political change was inhibited by the very doctrine and its explanation to which Development theorists were committed. The problem resided in the elitist interpretation of politics, in the revisionist approach to democratic theory. The view from the top, accepted as the only legitimate vision of politics, prejudiced the sympathetic interpretation of social and political forces opposing elite rule. This in itself did not preclude explanations of political change; it merely determined the direction in which such explanations would lead.

Development theorists, as exponents of the revisionist interpretation of liberal democratic theory, were affected by a more deeply rooted problem with respect to the theoretical interpretation of political change. Verba, in discussing the meaning of "crises and sequences" of Development, addressed exactly this question. Focusing attention on "certain significant phenomena and the relationships among them without presenting a coherent and interdependent set of propositions" did not constitute a theoretical explanation, he claimed.[78] The attempt to produce a theoretical interpretation of Development had in fact failed, he observed. Referring to the notion of sequence, he pointed out that it was a nonexplanation. To talk in terms of stages or sequences was to say little, Verba admitted, "unless one can make some statements about sequential ordering and about the consequences of various orderings. ... If one makes strong statements, one is likely to be wrong. If one allows flexibility—'there is no necessary ordering of stages, all sorts of variations are possible'—one will not easily be shown to be wrong, but one will not say anything much of interest."[79] What was to be done? The fall-back position, according to Verba, was the linkage of "pairwise statements." But that recommendation did not escape the weaknesses of previous efforts. Whatever the degree of their firmness, such statements offered no explanation of their linkage.

Verba argued otherwise. He maintained that something was implied in such statements. They represented the "necessary-condition model," a listing of conditions identified as essential for the emergence of yet another, succeeding phase or crisis in political change.[80] *Crises and Sequences* adopted this approach. Necessary conditions of political change were organized around various "problems areas," such as identity, legitimacy, penetration, participation, and distribution. The juxtaposition, linked to a historic image of state formation, provided no resolution of the problem. At best, it offered an impressionist collage of the elements of crises and their sequence.

The problem of explanation was embedded in Development doctrine. It was, finally, inseparable from the historical origins of Development studies and their incorporation of contemporary liberal democratic ideology. Students of Political Development proposed to explain political change by relying on an interpretation beset by theoretical problems that were magnified in this transfer.

Theorists of Political Development took as their starting point in the discussion of political change the justificatory theory of liberal democracy. What they accepted without question, namely, its view of politics and society, required explanation in the extension of liberal democratic theory to the analysis of political change in the Third World. In short, what Development theorists felt no urgency in addressing because they did not challenge its premises, assumed a different complexion in the context of Third World politics.

In their capacity as theorists of Political Development, scholars of political change were committed to the explanation of conditions leading to modern political systems. For some, the assignment was conceived in broader terms, as the debate over the meaning of Political Development suggests. Given the prevailing definition of Development as capitalist development, and the acknowledgment by Development scholars that such development was linked to the emergence of liberal democracy, the historical connection was a central element in discussions of political change. Yet the review of this historical experience proved to be problematic, since the history of socioeconomic transformation in the West disclosed the intensification of social conflict that accompanied the expansion of capitalist market societies.

If the process of socioeconomic change implicit in Development (policies, studies) was historically linked with social and political instability, its encouragement by those committed to the maintenance of political equilibrium and stability gave pause for consideration. If the same process was identified with equality and participation and these were implicated in the intensification of social conflict, what then? Interpretations of political change that were described as democratic theories of political change, yet subscribed to an elitist, pluralist, and equilibrium model of explanation, suggest the solutions that were found on the level of explanation.

The predicament of Political Development theorists makes sense of the conflicting positions of partisans of mass society. It explains the ahistorical bias that characterized interpretations of Development.

Development theorists dealt with this predicament by referring to the paradox of change, while assuming the validity of liberal democratic theories as self-evident and therefore requiring no historical examination. The discussion of change in terms of pairwise statements, or gaps, illustrated the tendency toward separatist explanations in which discrete but firm boundaries were drawn between social, economic, and political aspects of societal transformation. More striking was the bias in favor of explanations that focused on personality and culture, which characterized the various orientations among Development scholars.

The appeal of such an approach was widespread. It short-circuited the confrontation with the socioeconomic origins of Development and the deeper causes of its rampant instability. It offered what Development theorists believed to be an effective mode of describing as well as justifying apparent obstacles to Political Development. But the approach was misleading, as demonstrated by the illustrations in the "Key Texts" section to come. Relying on psychological, attitudinal, and cultural descriptions of political action, distorted the fundamental issues at stake in the analysis of Development. As explanations of political change, such interpretations confirmed the deadlock to which Development theories were subject.

Key Texts

The texts reviewed in this section are well known in the literature of Political Development. They are among the "classics" of the field often cited in discussions of Third World Development. But seldom, with the exception of Almond's essay, are they discussed as illustrating contemporary interpretations of liberal democratic theory. Yet, viewed in this light, their characteristics emerge—not as a function of descriptions of Third World realities but as an expression of the conservative and conditional interpretation of democracy that dominated political theory in the late 1950s and beyond.

The fear of participation, the inability to come to terms with the historic origins of liberal democratic theory and its reproduction in contemporary theories of Development, the reliance on culture and personality as alternative sources of explanation, these are intellectual habits that do not originate with the study of Third World societies so much as with the conservative trend of political thought in the United States.

In spite of the differences among them, the following texts reflect these positions and do so in a manner that conveys the continuing influence of the elitist interpretation. Lerner's work, outstanding in its overt identification of Modernization with Westernization, was most important for its commitment to a quasipsychological discussion of politics. Deutsch's essay, notable among students of Political Development for the identification of transition with "social mobilization," in effect underlined the feared potential of radicalization as a result of social change. Shils, advertising the widespread support for liberal democracy that he found among Third World leaders, used the criteria of such a system against which to measure the deficiencies of Third World regimes, and then situated these in the "spectrum of 'tradition' as opposed to 'modern' systems." And it was in Shils's essay that the idea of gaps emerged, as a device to describe and somehow "explain" the social differences that characterized the same states. Almond's introduction, appearing in one of the early theoretical statements on Political Development, was a direct illustration of the marriage of functionalism to status quo politics, as exemplified in the revisionist interpretation of democracy. In some respects, the essay by Huntington, published at a later date than the previous material, represents the most telling synthesis of all. Huntington's discussion of "Political Order and Political Decay" is often read as an example of the pessimistic criticism leveled at conventional views of Political Development. But it can be read also as a derivative essay, entirely conformist with the conventional approach to political analysis exemplified by the elitist approach to political change.

Daniel Lerner, The Passing of Traditional Society (1958)

As recently as 1973, Lerner's book was described in the *Handbook of Political Psychology* as applicable to "developing nations all over the world."[81] In the same volume, another writer described it as contributing an important example of the "psychic basis of the increasingly clearly explicated causal chain in democratic government."[82] Given Lerner's interpretation, these are revealing affirmations. Yet Lerner's antitheory of social and political change, his view of politics as inherently subversive, and his commitment to a blunt cold war perspective represented a disturbing analytic framework for the investigation of Third World politics.

From the beginning, Lerner announced that he was not interested in theory, or in those who assigned a "unique role to 'human nature' or to 'social determinism.' Having no taste for beating dead horses, we do not even acknowlege these as issues, but go directly to a 'behavioral perspective.' To wit: social change operates through persons and places. Either individuals and their environments modernize together or modernization leads elsewhere than intended."[83] This ominous statement contained the gist of Lerner's approach. Reliance on the behavioral perspective was designed as a counterbalance to excessively theoretical interpretations. Modernization was the product of individually determined change. If such change deviated from the accepted pattern, it was unacceptable. The choice facing Third World states, Lerner remarked, was to follow either a pro-Western path or a pro-Soviet one. Those who chose the latter were accused of "bolshevizing."[84] Further, they were described as representing a form of political deviation, since, in Lerner's words, "what the West is . . . the Middle East seeks to become."[85] There was little doubt that Lerner believed the position to be applicable to other regions as well.

In a rendering of modernity that acquired considerable support, Lerner described its features as including such diverse processes as those involved in urbanization, the emergence of the media, and the increase of literacy and participation. Those able to envision such conditions as legitimate goals for their society were viewed as the positive elements in the quest for social and political change. Although Lerner assigned no "unique role" to "human nature," his explanation for change was based on the interrelationship of personality and society in a manner that gave great weight to the former. Here was the key to Lerner's interpretation.

Lerner went on to say that "if new institutions of political, economic, cultural behavior are to change in compatible ways, then inner coherence must be provided by the personality matrix which governs individual behavior. We conceive modernity as a participant style of life; we identify its distinctive personality mechanism as *empathy*,"[86] Related to the so-called mobile personality, any individual possessed of the capacity for empathy was, according to Lerner's scheme, capable of imagining himself into foreign situations that previewed change. He was, in short, willing to chance new, unknown, and risk-laden situations. This kind of behavior and attitude, in Lerner's terms, was symptomatic of a premodern individual. Those incapable of such sympathetic imaginings were classified as nonrational. The classification was not only ethnocentric but indifferent, as well, to the degree of risk assessment that existed in so-called traditional societies, in which the maintenance of familiar patterns of production was the product of calculation and not only one of blind "tradition."

Although Lerner repeatedly affirmed the connection between the empathetic personality and societies that were "distinctively industrial, urban, literate and participant,"[87] it remained unclear as to how such personality types came about. What was the relationship between empathy and the particular culture and society in which it emerged? And how was one to explain the capacity of some individuals to empathize and the inability of others to do so? These questions went unanswered, although the connection between empathy and culture was repeatedly underlined.

On a different level, Lerner situated his interest in change in "the large historical movement," which he identified in the Middle East. In this context, he related, "our interest is to clarify the process whereby the high empathizer tends to become also the cash customer, the radio listener, the voter."[88] Evidence of this interest was sought in the investigation of individual case studies, notably those pertaining to Egypt, Syria, Jordan, Turkey, Lebanon, and Iran. Interviews as well as historical summaries of recent developments in these states were combined with an ideological litmus test that determined their political direction. On one end were countries described as on the path of economic change and political stability (Turkey and Lebanon); on the other were those considered to be deviants, the states with tendencies to "bolshevize" and otherwise stray from the accepted path of Development (Egypt and Syria). In the center were those that defied classification, according to Lerner (Iran and Jordan).

In the Syrian case, the political atmosphere was described as frustrating for the young, ambitious, and upwardly mobile. The result was the emergence of discontented elements, or "counter-elites," who aroused suspicion. Syrian malcontents, claimed Lerner, "begin by displacing their personal frustrations onto political objects; they continue by constructing extremist ideologies of the national welfare; and they end by tying national aspirations to the shifting of world politics."[89] Lasswell's language was echoed in this description.

With respect to Iran, Lerner claimed that "the mark of extremism is highly visible," especially among those affected by social change.[90] The very conditions associated with modernity, such as urbanization, education, and the media, were now described as factors contributing to alienation. Those who exhibited an enthusiasm for social change, previously considered a sign of empathy, were now castigated as troublemakers suffering from alienation and "relative deprivation." At issue was not their activity but the direction it took, as Lerner made clear in his identification of the dangers of excessive political activity, which was linked first to organized political movements and then to extremism.

Among the reasons frequently given for the acclaim that *The Passing of Traditional Society* received was its reliance on quantitative data, a pioneering move on the part of students of the Middle East.[91] But the research on which these data were based gives pause for concern. Lerner relied heavily on the "Index of Social Dissociation" compiled by the Bureau of Applied Social Research at Columbia University. It was his source for the correlation of personality to politics; but it was also a source that he used to suit his purpose.

The "Index of Social Dissociation," a behaviorist contribution to political study, included the following as factors leading or relevant to political discontent: the limitation of traditional ties of friendship, the presence of so-called individual recreational patterns, and unemployment. Of these Lerner omitted the last while elaborating on the other two, the least persuasive and most open to criticism.[92] Ironically, the traits listed for alienated personalities in this index were the same that Lerner had himself proposed as descriptions of "modern" personalities. Thus, the "mobile personality" type would most likely have exhibited the kind of initiative that involves breaking with traditional ties and creating new ones, based on common interest as opposed to family.

In the Iranian case, the index was used to support evidence of the existence of "an underlying psychic structure of political extremism . . . which combines a high dissociation from institutions and ideologies with a high degree of interaction among people."[93] This, in turn, was read as confirming the existence of the "logical structure of a revolutionary counter-elite. . . ." Such an elite, Lerner argued, was involved in the "bi-polar external conflict between Communists and Free World."[94] What this meant in translation was that Lerner had found a high degree of discontent with institutions and their ideological cover, such that those dissatisfied turned to political organization.

Karl Deutsch, "Social Mobilization and Political Development" (1961)

First presented at the Dobbs Ferry Conference of the Social Science Research Council Committee on Comparative Politics in 1959, Deutsch's paper[95]—a landmark event in the history of Political Development studies— subsequently acquired an independent reputation among scholars of political change.* Its central thesis focused on precisely the connection that was at the center of the Development predicament, namely, the relationship between fundamental social change and its political repercussions.

As in Lerner's text *Traditional Society,* though more sophisticated from a methodological viewpoint, Deutsch argued that modernity was a system. Unlike Lerner, however, Deutsch was not inclined to classify states according to their propensity to plan or pursue a Western path of development. He made no attempt to support the reproduction of such a path, which was considered historically unlikely. On the other hand, Deutsch shared with Lerner and other theorists of Modernization and Development a compatible world view in which the future of Third World states was a subject of major concern. As he observed, "to rely upon automatic developments in economic and political life in those countries of the Free World to which the assumptions of our model apply, would be to court mounting instability, the overthrow of existing governments and their replacement by no less unstable successors, or else their eventual absorption into the Communist bloc. Deliberate political and economic intervention into the social mobilization process, on the other hand, might open some more hopeful perspectives."[96]

The nature of this "social mobilization process" is what interested students of Development, among others. What Deutsch argued was that the dynamics of profound social change affected a transformation on the individual level that manifested itself in social and political terms. How this occurred, the nature of the causal relationship between social, individual, and political change, remained—as in Lerner's case—difficult to grasp. The appeal of Deutsch's argument rested on its attempt not only to relate individual to social changes but also to interpret these in an historical context. The relevance of this argument to the work of students of Political Development is obvious. Concerned with the nature and direction of the societal changes occurring in Third World states, Development scholars sought to map these changes in an effort to predict their outcome.

The premises of Deutsch's argument were as follows: Individuals undergo change, particularly in the period between the ages of fifteen and sixty-five. Important on the individual level, these changes are translated in ways that affect the community and, ultimately, the political character of society. How this process of translation occurs, how the very different kinds of changes that were identified are related to one another, was unsat-

---

* What follows is a brief discussion of certain aspects of Deutsch's paper alone. It is not meant as a commentary on the extensive literature of social or political mobilization.

isfactorily explained. But there was no doubt that the linkage between fundamental social change and its political potential and manifestation exercised enormous appeal. It spoke to a central concern, namely, the fear of radicalization.

"Social mobilization" was the descriptive term by which Deutsch referred to the processes of change occurring among people whose societies were in transition. It evoked the drama of change, the implication of its manipulation. In Deutsch's words, it referred to

> a concept which brackets together a number of more specific processes of change, such as changes of residence, of occupation, of social setting, of face to face associates, of institutions, roles, and ways of acting, of experiences and expectations, and finally of personal memories, habits and needs, including the need for new patterns of group affiliation and new images of personal identity. Singly, and even more in their cumulative impact, these changes tend to influence and sometimes to transform political behavior.[97]

The description begged for explanation. The changes listed were so all encompassing and so varied in nature as to defy common classification. How were they correlated? What did it mean to bracket such changes together? How was the transfer effected between individual and social change? And how was the connection between such changes, their social meaning, and their political outcome negotiated? Whatever the intent of Deutsch's original discussion, the notion of social mobilization was susceptible to a wide variety of interpretations.* It served to flatten experience, to assimilate dissimilar forms of experience, and, in the end, to further an apolitical mode of discussing the basis of political change. Yet Deutsch himself was not vague about his intentions with respect to social mobilization. The concept, he indicated, was more than a way of referring to a congeries of interrelated changes. "It implies that these processes tend to go together in certain historical situations and stages of economic development; that these situations are identifiable and recurrent, in their essentials, from one country to another; and that they are relevant for politics."[98]

Turning to the broader historical view, Deutsch pointed to the example of France in 1793 and Germany in the period from 1914 to 1918. Referring to Shils on Mannheim, Deutsch noted that in Mannheim's usage of the term

---

* C. H. Moore applied it to the description of French colonial policy in North Africa (*Politics in North Africa* [Boston: Little, Brown and Company, 1970], p. 53).

mobilization, there were two phases of the process that were identified.[99] The first referred to the break with a particular style of life; the second involved "the induction of the mobilized person into some relatively stable new patterns of group membership, organization and commitment."[100] Mannheim's discussion of "fundamental democratization of society," however, involved additional considerations. In his work published during World War II, *Man and Society in an Age of Reconstruction*, Mannheim was concerned to expose the dangers in "modern social structure," including those that stemmed from "a certain disproportion in the distribution of rationality and moral power," a condition he regarded as intolerable and untenable.[101]

The thrust of Mannheim's discussion was, in fact, at odds with the prevailing interpretation of social change common to Development theorists. Discussing the course of capitalist industrialized societies, he noted that the movement for democratization was accompanied by a movement for increased interdependence. Unless the masses were integrated into the political system, Mannheim warned, the results would be incompatible with democracy. Unlike revisionist theorists of democracy who feared this integration, Mannheim counseled that democratic systems be extended, not that their political elites be contained in the support of a status quo policy. Even where he discussed the dangers of "irrationalism in mass society," his approach led to the consideration of measures designed to counter the causes and effects of the "latent insecurity in mass society." Such measures, according to Mannheim, would revitalize society and so perhaps spare it the turmoil of recent history. What Mannheim described as the "spiritualization or refinement of passion at all levels of human action and cooperation"[102] was designed to contain and transform the effects of such turmoil. Moreover, in a comment of particular relevance to Development studies, Mannheim warned against psychological interpretations of "the irrational elements in mass society" and further cautioned that these ought to be interpreted according to sociological terms, not psychological ones.[103]

Edward A. Shils, Political Development in the New States *(1962)*

Like Deutsch's essay on social mobilization, an early version of Shils's text was presented to the Dobbs Ferry conference of the SSRC Committee on Comparative Politics in 1959. And like the Deutsch work, its influence on those interested in Third World change was notable. Shils's perspective was molded both by contemporary liberal democratic theory and by the synthesis of Weber and Parsons that he translated into his own interpretation of the dynamics of political change.

At Dobbs Ferry, Shils's paper served as an agenda for discussion and research, influencing the course of Political Development study. In its book form, the work marked the approach to the field, with its tradition/modernity dualism, its "gap" thesis, and its classification of states and political options.

Given its place in Shils's essay, this tradition/modernity dualism merits interpretation. It is instructive to note, as well, that virtually from the outset, when discussion of change in terms of the tradition/modernity polarity became current, there were social scientists sympathetic to the conventional interpretation of change who rejected it as reductionist.[104] Shils nonetheless held to the validity of the distinction. In some respects he echoed Lerner's view that change was a matter of attitude and that those marked by a traditional perspective inhibited progressive change. Among such people, according to Shils, there was a "general disposition to accept what has been accepted in the past."[105] As evidence, he cited the attitude of "the ordinary peasant or recently recruited factory worker, handicraftsman, small scale trader, or old style money lender." What these people lacked were the characteristics associated with the opposite tendency, one directed toward modernity. This latter tendency included such qualities as "individuality, an indifference to or disbelief in the efficacy of supernatural forces, the freedom of the individual, economic progress, a concern for national unity and dignity, and an interest in the larger world. . . ."[106]

How selective was the designation of this tendency toward modernity becomes clear in one of Shils's own essays, "The Meaning of the Coronation," written with Michael Young and published several years earlier than the aforementioned essay.[107] The context differed. What was described sympathetically as a meaningful ritual with communal and historic significance—that is, the coronation—might well have been appraised by an outsider using the criteria of the tradition/modernity dualism as evidence of atavistic behavior. There was apparently more to the classification, which indeed became clear from Shils's discussion. The definition of tradition and/or modernity was closely linked to socioeconomic changes implicit in the meaning of Development and Modernization.

In what must have appeared to be a break with the position he dogmatically espoused at the Milan Conference of the Congress for Cultural Freedom, Shils now argued that without meaningful economic growth progressive political change was unlikely. Under such circumstances, the states of the Third World "could never become genuinely democratic. Extremely poor, traditional people with a primitive technology would not develop the social differentiation and personal individuality necessary for democracy."[108] But no illusions were to be had with respect to the nature of social changes that would accompany such economic growth, Shils noted. They would accelerate class differences and intensify "alienation between the extremes," and this might be "transformed into hostility through 'politicization' engendered by universal suffrage and by the propaganda of modern oligarchical regimes."[109]

The argument was not pursued. Instead, there was a detour into the problem of "gaps," as well as the question of obstacles to progressive change, in which personality and culture were introduced.

The discussion of gaps was remarkable for the elasticity of the term. Gaps were used to describe social differences and to suggest their causes. On every level of society, Shils argued, there were gaps between the rich and poor, "between the educated and the uneducated, between the townsman and the villager, between the cosmopolitan or national and the local, between the modern and the traditional, between the rulers and the ruled."[110] In the same passage, he joined the description of such differences to the existence of the tradition/modernity contrast. "It is the gap between a small group of active, aspiring, relatively well-off, educated, and influential persons in the big towns and an inert or indifferent, impoverished, uneducated and relatively powerless peasantry." In still another passage, Shils described the difference between an "exotic—usually Western—political culture, on the one hand, and the traditional societies ... of which a large segment of the population continues to be socialised, on the other."[111] Discussions of Third World societies in these terms left the question of causality unanswered. Useful perhaps as a graphic description, gaps were assigned a more ambitious function in Shils's interpretation. They appeared to allude to reasons for social differences. In a recent work, Clifford Geertz, another scholar of Third World change, took up the same usage.[112]

Shils's classification of Third World states and the assessment of their political trends attracted even more attention among students of the field. In most such states, Shils claimed, there was enormous support for the Anglo-Saxon model of political systems.[113] In detailing the characteristics associated with such systems, Shils provided a trait list of liberal democracies: representative institutions, public liberties, civilian rule, pluralist institutions and parties, effective and responsible political elites, loyal opposition members, and reliable members of the civil service.

In addition, Shils provided an explanation of the conditions he considered essential to achieve and maintain such systems, discussed in terms of culture, political culture, and personality. "Widespread dispersed civility," Shils wrote,[114] was the condition necessary to achieve the kind of political climate that Almond and Verba would later identify with "civic cultures." With respect to individual participation, this meant moderation—that is, support without excessive interference in the work of ruling political elites. Thus, for a "widely dispersed civility" to exist, according to Shils, there was the need for a reasonable "degree of interest in public affairs sufficient to impel most adults to participate in elections and to follow in a very general way what is going on in the country as a whole, with a reasonable and temperate judgment of the quality of the candidate and the issues."[115] In such circumstances, elites might be able to lead in the task of national reconstruction, and even to disperse their power so as to create support for a meaningful "political society."[116]

Gabriel Almond, Introduction to The Politics of the Developing Areas *(1960)*

In his opening to the work that Almond co-edited with J. S. Coleman, one of the first major collections in the conventional interpretation of Political Development, Almond made reference to Shils's presentation at Dobbs Ferry.[117] Shils's proposed classification of states served to illustrate one of Almond's principal arguments, namely, that the study of non-Western areas required a new political vocabulary.

Almond's response to this situation was an ambitious one. In the introduction to the 1960 volume he noted that "we are not simply adding terms to an old vocabulary, but rather are in the process of developing or adapting a new one. And, to put all of our cards on the table, this is not only a matter of a conceptual vocabulary; it is an intimation of a major step forward in the nature of political science as science."[118] The formulation reflected the temptation of the natural sciences, to which Almond and a good many other political scientists of this period ceded. But on examination, this "major step"—that is, Almond's attempt to invent a new language with which to discuss political change—incorporated a view of politics that was less scientific than suggested. At its core was the elitist and pluralist interpretation of democratic theory wedded to a vocabulary with universalist pretensions.

The innovations claimed by Almond—and disputed by his critics[119]—revolved around the notion of systems, roles, political culture, political socialization, and the interdependence of systems. Such an approach, Almond argued, avoided the evident limitations of interpretations that were described as excessively rigid and monistic in character.[120] In their place a rather different formulation was suggested that, in effect, mirrored the conventional definition. "What we propose is that the political system is that system of interactions to be found in all independent societies which performs the functions of integration and adaptation (both internally and vis-à-vis other societies) by means of the employment, or threat of employment, of more or less legitimate physical compulsion. The political system is the legitimate, order-maintaining or transforming system in the society."[121] In the ensuing discussion it became clear that the analysis of the structures and functions of the political system were dependent on the accepted definition of its legitimacy. Such an assumption figured in the interpretation of political socialization, interest articulation, and aggregation.

Almond placed great emphasis on the role of political socialization. Not only was it indispensable to the functioning of any political system, but it was critical also, he claimed, to "the whole field of political analysis, since it not only gives us insight into the pattern of political culture and subculture in that society, but also locates for us in the socialization processes of the society the points where particular qualities and elements of the political culture are introduced, and the points in the society where these components are being sustained or modified."[122] In short, political socialization was relevant to the reproduction of values essential to the functioning of a particular political system. Any political leadership committed to its own maintenance in power would be concerned to identify "the points in the society" in which its basic "components are being sustained or modified." And, in fact, Almond supported this interpretation, insofar as his discussion of political socialization was followed by a description of its relationship to "the political recruitment function" in society. This function, he noted, recruits members of "particular subcultures . . . and inducts them into the specialized roles of the political system, trains them in the appropriate skills, provides them with political cognitive maps, values, expectations and affects."[123]

Where description faded into legitimation, the neutrality of the former came into question. Thus, in discussions of interest articulation—that is how political systems deal with conflicting interests—the elitist bias of the approach was apparent. Almond maintained that four principal kinds of structures were involved in this process: "(1) institutional interest groups, (2) non-associational interest groups, (3) anomic interest groups, and (4) associational interest groups."[124] It was the third kind that revealed the vantage point of the discussion. "By anomic interest groups we mean more or less spontaneous breakthroughs into the political system from the society, such as riots and demonstrations. Their distinguishing characteristic is their relative structural and functional lability."[125] Almond went on to say that "even when organized and controlled they have the potentiality of exceeding limits and norms and disturbing or even changing the political system."[126] Demands articulated by different groups, Almond noted, were general and particular. And they could be described as "instrumental or affectively neutral or affective."[127]

There was nothing neutral about the ensuing description of the relationship of anomic interest groups, their demands, and the given political system.

> For example, a high incidence of anomic interest articulation will mean poor boundary maintenance between the society and the polity, frequent eruptions of unprocessed claims without controlled direction into the political system. It will affect boundary maintenance within the political system by performing aggregative, rule making, rule application, and rule adjudication functions outside of appropriate channels and without benefit of appropriate process.[128]

The proposition that demands made by such groups would lead to "poor boundary maintenance," "eruptions of unprocessed claims," and activities carried on outside the "appropriate channels" had much in common with Kornhauser's discussion of the unconstitutional and antidemocratic character of political opposition. It suggested a judgment about the legitimacy of such demands that stamped them as threatening to political systems and the legitimate process of "interest articulation."

Discussions of the relationship between political systems and style, an approach to which other conservative theorists contributed, exhibited the same characteristic defects. In the 1960 "Introduction," Almond set forth the proposal that three different kinds of parties, described as "(1) secular, 'pragmatic,' bargaining parties; (2) absolute value-oriented, Weltanschauung or ideological parties; and (3) particularistic or traditional parties," could be associated with particular styles of political behavior.[129] More is noted with respect to this proposition in Chapter 7 of this text, in which Verba's elaboration of the scheme is discussed. But for now it should be noted that the notion of political behavior, which exploited a behavioral perspective and its reductionist tendency, was allied to a classificatory scheme that belied the claims of neutrality or objective analysis.

In the second edition of *Comparative Politics* (1978), Almond and Powell conceded that their tendency to emphasize process at the expense of "performance and productivity" had limitations.[130] The comment, applicable to the analysis of political systems in Almond's 1960 "Introduction," omitted any reference to the relationship between interpretation of process and the resulting view of "political products"—as notable a limitation as the aforementioned omission and one applicable to both works.

Samuel P. Huntington, "Political Order and Political Decay," in Political Order in Changing Societies (1968)

The relationship of this essay to the previous works discussed has already been remarked upon in the introductory notes to this "Key Texts" section.[131] The very notion of "political decay," which symbolized Huntington's pessimistic view of the prospects of political change, can be understood not as a reflection of his interpretation of Third World politics alone but as an expression of the views of mass society critics who feared that the expansion of participation would undermine democracy. As Huntington observed, the effects of "modernization and social mobilization, in particular . . . tend to produce political decay unless steps are taken to moderate or to restrict its impact on political consciousness and political involvement."[132] The debt to revisionist interpretations of political change was evident even in Huntington's criticism of earlier interpretations of Development. These, he argued, had erred in an overly optimistic direction. They had assumed that economic growth would be accompanied by development and stability.[133] The assumption was incorrect, Huntington maintained. The relationship between these factors was such that no equation of the kind occurred in practice. Huntington offered an alternative formulation. He linked participation with institutionalization, thereby indicating the forces he considered responsible both for the maintenance of and the threat to stability and order.

The argument central to Huntington's essay was developed in five steps that reproduced arguments previously encountered in the works of elitist theorists of democracy. The first of these related institutions to the public interest; the second introduced the ideas of trust and political organization; the third identified Modernization as the cause of instability; the fourth pointed to participation as the root problem of sociopolitical change; and the fifth correlated the relationship between participation and institutionalization and the nature of the political system.

Institutions and the Public Interest. Political institutions, Huntington claimed, had moral as well as structural dimensions. As a result, intentionality and values could be attributed to them. They were viewed as having interests different from those of the public, although obviously related to it.

Thus, in "Political Order and Political Decay," Huntington argued that "a government with a low level of institutionalization is not just a weak government; it is also a bad government."[134] Earlier, he had observed that societies that were weak were evidently lacking in will. "A society with weak political institutions lacks the ability to curb the excesses of personal and parochial desires. . . . Without strong political institutions, society lacks the means to define and to realize its common interests. The capacity to create political institutions is the capacity to create public interests."[135] The last phrase indicates that Huntington believed the initiative to lie justly in the definition of the public interest. Public institutions, with their own interests "apart from all other groups,"[136] had this capacity.

The Trust Quotient and Its Sociopolitical Meaning. Turning to the question of the purpose of public institutions, Huntington cited de Jouvenel to the effect that the purpose of "public authorities" was "to increase the mutual trust prevailing at the heart of the social whole."[137] But whereas de Jouvenel referred to the obligations of the public authority to the community, Huntington inverted the formula and questioned the obligations of the community to public authority.

Introducing the matter of trust and its relationship to the capacity for social and political organization, Huntington proposed that societies with unstable and ineffective governments were also those in which trust among the subjects of the state was lacking. Such societies were described as having political cultures "marked by suspicion, jealously, and latent or actual hostility toward everyone who is not a member of the family, the village, or perhaps, the tribe."[138] The Arab world and Latin America were said to exemplify the characteristics of such societies. The ability to create complex organizations, considered a sign of development, was therefore entirely lacking in such states. Pye was quoted in support of the first part of this claim.[139] But the analysis bore a distinct resemblance to the approach found as well in *The Civic Culture* by Almond and Verba, in which the manifestation of trust, as opposed to the conditions inspiring or negating it, was considered. The conclusions to which such an interpretation led were detrimental to the states concerned. The absence of trust was read as proof of weaknesses that were translated into underdevelopment. "Mutual distrust and truncated loyalties mean little organization. In terms of observable behavior, the crucial distinction between a politically developed society and an underdeveloped one is the number, size, and effectiveness of its organizations."[140]

Modernization, the Cause of Instability. The search for the reasons leading to such conditions led to the problem of change and the interpretation of Modernization. In this connection, Huntington accepted the definition proposed by Lerner, although the aspects of it he found to be "relevant to politics"[141] were those identified by Deutsch in his discussion of "social mobilization" and, more specifically, those identified with economic growth.

It was imperative to distinguish between descriptions of the direction as opposed to the political effects of the transition process, Huntington suggested.[142] Most theorists of Development, he argued, paid attention only to the first, thus propagating unrealistic descriptions of the process. In Third World states, it was "only the concept of political modernization as mobilization and participation" that applied. "Rationalization, integration, and differentiation, in contrast, seemed to have only a dim relation to reality."[143] According to Huntington, then, the concepts of Modernization, mobilization, and participation conveyed the traumas inherent in the actual practice of change. But references to "rationalization, integration, and differentiation" were misleading. They referred to processes that were more orderly and rational than was warranted by the facts of Third World change.

Participation, the Root Problem. By linking Modernization to social mobilization and participation, Huntington indicated its destabilizing aspects. These he proceeded to discuss in greater detail in the analysis of participation, clearly perceived as the root problem in conventional discussions of Political Development and in revisionist interpretations of democracy.

In this connection, it was Kornhauser and Lipset, among others, who provided evidence of the adverse relationship between the process of social change and the degree of instability it provoked. Emphasis was put on the rate of change. That, according to the present interpretation, determined the ability of institutions to resist pressures for change. The rate of change was also related to the tempo of socioeconomic development and its acceleration of political participation.

Huntington's observations on the subject were particularly revealing. Like other theorists of Political Development, he underlined the inextricable connection between modernity and participation as well as that between increased participation and instability. "More than by anything else, the modern state is distinguished from the traditional state by the broadened extent to which people participate in politics and are affected by politics in large-scale political units."[144] The negative aspects of the relationship followed: "Not only does social and economic moderniza-tion produce instability, but the degree of instability is related to the rate of modernization. The historical evidence with respect to the West is overwhelming at this point. 'The *rapid* influx of large numbers of people into *newly* developing urban areas,' Kornhauser observes, 'invites mass movements.'"[145] Following upon Kornhauser's arguments regarding mass society, and then distinguishing between the Euro-American experience and that of the Third World, Huntington argued that in the former areas the disruptive effects of the transition process had been contained. They had been spread out over time and "in general, one issue or one crisis was dealt with at a time."[146] Some years later Charles Tilly, in his anthology on state formation (1975), exposed such claims as historically false. The experience of Europe and the United States did not support the claim that a moderate, evolutionary path to "modernity" and development had been pursued. The position proposed by Huntington, however, was essentially similar to that repeated by other Development theorists. Among those cited in this text, Lerner (1958) supported the argument.

But the relationship of speed of change with stability pointed to the central question that preoccupied Huntington and other Development theorists— the question concerning the dangers of participation. The interpretation offered in "Political Order and Political Decay" identified participation as the root problem. This approach bore a distinct resemblance to the discussion of the relationship of elites and nonelites in Kornhauser's work as well as to accounts of political socialization and recruitment found in *The Civic Culture*. Emphasis, in short, was on the capacity of political institutions to absorb rather than to be challenged or undermined by increased pressures for political participation and, perhaps, by a change in the political order. As Huntington explained, "In every society affected by social change new groups arise to participate in politics. Where the political system lacks autonomy, these groups gain entry into politics without becoming identified with the established political organizations or acquiescing in the established political procedures. The political organizations and procedures are unable to stand up against the impact of a new social force."[147]

In explaining why the dangers of the transition process should be more extreme in Third World states than in the West, Huntington offered what appeared to be a revision of his earlier statement comparing the experiences of Europe, the United States, and Third World states in the process of change. Capitalist development and industrialization, he noted, had resulted in feelings of "alienation and anomie, normlessness generated by the conflict of old values and new."[148] The same conditions were responsible for an increased political consciousness. And here the direction of the argument changed. Turning to the issue of support for state planning in Third World states, Huntington suggested that its anticapitalist character was responsible for a more intense politicization than had occurred in the Western experience. Acknowledging the existence of limited economic opportunities that accelerated the instability of Third World urban areas,[149] Huntington observed that economic change was further hampered by a tradition-bound oligarchy.[150] Under the circumstances, the initiatives taken by the state were all the more compelling—and, in this interpretation, adverse—since they favored noncapitalist modes of production. "In addition, the modern values and ideas which are introduced into the system often stress the primacy of government (socialism, the planned economy), and consequently may also lead mobilized individuals to shy away from entrepreneurial roles."[151]

But Huntington was not prevented from candidly observing that economic growth, in itself, accelerated "income inequalities."[152] More telling was the proposition that "economic development increases economic inequality at the same time that social mobilization decreases the legitimacy of the inequality. Both aspects of modernization combine to produce political instability."[153]

The obvious question, then, was how economic growth could be encouraged if political stability was the highest priority. The answer lay in the strength of political institutions to curb the demands of would-be participants. And states were identified according to their ability to act on this score.

On the "Distinction Between Civic and Praetorian Polities." Reviewing the crucial connection between political participation and institutionalization, Huntington noted the importance of distinguishing between different kinds of political systems. Those "with low levels of institutionalization and high levels of participation are systems where social forces using their own methods act directly in the political sphere. . . . Such political systems are appropriately called praetorian polities."[154] Those in which the relationship was reversed (i.e., such that the greater weight was in the hands of those controlling institutions) were described as "civic polities."

Taking a historical detour that went back to ancient times and returned to the present by way of Kornhauser, Huntington argued that "the distinction between civic and praetorian polities corresponds roughly to the difference postulated by Plato, Aristotle, and other classical writers between legitimate or law-abiding states, where the rulers acted in the public interest, and perverted or law-neglecting systems, where the rulers acted in their own interests rather than those of the polity."[155] Kornhauser's analysis of mass society, according to Huntington, provided a modern expression of the same problem. Hence, the citation of Kornhauser's proposition that danger exists where "elites are accessible to masses and masses are available for mobilization by the elites. . . ."[156]

Again citing Kornhauser, Huntington repeated his words to the effect that where the previously existing authority had been autocratic, "rapid and violent displacement of that authority by a democratic regime is highly favorable to the emergence of extremist mass movements that tend to transform the new democracy in antidemocratic directions."[157] By contrast, civic polities exhibited none of these erratic movements, a factor interpreted as a sign of the inherent strength of their institutions. The point, as Huntington observed, was that "the institutions impose political sociali-zation as the price of political participation. In a praetorian society groups become mobilized into politics without becoming socialized by politics."[158]

According to this argument, the prognosis for societies in transition was as follows: If they were autocratic, the process of change to a more democratic system was fraught with danger. Mass movements, most likely involved in such transformations, were suspected as being inherently antidemo-cratic. Political change in such societies was therefore viewed as entailing considerable political risks. Only where strong political institutions existed and could control change was the possibility of change positively conceived. This approach ignored the question of how significant political opposition and fundamental political change could legitimately occur in the absence of manipulation by the state. The answer was implicit in the opening line of *Political Order in Changing Societies,* in which Huntington argued that "the most important political distinction among countries concerns not their form of government but their degree of government."

7

The Impossible Task of Theories of Political Development

Paradoxes and Predicaments

The key texts indicated in the previous chapter illustrate the dominant approach to the interpretation of political change found in conventional analyses of Political Development. They also illustrate the predicaments at the root of such analyses. Directly related to the prevailing view of politics found in the elitist theory of democracy, these predicaments were central to the meaning of Political Development. They informed the on-going debate over the term. They make sense of the reference to Development as a paradox. They explain the place of participation, the major symptom of the impossible task of Political Development theories.

There were two interrelated problems that surfaced in discussions of Political Development. The first was implicit in the attitude toward political change; the second concerned the nature of capitalist development, the accepted form of change in Development theories. The fear of change, a consistent theme in Development studies, was met by an interpretation of politics that appeared to offset it. The adoption of the elite, pluralist, equilibrium model was, in this sense, an appropriate choice. But if it appeared to explain political change in a manner that stressed the maintenance of stability through reliance on carefully chosen elites, it did not offer a resolution of the deeper problem at the source of Political Development theories. This deeper problem was based on the nature of capitalist development itself.

As numerous students of Development have recognized, capitalism generated the very social and political instability that was most feared. Moreover, although it was associated historically with the emergence of liberal and liberal-democratic states, its subversive tendencies were unacceptable in the present context as far as Development theorists were concerned. The expansion of capitalist market systems had the effect of delegitimizing the very class differences that it promoted.

For Political Development theorists, the combination was unmanageable. Given the premises that led to support for the elitist interpretation of democratic theory, the implications of supporting capitalist development as the motor force behind social and political change appeared to be paradoxical. The former emphasis on elite theory was geared toward controlling conditions that the latter systematically generated.

What, then, was to be done? The confrontation with this paradox and the predicaments in Development theories that it addressed led to a nearly permanent debate on the meaning of the term. Did Political Development imply democracy, equality, and participation? Or did it refer primarily to economic change? And what were the consequences of choosing the one or the other of the two definitions? Far from reflecting a confusion over the meaning of Political Development, these debates circled around the impossible choice clearly understood by Development theorists. To define Political Development in terms of democracy and participation meant accepting the contradiction implicit in the interpretation of political change in Development theories. To reject such a definition meant severing the connection with democracy, which would render theories of Political Development nothing more than instruments for the management of political change. Unmasked, such instruments represented a form of social and political engineering that could hardly be expected to attract the kind of support implicit in the first project.

Not all theorists were prepared to take this step. For those who resisted its implications—and they constituted the majority of conventional theorists of Development—the "solution" was an interpretation that shifted the focus from the *process* of socioeconomic change to the *actors* involved in it. This interpretation offered a way out. Attention was directed at personalities and cultures as the obstacles and/or the instruments of an acceptable mode of change. Such an interpretation offered a rationalization for the tutorial approach to Development in keeping with that to be found in elitist theories of democracy.

Those who counseled less ambiguity called for a different course. Their path was, for the most part, unacceptable. It undermined the enterprise of Political Development theories and replaced it with a more naked interpretation of change as the vehicle for economic growth. But even such "solutions" were problematic. Justified as offering a more neutral interpretation of the relationship between socioeconomic and political change, in place of one predicated on the positive direction of Development as democracy, such interpretations introduced the mystification of change as a technocratic phenomenon free of political consequences.

Historical Precedents

That the process of Development was problematic has been recognized by Development theorists. There was talk of the paradoxes at work in David Apter's discussion of Third World leaders promoting reforms that had the capacity to undermine their power (1965). There was recognition by S. N. Eisenstadt of the permanence of instability in forms of change that led to constant "system transference" (Eisenstadt, 1966). The very idea of a "development syndrome" pointed to the various levels and internal dynamic at work, according to James S. Coleman (in Binder et al., 1971). And finally, Samuel Huntington put the matter bluntly in his observation that "economic development increases inequality at the same time that social mobilization decreases the legitimacy of that inequality. Both aspects of modernization combine to produce political instability."[1] On the other hand, a major historical study that produced a scrupulous account of the complexity of *Social Origins of Dictatorship and Democracy*, by Barrington Moore, Jr. (1966), received little recognition in this circle. If individual theorists were moved by its interpretation, that outcome does not appear to have manifested itself in changes in conventional writings on Development. Almond, who wrote a brief review of the work, described it as a "most useful corrective for those of us who sometimes permit hope to carry us away."[2] Almond further noted that Moore was pessimistic about violence, coercion, and the "unequal distribution of burdens in the process of industrialization and democratization," but he regretted that the author had not paid more attention to the role of political elites and "international pressures as the independent variables when appropriate."[3]

Several years later an anthology appeared that had been commissioned by the SSRC Committee on Comparative Politics and edited by Charles Tilly. Impossible to ignore within the circle of Development scholars for these reasons alone, the anthology undermined the myths of Development theories. It criticized the historical fallacies that colored such theories, directly and indirectly. As Tilly and his collaborators noted, the process of state formation in the West bore little in common with the allegedly historical accounts to be found in some Development studies. Furthermore, the relationship of capitalism to liberal democracy discussed in this text disclosed a different history than that advertised in traditional accounts of Political Development. Tilly referred to the connection between the expansion of capitalist market systems and the emergence of liberal theory—a connection he did not pursue—although Tilly observed in passing that writers such as C. B. Macpherson and Karl Polanyi had much to say on the subject.[4]

In fact, the connection between the expansion of capitalism and the emergence of liberal theory is exceptionally relevant to the predicament of contemporary theorists of Political Development. What the political theorist C. B. Macpherson found with respect to John Locke and his "main theoretical weaknesses"[5] is instructive as a guide to the nature of Development theories. Such an approach goes beyond chronicling the paradox on the surface, the permanence of change, the instability of reform, the contrary quality of Development, and the maintenance of the status quo. It points to the deeper incompatibility that is the root tension in the very nature of Development as process. And it suggests an unexpected comparison between the ability of Locke to provide the "moral basis for capitalist society"[6] in his justificatory theory and the moral claims with respect to Development produced by conventional theorists of contemporary capitalist development.

Locke, in Macpherson's lucid reading of his work, was confronted with an emerging bourgeois society that he sought to explain in terms of a system of morality and political obligation derived from another, prebourgeois order. Locke was unable "to surmount an inconsistency inherent in market society. A market society generates class differentiation in effective rights and rationality, yet requires for its justification a postulate of equal rights and rationality."[7] Recognizing class differences in the society in which he lived, Locke read these "back into natural society. At the same time he maintained the postulate of equal rights and rationality."[8] Where is the analogy with the situation of Development theorists? They were not faced in their own societies with the conflicts between traditional and bourgeois values. On the contrary, their starting point was the validity of a liberal theory akin to that evolved by Locke. But their projection of that theory onto a particular vision of Third World society in the midst of a transition process evoked problems similar to those faced by Locke with respect to his own society.

As theorists of capitalist development in Third World states, Development scholars were beset by the same inconsistencies in different circumstances. Class differences and the intensification of social conflict generated by capitalist development were read "back into natural society" at the same time that the commitment to equal rights and rationality was retained. Therein lay the contradictory tensions at the source of contemporary Development theories. To ignore the increasing instability that accompanied social change, as interpreted in conventional discussions of Modernization and

Development, was scarcely possible. Instability was one of the recurring themes in the literature. But to remain indifferent to "a postulate of equal rights and rationality" was to rationalize capitalist development in coercive terms, at odds with the claims of Development theories to be democratic.

The analogy does not rest here. Just as Locke relied on certain assumptions with respect to "class differentiation in rights and rationality" in order to be able to justify the inconsistencies in market systems, so did theorists of Political Development. Whereas in the case of Locke the results allowed him to provide "a positive moral basis for capitalist society,"[9] in the case of Development theorists the result permitted the expression of a moral claim for Development as process.

Locke accomplished this in his interpretation of the social order and in his description of the basis of "rational behavior" and the behavior of the "labouring class." His interpretation altered the way in which capital accumulation had previously been rationalized. Locke, in effect, erased "the moral disability with which unlimited capital appropriation had been handicapped."[10] This he accomplished by means of two interrelated steps in his argument. The first assumed "that while the labouring class is a necessary part of the nation its members are not in fact full members of the body politic and have no claim to be so; and secondly, that the members of the labouring class do not and cannot live a fully rational life."[11] The notion of the "moral delinquency of the labouring class," found in the writings of the post-Restoration period, was further expanded by Locke. He assumed "a class differential in rationality which left the labouring class incapable of a fully rational life, i.e., incapable of ordering their lives by the law of nature or reason."[12] The ability to do this was a function of Locke's understanding of rationality and its changed meaning. The shift was from a definition of rationality in terms of an "industrious appropriation of that modest amount of land that a man could use to produce what he and his family needed, to appropriation of amounts greater than could be used for that purpose. And when this unlimited accumulation becomes rational, full rationality is possible only for those who can so accumulate."[13]

And what of those who failed according to this standard? If the starting point was the assumption that all were capable of managing their lives,[14] clearly those who did not were judged, according to this calculus, as negligent or incapable. The difference between rich and poor was thus read as "a difference in men's ability to order their lives by moral rules as such."[15] This interpretation followed from a contemporary view of man that assumed not only the ability of each to manage for himself but also his moral obligation to do so.[16] This assumption in turn, Macpherson concludes, reflected "the ambivalence of an emerging bourgeois society which demanded formal equality but required substantive inequality of rights. The leaders of that society were not prepared, as the chilly reception of Hobbes' doctrine on all sides had shown, to abandon traditional moral law in favour of a fully materialist doctrine of utility. Rightly or wrongly, such a doctrine was thought to be too dangerous to the fabric of society."[17]

The implications of this set of arguments for interpretations of Political Development are striking. The notion of a "class differential in rights and rationality" had its counterpart in the writings of Political Development theorists.[18] Psychological interpretations of politics and the transition process that delegitimized political differences by reducing them to personality problems, or to expressions of political cultures, accomplished the same end. Claims that Development was a result of individual attitudes, empathy, and the emergence of certain compatible personality types were not so much idiosyncratic as expressive of a particular mode of rationalizing the social order. In a period when arguments in terms of natural law were no longer credible, the law of personality fulfilled the same end. In short, it placed the subject—Development—beyond history.

The ensuing marginalization of the poor, the suspicion of those outside the established system, and the fear of dissidence were rationalized in contemporary interpretations of Political Development in a manner similar to that found in Locke's writings. Stigmatized as incapable of leading "fully rational" lives, the modern-day members of the "labouring class" were not considered to be politically trustworthy. The blatant fear of increased political participation and the changes it might provoke corresponded to this social portrait.

As market society changed with the emergence of a working class that was both more cohesive and more articulate than at any previous time, the justification of inequality in terms of "class differential in rights and rationality" wore thin. It was no longer acceptable. The inevitability of subjection to the law of the market was no longer passively tolerated. By the mid-nineteenth century, not only market systems and societies but their justificatory theories as well had undergone significant changes.

By the mid-twentieth century, theories of Political Development reflected these transformations. Moreover, their weaknesses were amplified by conditions existing in many Third World states in which social change had intensified the demands of the "labouring class" as well as incumbent elites bent on staying in power. Yet to judge by the rationalizations of Development theorists, the defense of capitalist market systems was accomplished in terms of "class differential in rights and rationality." The fear was the same as that articulated by Locke and other liberal theorists—namely, that the movement toward democracy would actually take root. Arguing in terms of the assumptions of "possessive individualism," theorists of Political Development were unable to cope with the disintegration of the social consensus that was the product of Development. They were similarly ill equipped, given their interpretations of political change, to articulate a valid theory of political consent.

There was no connection made by Development theorists between their interest in psychology and politics and the kinds of arguments just cited. Nor was there a comparable connection made in deliberations on the meaning of Political Development and the challenge of participation. Yet it takes little effort to discern such connections, particularly since theorists of Political Development defined their political position in terms of contemporary liberal democratic theories, thus identifying their approach with the experience of earlier exponents of liberalism—Locke among them.

Deceptions of Development: The False Promise of an Explanation

The study of personality and politics represented a common interest among social scientists working on problems of Development. Few were indifferent to its significance, although how they chose to combine the interrelationship of personality, society, culture, and politics accounted for dramatically differing interpretations.

In *Politics and Markets* (1977), Charles Lindblom pointed out that social theorists, such as Talcott Parsons and Abram Kardiner, had long been interested in the question of culture and social systems.[19] Such interpretations were not necessarily in conflict with those that focused on class and social structure, Lindblom observed. But in the work of elitist theorists working on problems of Political Development, there was no such compatibility. If anything, emphases on personality and culture were used as substitutes for interpretations that recognized the importance of materialist considerations in the analysis of politics or social structure.

Leading exponents of Political Development studies were among the most vocal supporters of the integration of psychology with political analysis. Some, like Almond, explained the phenomenon in terms of the interdisciplinary elan that characterized postwar political science, with its opening to sociology, social psychology, and psychology, as well as psychoanalysis.[20] Almond himself repeatedly acknowledged the importance of psychology and social psychology in interpretations that influenced contemporary political theory. In *The Civic Culture Revisited*, he referred to such works as *The American Soldier* (1949) and the more controversial *The Authoritarian Personality* (1950) as illustrative of this movement.[21] It is interesting to note, however, that in 1963 Almond and Verba referred to "authoritarian personality" studies in a more general way. Among their citations were critical evaluations of the Adorno et al. work, by Shils and Lasswell, among others. In short, although it was not the approach in the Adorno et al. work that characterized interpretations of Political Development in which psychology played a role, there is no doubt that an interest in exploring the connection of politics and psychology was present. For the most part, such an interest assumed an apologetic character. And in this connection, the work of H. D. Lasswell offered a dramatic guide.

That Lasswell played a role in the prehistory of Political Development studies has already been emphasized. But in addition to his well-known work in the areas of propaganda and communications, and the "policy sciences," there were his writings on the psychology of politics.[22] Lasswell had worked on problems of propaganda in the period between the two great wars. Later, at Harvard, he studied with Elton Mayo. As he became more interested in psychoanalytic theory, he launched into the field. Psychoanalyzed himself, he recommended the process to his colleagues. He became a lay analyst and contributed to professional journals, such as that associated with the Frankfurt School Institute for Social Research—the very institution whose members were so caustically attacked by Shils in his deliberations on mass society.

At the time, Lasswell was interested in Fromm, Mead, and Malinowski and attempted to integrate their psychoanalytic and anthropological insights with a Marxist perspective.[23] That approach was difficult to discern in the work that sealed Lasswell's reputation among psychologically oriented American social scientists, *Psychopathology and Politics* (1930). It was in this essay that Lasswell set out to expose the psychological motives of public figures.[24] "Political man," he claimed, is a deceptive creature; he imposes his private motives on public objects, but he does so in a manner that few can see through. Following is the formula that conveyed Lasswell's view:

$$P \} d \} r = P$$

where the initial P refers to "private motives; d equals displacement onto a public object; r equals rationalization in terms of public interest; P equals political man; and $=$ equals transformed into."[25] Politicians, according to Lasswell, were really actors in disguise. They engaged in ritualistic displacement of motives. Thus, Lasswell argued, "political prejudice, preferences, and creeds are often formulated in highly rational form, but they are grown in highly irrational ways."[26]

If the innocent were duped by this performance, what was to be done? Lasswell's solution was worse than the condition he diagnosed. The answer, he suggested, was "preventive politics," a form of political pacification that was based on assumptions common to revisionist theorists of democracy. "The ideal of a politics of prevention is to obviate conflict by the definite reduction of the tension level of society by effective methods, of which discussion will be but one. The preventive point of view insists upon a continuing audit of the human consequences of social acts, and especially of political acts."[27] Who were the auditors, and what political acts were to be so monitored? The possibilities, as later students of "mind control" suggested, were terrifying.[28]

Lasswell believed that in the past politics had been thought of in terms of conflict and struggle. That approach, he claimed, was a waste of time. He further claimed that democratic theorists assumed that "social harmony depends upon discussion, and that discussion depends upon the formal consultation of all those affected by social politics."[29] But this was to misunderstand the objective of politics, according to Lasswell. It was less important to resolve differences than to prevent them.[30] Moreover, the proposition also accepted by democratic theorists, to the effect that individuals were the best judges of their own interests, was similarly viewed as erroneous.[31] Personality research, Lasswell claimed, had shown the opposite. The individual who expressed political choices was subject to the same vicissitudes as beset the professional politician. This individual was most likely manifesting internal disorders that were masked in political terms. "An examination of the total state of the person will frequently show that his theory of his own interests is far removed from the course of procedure which will give him a happy and well adjusted life."[32] But if the individual was not the best judge of his interests, who was to assume that responsibility?

Applying the same line of reasoning to social and political groups and movements, Lasswell's approach reduced politics to a form of catharsis.[33] Those he identified as leaders capable of avoiding the pitfalls of such a condition were drawn from "medicine, psycho-pathology, physiological psychology, and related disciplines. Its practitioners will gradually win respect in society among puzzled people who feel their responsibilities and who respect objective findings."[34] Having concluded that politicians tended to objectify their private psychological problems, Lasswell assigned political work to psychologists and psychologically oriented "practitioners." Implicit in Lasswell's approach was not only the elitist view of democracy but an interpretation of politics that defined conflict in psychological terms.

One critical political scientist noted that it was difficult to take Lasswell's writings seriously. Otherwise, their totalitarian implications would be alarming. At the least, noted Bernard Crick, "its negative consequences for American political education are . . . worrying."[35]

Ironically, Lasswell himself warned against the dangers of what he termed "the garrison state." As early as 1941 he insisted on the urgency of considering the changing nature of the state, the growing power of state bureaucracies, and the increasing isolation of the individual. He described the possible marriage of science and politics as awesome. The garrison state, in his opinion, would usher in an "age of physiology in polities [that] may be expected to amplify the cruder dialectic of missiles and missives with the methods of sterilization and inoculation. Machiavelli, M.D., therefore, will become a more distinct figure as contradictions sharpen and new knowledge is drawn into the struggle against dissent."[36] This prospect would be particularly dangerous, Lasswell observed, for the skilled, the semiskilled, and the intellectuals.

Some years later, in 1950, Lasswell expressed concern about the possible confusion between the analytic value of studying the psychological aspects of politics and the reductionist interpretations to which such studies might lead. The warning came late.

Searching for the "Spirit of Capitalism"

A documentation of Max Weber's influence on the political scientists who wrote of Political Development is beyond the scope of this essay. The task would be enormous. Weber, after all, was the grand master of American social science. His influence among social scientists preoccupied with problems of socioeconomic change and the maintenance of social order was paramount. But among Weber's works, one essay has special significance for students of Political Development. This is *The Protestant Ethic and the Spirit of Capitalism*, which offers an interpretation of the relationship among culture, values, and economic change that seemed destined to be taken up by students of Development.

Reviewing the intellectual background of Development theories, Pye credited Weber with "elaborating, with great erudition and profound historical insight, the distinctive qualities of the traditional and the rational-legal forms of authority." He also cited Weber for the identification of the "charismatic form of authority with its emphasis upon the affectual type of social action."[37] But beyond this, according to Pye, "an even greater contribution" was Weber's belief that there was an inner coherence in all societies. It was manifest "in the form of a systematic relationship among the social, economic, legal, and political forms of behavior on the one hand, and the nonrational spirit or ethos of the society, as best expressed in its religion, on the other."[38] What Weber achieved in his study of Calvinism and capitalism, Pye continued, was nothing less than the correlation of the individual and the social, the psychological dimension and the social system. In Pye's words, "The social, economic, and political realms were seen as no more than different aspects of basic human acts, all conditioned and given coherence by the psychological makeup of man. Weber thus set the stage for relating questions of social structure to the profound psychological insights of Freud."[39] But whether Weber set out to do what Pye described is another matter. Psychological insights were not a primary consideration of Weber's analyses. But Pye's account conveyed the manner in which Political Development theorists read Weber's study of Calvinism and capitalism.

No doubt Weber's *The Protestant Ethic* raised issues that were well within the mainstream of contemporary Development studies. The relationship between capitalism and rationality, central to Weber's essay, was reproduced with few changes in interpretations of Development. It was opposed to nonrational "traditionalism," described as the "most important opponent with which the spirit of capitalism, in the sense of a definite standard of life claiming ethical sanction, has had to struggle. . . ."[40] Weber's comments on this worthy opponent presaged what Development theorists were to write about "traditional" society. In Weber's terms, modern capitalism repeatedly "encountered the immensely stubborn resistance of this leading trait of pre-capitalist labor. And today it encounters it the more, the more backward (from a capitalist point of view) the labouring forces are with which it has to deal."[41]

Weber's explanation offered inspiration to Development theorists seeking confirmation of the importance of nonmaterialistic factors in social analysis. Weber referred to the "anthropological side of the problem," although he quickly modified this by asserting that there was not enough research to sustain such an emphasis.[42] Modern capitalism emerged in certain areas, according to Weber, because of internalist reasons. What was lacking where it failed to appear was "the development of the spirit of capitalism."[43] Education was required to arouse it. Then, the Calvinist ethic would emerge and play its role. This role Weber referred to as "a calling," which in time became an end in itself. Far from describing it as rational or as a source of personal happiness, Weber was more critical of its effect. Indeed, he described the internalizing of such a calling as a deformation. How else to describe a situation in which, as Weber noted, "a man exists for the sake of his business, instead of the reverse."[44]

In conventional interpretations of Political Development, the behavior associated with this "calling" was described as rational. Its absence, accordingly, described nonrational behavior, an important ingredient in the arbitrary definitions of traditional as opposed to modern societies that appeared in the writings of Development theorists. Whether students of Political Development were faithful to Weber's spirit is another question, however. They certainly did not heed his warning against substituting "for a one-sided materialistic an equally one-sided spiritualistic causal interpretation of culture and history."[45] And they ignored his warning that a lopsided interpretation of this relationship "accomplishes equally little in the interest of historical truth." Generally, critical commentaries on the Weber thesis, which abounded, were scarcely acknowledged by Political Development scholars. Hence the proposition that the emergence of capitalism was not a function of the Calvinist ethic alone, as the European and the Third World experiences indicated, was ignored.[46] In the late 1960s, S. N. Eisenstadt attempted to bring the Weber thesis and its related arguments up to date.[47]

Given the general thrust of Development studies, it was scarcely surprising that the Weber thesis received such a warm welcome. Weber's work was cited as an inspiration in the works of various social scientists concerned with the conditions of economic growth. Those like Bert Hoselitz, founder and editor of *Economic Development and Cultural Change* (EDCC), conceptualized the problem posed by Weber in broad terms: "Does economic development mean only a change in certain aspects of overt behavior, notably the acquisition of new skills or the exercise of new forms of productive activity, or is it accompanied by or contingent upon more basic changes in social relations, and even the structure of values and beliefs of a culture?"[48] Hoselitz raised the question in other works as well. His conclusion was that it would be useful to be able to determine the "culture traits" compatible with, as well as antagonistic to, economic and technological growth.[49] Critics of conventional interpretations of Political Development and Modernization argued against the limits of such theses, notably those propagated in Hoselitz's journal.[50]

There were other works, however, that were far more extreme in their application of the Weber thesis. Titles such as *The Achievement Motive* (1953) and *The Achieving Society* (1961), by David McClelland, which were often cited in Development studies, carried the general thrust of the Weber thesis considerably further. McClelland indicated a general dissatisfaction with existing interpretations of social change. He felt that they were too materialist in character. In comparison, his own work dwelled on the impact of early childhood training and its implications for the emergence of the entrepreneurial spirit.

Everett Hagen argued from a similar perspective, claiming that the explanation of social change could be located in "the internal structure and functioning" of societies. In his interpretation, "both the barriers to growth and the causes of growth seem to be largely internal rather than external."[51] Finding inspiration and confirmation in the work of psychoanalysts and sociologists,[52] Hagen insisted that the key to social change was to be found in the relationship of "personal to social structure."[53] Another writer put the matter more crudely: "Change in underlying material conditions usually presupposes changes in the contents of the mind, since material conditions are passive whereas mental conditions are potentially dynamic."[54]

It was not the significance of the relationship between personality and society that distinguished the writings of various social theorists on Development, but the weight these writings attributed to the interrelated elements and the manner in which their interrelationship was conceived. Parsons, for example, who wielded an inordinate influence on postwar American social science, was preoccupied with this very subject. He continually sought to define the boundaries between individual, culture, and society and the nature of their reciprocal relations. From his reading of Freud, Durkheim, and Weber, Parsons elaborated the concept of internalization, which he described as far more radical than most people recognized.[55] Internalization, according to Parsons, described the integration of socially sanctioned structures of meaning. It was a key to the process of socialization;[56] which, in turn, was an essential element in the political vocabulary of theorists of liberal democracy and Political Development. *The Civic Culture, Political Culture and Political Development,* and *Comparative Politics,* all works previously discussed under the rubric of changes in political science and interpretations of Political Development, elaborated on this concept.[57] But the tensions that Parsons recognized as central to the relationship of individual to society were muted in such interpretations. It was the conformist aspect of internalization that was reproduced in the studies on Political Development.

Politics, Personality, and the Question of Political Style

Where do Lasswell, Weber, and Parsons fit in the annals of Political Development studies? From the perspective of their contribution to the analysis of the relationship of personality to politics, what was the legacy that theorists of Political Development inherited and exploited?

Not all students of Third World politics were interested in psychology, psychoanalysis, or social psychology. But among those who accepted the conventions of conservative political theory implicit in the elitist interpretation of democracy, the tendency to adopt psychological explanations of politics was commonplace. In this circle, the habit of discussing fundamental social and political change in terms of stress was widespread. Similarly, the tendency to analyze dissident political movements in terms of their appeal to those identified as psychologically unbalanced found a warm reception. The reasons for these responses are not difficult to find. By displacing political analysis from the political to the personal level, political differences and conflicts were reduced to matters of deviance and other personality malfunctionings. The approach was convenient, albeit a distraction from the ostensible purpose of political explanation.

Lerner's exploitation of this approach was evident in *The Passing of Traditional Society* (1958). But he applied the approach to European conditions in an earlier essay on neutralism, in which he claimed that "the psychological mechanism underlying neutralist sentiment is neither apathy nor apoplexy, but ambivalence. . . . When this inability to choose persists against all considerations of greater good or lesser evil in an actual situation, a new conception of reality may be internalized which ignores or denies the need to make a choice at all."[58] There was no attempt to mask the underlying ideological thrust behind this form of mystification. As Lerner wrote in his conclusion, "Either way, as privatized apathetics or apoplectic antagonists, the neutralists would represent a total loss to the Free World, a serious and unnecessary loss. . . ."[59] The description did not contradict the view of neutralism current among scholars of Political Development, particularly those who were policy oriented. Lerner's approach demonstrated how a psychological or pseudopsychological language might be used to target an undesirable political position. But in other works dealing more directly with Political Development, another dimension of this approach emerged. By describing the process of social change in terms of pathology,[60] a breakdown occasioned by the rupture with traditional lifestyles, theorists of Development injected a reductionist element into the discussion of social and political change. Treading the line between individual, societal, and political change, some Development theorists concluded that Third World change was best understood in terms of the quest for personal and political identity.[61] Although buttressed by references to the works of various psychologists and social psychologists (Erickson among them), the notion of political identity emerged as an impressionistic and ahistorical phenomenon.

Lucian Pye presented just such an interpretation in *Guerrilla Communism in Malaya* (1956), a work in which he argued that Third World populations in search of political identity were likely to interpret their quest in personal terms.[62] In a subsequent essay on the "non-Western political process" (1957), the approach was extended to the discussion of politics in Third World societies. In Third World states, Pye argued, there was a mix that revolved "around issues of prestige, influence, and even of personalities, and not primarily around questions of alternative courses of policy action."[63] Parsons's discussion of dichotomous schemes characterizing societies at different stages of evolution recommended such an interpretation. In Pye's essay the implications of such an approach were evident. Third World societies were viewed as apolitical and, more precisely, as departing from the political norms of modern, Western, liberal democratic states.[64]

It was in *Politics, Personality and Nation Building* (1962), a work dealing with Burma, that Pye elaborated on these themes at great length. All politics had a psychological dimension, Pye argued. But the politics of transitional societies was the most affected by psychological conditions, he claimed. It was in some significant degree more personal than the politics of developed societies—presumably because the transition process uncovered deep-seated psychological problems. Pye made his position known in the opening pages of his book, where he explained that, in his estimate,

> there is, of course, a psychological dimension to politics in all societies; but in transitional countries the political process often has to bear to an inordinate degree the stresses and strains of people responding to personal needs and seeking solutions to intensely private problems. People who are caught up in all the uncertainties of social change may turn to political action to gain an element of individual security, to re-establish links with their fellow human beings, and to find a sense of personal identity.[65]

Given the assumption that political change was inextricably related to considerations of personality, the nature of such change was directly dependent on personality types. Once understood, the task of the social scientist was essentially to investigate personality in particular political cultures.[66] The

Burmese case offered Pye the opportunity to test his hypothesis that nation building was a function not only of political development but also of transformations on the level of personality.

Eager to explain the sequence of developments that had transpired in the aftermath of the British withdrawal from Burma, Pye observed what the British had accomplished: "History contains few more dramatic examples of the extraordinary power of economic motivations to change a society than the development of the Delta regions of Lower Burma under British rule."[67] Contrary to conventional interpretations of Third World society as paralyzed by "tradition," Pye described the response of the Burmese peasant as one of energetic support for a form of economic activity that reflected well on the Burmese character. "Once the logic of the situation was clear to him in economic terms, he recognized with amazing spontaneity both the rational and nonrational components of the calculus of the market. He quickly came to appreciate the short-run principles of supply and demand and the long-run principle that resources invested rather than immediately consumed would in time produce even more resources."[68]

Change, far from being resisted, was actually supported at this time, although some were displeased with the transformations that followed. Emphasizing the response of those who benefited from the changes introduced, Pye noted that these people exhibited an appreciation of "the function of capital, the importance of indebtedness, and the fact that only the indebted peasant could become the rich peasant."[69] With the end of the British occupation the transformation came to an end, according to Pye. As Pye turned to the reasons for this shift, he turned away from the social character of economic change to a psychological description of its meaning.

The withdrawal of British initiative and support, according to Pye, set the stage for the negative changes in Burma's economic life. The Burmese were unable and/or unwilling to keep up modes of production introduced under the British. Why? The most satisfactory explanation, Pye suggested, was to be found in the connection between personality and politics. Personality, it was argued, affected political choice. Political choice, in turn, was affected by the search for identity, on both the personal and political levels.[70] The purpose of Pye's investigation was described as the search to uncover "the complex and ambivalent ways in which psychological reactions to social change can so affect the political culture as to impede its collective action."[71] The way was now open to search for the inner meaning of outer disarray. Having situated the root of political and economic change in personality, personality became the focus of investigation.

Childhood rearing patterns were examined and linked to socialization processes. And these were matched against the general perception of Burmese politics as erratic, masked, and dissimulating.[72] The excessive sensitivity betrayed in the process of social change, according to Pye, was attributable to deeply felt sentiments of distrust. Hence the conclusion that "when people are being changed from traditionals into moderns, they are likely to be hypersensitive to the deeply felt sensation of being changed and manipulated by others who always protest that they are only being helpful."[73] The Burmese, in this account, were said to suffer from a fearful, anxiety-ridden personality type. They were prone to anticipate deception—and fearing it, they provoked its appearance. It was to be expected that the Burmese would therefore seek protective disguises enabling them to meet adversity by evading it.[74] And, indeed, evasion and ambivalence loomed as attractive options in this interpretation.

Foreign policy provided an illustration for Pye's thesis. The Burmese wanted independence, Pye claimed, but they were moved by contrary feelings. "The only well-recognized roles in Burmese politics are those of the personal leader and the devoted disciple, either complete independence or complete submission."[75] Neutralism satisfied the personal cravings of the Burmese, according to Pye's interpretation. It expressed the search for "a warm dependent relationship in which they would be fully protected from all dangers."[76]

It was a long way from the earlier descriptions of Burmese peasants engaging in productive and rational economic activity to such descriptions of a politics of fear, anxiety, and paralysis. The reception accorded Pye's work, however, suggests that few objected to his method or his findings. Based on an extremely limited number of sources, its delegitimation of politics and political analysis met with little challenge from Development scholars. The Burmese case inspired other works. Pye and Verba's contribution to the SSRC Committee on Comparative Politics series on Political Development, *Political Culture and Political Development* (1965), involved a further elaboration of the notion of political identity and its relevance to Third World politics. Not only did Pye trace the notion in the works of contemporary psychologists,[77] but ironically, he expressed great misgivings about possible reductionist tendencies to which interpretations based on psychology could lead.[78]

The Matter of Political Style

The exploitation of a psychological and psychoanalytic vocabulary contributed to the depoliticization of political analysis in Development studies. Behaviorism contributed to the same end. Far less defined, behaviorism lent itself to the most impressionistic claims about the relationship of attitude to politics. In discussions of political identity, the conformism that the behaviorist approach endorsed was evident. In discussions of political style, investigations of attitudes and their labeling became a substitute for the analysis of political differences.

The question of political identity and its subtle shift of emphasis from the political community to the actor and his attitudes was illustrated in *The Civic Culture*. There, political identity was associated with legitimacy; that, in turn, was described as a response resting on shared values in—rather than about—the work of political elites.[79] Attention was focused on the respondent, his attitudes, his conformism, his integration of existing political norms. A similar usage was apparent in some of the essays collected in the Pye and Verba volume.[80]

Discussions of political style elaborated on previous descriptions of political identity. From a common-sense perspective, the proposition that individuals possess distinct political styles appears reasonable—provided that style refers to modes of political expression. But discussions of political style found in Development studies did not rest on such simple propositions. Style became a synonym for political positions of various kinds. Differences in political styles—interpreted as attitudes—were then read as equivalent to differences in substantive political positions. And, accepting the validity of this approach, political style and substance became interchangeable. If you identified an individual's political style, you presumably knew his politics, whatever the context. But the dangers of such an approach are clear. Not only are political differences reduced to questions of style, but the identification of political style (i.e., attitude) becomes a substitute for the investigation of political content.

Political style, as Verba explained in his conclusion to the Pye and Verba volume (1965), was associated with "two aspects of political belief systems." The first referred not to "the substance of beliefs but the way in which beliefs are held. The second aspect lies on the border between the system of political culture and the system of political interaction, and involves those informal norms of political interaction that regulate the way in which fundamental political beliefs are applied in politics."[81] What does it mean to separate substance and style in this manner? If "the way" beliefs were supported presented difficulties of analysis, even more difficult was the clarification of "informal norms of political interaction." Yet these categories, in fact, referred to familiar forms of classification. As developed in Verba's essay, the underlying distinction between the two views of politics was between the "ideological and the pragmatic," a familiar breakdown in contemporary elitist theories of democracy.

According to this scheme, individual styles were linked to particular political doctrines. Inverting the approach, doctrines were then associated with particular styles so that the identification of one was a key to the other. Pragmatism was identified with moderation, ideological politics with fanaticism. The pragmatic approach suggested a piecemeal view of politics; the ideological was linked to a totalitarian conception. The assimilation of style and substance proceeded as follows: The "ideological style" was defined as involving a "deeply affective commitment to a comprehensive and explicit set of political values which covers not merely political affairs but all of life, a set of values which is hierarchical in form and often deduced from a more general set of 'first principles.'"[82] By contrast, the pragmatic approach was described as assuming an evaluation of problems "in terms of their individual merits, rather than in terms of some preexisting comprehensive view of reality."[83]

Whatever the formal intention of such analyses, they were selectively applied. Even so sympathetic a reader as Alex Inkeles, a contributor to Development and Modernization literature (A. Inkeles and D. Smith, *Becoming Modern*, 1974), argued that the approach obscured differences between attitudes and evaluations of politics.[84]

In Anticipation of "Participation Crises": The Idle, the Poor, and the Elites

The reliance on psychology and the exploitation of behaviorism in the analysis of politics were crude tools common to some interpretations of Political Development. In spite of claims to the contrary, such interpretations did not define the process of Development so much as identify the fears it inspired. These emerged in other kinds of interpretations that concentrated on delineating, in however impressionistic a fashion, the social forces unleashed by Development. These diverse interpretations were mutually reinforcing. They represented a common strategy vis-à-vis the process of social and political change implicit in Development: an intellectual strategy of "containment" designed to restrict participation pressures and to immobilize radical movements.

Efforts to distinguish between the politics and the "logic" of Development offered no challenge to this approach. Such a choice reflected an ahistorical vision of the interrelated character of social and political change that was self-serving. Without minimizing the importance of the autonomy of the state, such interpretations signified no fundamental departure from the prevailing view of politics and the Development process.

At about the time when students of modern European social history were discovering the significance of social groups they had previously dismissed as outside of history, theorists of Political Development were propagating the old myths about "urban mobs" and masses. The contrast was not a function of different stages of political development but one of different stages of intellectual analysis. There was no work analogous to that of Hobsbawm (1959, 1969) or Rudé (1969) among conventional scholars of Political Development.[85] And while Rudé was finding evidence that the "crowd" in the course of the French Revolution was not as uninteresting as had once been thought, major theorists of Development persisted with descriptions of inchoate mobs unleashed by the pressures of social changes identified with Modernization and Development. There was no counterpart for the discovery (in the work of Rudé, for example) that "the popular elements composing the sans culottes—the peasants, craftsmen, journeymen, and labourers" had acquired a new look.[86] They had begun, Rudé explained, "to appear as social groups with their own distinctive identity, interests, and aspirations, whose actions and attitudes can no longer be treated as mere echoes or reflections of the ideas, speeches, and decrees of the journalists, lawyers, orators, and politicians established in the capital."[87] In the literature of Political Development, some of the same social elements continued to appear without identity, interest, or aspiration. If there were expectations, they were largely negative in character.

By contrast, the elaboration of the role of political elites was of an entirely different kind. Although the investigation of such elites was relatively undifferentiated, the support they aroused was clear and coherent.[88] In coordination with the military and with conformist intellectuals, political elites were viewed as the instruments for responsible political change. It was through their eyes that Development theorists considered the pressures stemming from the Development process. It was from an identification with their perspective that opposition and political dissent were assessed. Nonetheless, political elites were susceptible to different political outlooks. Those who leaned toward statist programs were regarded critically. Their choice represented a deviation that was considered significant.

Democratic and oligarchic states of the Third World, wrote Shils, possessed a common social phenomenon, namely, the "urban mob" referred to earlier. It consisted "partly of menials, servants, and workers away from their families, of refugees and displaced persons, and partly of restive students and discontented high school and university graduates."[89] The active element in this grouping, Shils observed, passed for public opinion in some of the "new" states.[90] In the conclusion to *The Politics of the Developing Areas*, Coleman described the urban mob as part of the "anomic movements" that were found in transitional societies. Animators of such movements tended to be "newly urbanized elements not fully integrated into either the modern or the traditional sectors of society. The most characteristic type of anomic movement is the highly suggestible urban mob whose passions are readily ignited and whose energies are frequently manipulated by those out of office."[91]

What accounted for their movement? The answer was often to be found among intellectuals, according to theorists of Political Development. In the annals of Development studies, no social group was more open to diversity of interpretation than this one. Viewed by some as leaders of and guides to the process of change, they were regarded by others—and sometimes by the very same interpreters—as subversive elements responsible for the radicalization and manipulation of the transition process. Shils evoked both images. Intellectual elites, he claimed, possessed uncommon powers. They were at the source of the foundation of new states. "The gestation, birth, and continuing life of the new states of Asia and Africa, through all their vicissitudes, are in large measure the work of intellectuals. In no state formations in all human history have intellectuals played such a role as they have in these events of the present century."[92] In this capacity, Shils suggested, they might become a force for East-West understanding; an instrument for the diffusion of Western liberal democratic values; bearers of a Western concept of rationality.[93]

That was the positive view. The negative emphasized the questioning attitude of intellectuals, their tendency to opposition, their political unreliability from the vantage point of existing elites. Some writers noted that Soviet analysts adopted a similar interpretation of Third World intellectuals.[94] Among Development theorists, Shils took this position as well. Intellectuals, he argued, were often "extremely critical of practically all politicians and they are contemptuous of party leaders. A large part of the intelligentsia incline toward opposition—as if by their very nature."[95] This inclination manifested itself in the "disproportionately high readiness [of intellectuals] to associate themselves with alienated movements aspiring to extremist solutions of the problems of their societies."[96]

Shils's interpretation was shared by other Development theorists. Where intellectuals criticized or disparaged existing political systems, they were described as politically naive or even as political. On the other hand, the question as to why intellectuals should have been in sensitive positions and able to take advantage of their articulate views led to an investigation of the effects of education on the political order. Education, some Development theorists argued, was subversive. Identified with alienation and protest movements, education was associated with political activism and therefore regarded as dangerous.

Fred Riggs, known primarily for his work on bureaucracy, had some revealing things to say on the matter. He underlined the discrepancy between the enthusiasm for education, literacy, and schooling, and the results thereof. "Combined with other developments in the new technologies of transport and communications, the result is explosive social mobilization, the sudden entry of new populations into political participation. Unfortunately, assimilation cannot proceed as rapidly, and little enough attention is given to the need for bringing the newly mobilized into community with the elite. Yet this is precisely one of the most acute problems of political development."[97] Riggs's statement focused on the key problem of Political Development—the assimilation of newly mobilized political elements.

Among established theoreticians of Political Development and Modernization, this theme was a prevalent one. Lerner (1958), Coleman (1965), Eisenstadt (1966), and Huntington (1968) stressed its implications in their various works. In *Education and Political Development*, J. S. Coleman and Bert Hoselitz called attention to the problem of education and social change. They pointed to the existing imbalance between resources allocated to different educational levels and the corresponding unpreparedness to assimilate those so educated into the community. They cautioned against a rapid increase in the number of graduates without a similar increase in employment opportunities. Lerner's work, *The Passing of Traditional Society* (1958), was cited as a confirming source that addressed the import of phased educational planning. Hoselitz argued in favor of slowing down the educational process given the lack of "necessary non-human capital in new agricultural and industrial enterprises and the change in values and beliefs which makes traditionally or previously low-ranked occupations compatible with the acquisition of some education."[98]

As Hoselitz went on to argue, in societies with high levels of illiteracy, "the acquisition of primary education has chiefly an impact on consumption and aspirations for higher levels of consumption. . . ."[99] With the inadequacy of employment opportunities, the acquisitive instinct might lead to difficulties. Unemployed citizens would be prone to organize their discontent. Hence, the danger. What was to be done? Hoselitz's description of the situation conveyed the alarm with which other theorists of Political Development regarded these trends. The unemployed became the focus of attention. Instead of turning to the conditions responsible for it, they viewed the relationship between education and unemployment as constituting an explosive combination.

In Hoselitz's terms, the "basically hopeless educated unemployed become the members of the cadres of various messianic or revolutionary political movements. The leadership is provided usually by persons whose training and education has been even more extensive, but who have been unable to find suitable employment or who have become disillusioned with the more regularized employment they might have secured."[100] Coleman, writing in the same volume on education and Political Development, agreed that advanced students were often to be found at the "core of political opposition in new states," and that intellectuals who were "usually disesteemed by the political elites" were often active as leaders of radical movements."[101]

Some years later, in 1968, Huntington contributed to the same arguments. He seconded the proposition that intellectuals were prone to support opposition movements, singling out middle-class intellectuals in particular. He approved the view that those inclined to opposition were apolitical— that is, nonconformist. Writing about middle-class, urban intellectuals in *Political Order in Changing Societies,* Huntington maintained that they were moved by "psychological insecurity, personal alienation and guilt, and an overriding need for a secure sense of identity."[102] This argument was designed to explain their sympatheitc endorsement of political goals described as Utopian in character, such as the search for "national dignity, a sense of progress, a national purpose, and the opportunity for fulfillment through participation in the overall reconstruction of society. These are Utopian goals. They are demands which no government can really ever meet."[103] Faced with such demands, Huntington suggested, "the appropriate response to middle-class radicalism is repression, not reform."[104]

As in other works in which education was identified as contributing to political instability, Huntington questioned the origins of political discontent and located it, among other places, in education. The belief that education magnified discontent was emphasized. Increased education was viewed as increasing the potential for alienation and subversion. As Huntington observed, "In general, the higher the level of education of the unemployed, alienated, or otherwise dissatisfied persons, the more extreme or destabilizing behavior which results. Alienated university graduates prepare revolution; alienated technical or secondary school graduates plan coups; alienated primary school leavers engage in more frequent but less significant forms of political unrest."[105] It followed from this argument that political stability increased with illiteracy. Writing about India, Huntington declared that "political participation by illiterates . . . may well . . . be less dangerous to democratic political institutions than participation by literates."[106] Similar arguments pertaining to American society were offered in Huntington's contribution to *The Crisis of Democracy* (1975) and, in a somewhat different vein, in *American Politics, the Promise of Disharmony* (1981).

Parenthetically, it may be noted that the discussion on education and political instability was echoed in the writings of certain counterinsurgency students, such as John Pustay. Observing the existence of disenchanted intellectuals in such countries as Pakistan, India, Egypt, Korea, and Burma, as well as in Latin America, Pustay questioned the danger they posed given their positions in society. Moreover, he noted, "they may be disenchanted with the apparent inefficiency of a mixed economy or impatient with the democratic process."[107] The argument was entirely similar to that found among Development theorists whom Pustay quoted.

The Political Elites

Whereas intellectual elites held the promise of moral leadership and the threat of moral subversion, according to Development theorists such as Shils and Huntington, political elites were the rock on which the process of state formation was believed to depend. The rock was susceptible to cracks, however. These, in the form of demands for participation, exercised a constant attraction and repulsion in analyses of Development.

The study of elites, in the manner of Pareto, Mosca, and Michels, was widely appreciated in the circle of contemporary political scientists writing on Development. Lasswell and Lerner, two scholars familiar by now to readers of the present text, contributed to the tradition in the 1950s. Both were among those persuaded that elite studies furthered the understanding of society and its political direction. They argued that "changes in elite structure are . . . indices of revolution."[108] They were also persuaded that elite studies were not elitist. In fact, Lasswell and Lerner justified their approach in the terms of revisionist theorists of democracy. They maintained that elite studies provided a necessary corrective to the "democratic fallacy, that governments are run by the governed."[109] That such an approach, particularly if not acknowledged as the governing perspective in an analysis of politics, might have a prejudicial effect on understanding its functioning was not overlooked. Verba, for example, in his concluding comments in *Crises and Sequences*, noted that differences in perspective were not to be ignored. "It is quite likely that most problems—especially those involving conflict—are problems to which there are alternative perspectives that would lead to different 'codings.'"[110]

The dominant coding pattern in conventional studies of Political Development was of the elite type. It illustrated Lasswell and Lerner's outlook, supporting the proposition that elitist studies were the principal focal point from which to understand the functioning of the "new states."[111] But it did so by merging this standpoint with a normative judgment as to the nature of political change in the same societies. This bias was evident in the discussion of mass versus elite political cultures.[112] It was apparent in the more intricate deliberations on the course of "participation crises"[113] and in the definition of the "development syndrome."[114]

Shils, writing about new states, claimed that their elites were the hope of the future. "No new state will modernize itself in the present century without an elite with force of character and intelligence. No new state can modernize itself and remain or become liberal and democratic without an elite of force of character, intelligence and high moral qualities."[115] Shils described political elites in Third World states as committed to the ideals of liberal democracy, sympathetic to a "regime of civilian rule through representative institutions in the matrix of public liberties." Their ability to implement such conditions, however, was in doubt. One index of the problem facing elites was the disparity in social, cultural, economic, and political conditions. This disparity was described in a diagrammatic form. Shils referred to a succession of "gaps" that became signs of underdevelopment in his account and in the accounts of those who adopted the catchword.

In *Political Culture and Political Development*, Pye argued that such gaps were significant as indices of different forms of political culture. And such differences, in turn, were read as indicative of the political health of a community. Pye claimed that in order to study the political culture of elites, it was essential to interpret their ideologies and their operational codes and to define "the spirit and calculations that lie behind high-risk political behavior."[116] Mass political culture, on the other hand, perceived as largely responsive in character, required less demanding forms of research. Public opinion surveys were adequate to assess the direction of mass sentiment. The disparity in the approaches to mass and elite cultures was a reflection of the assessment of the sources of power in society. Under the circumstances, greater effort went into the analysis of the thinking of elites. The implications of this were not considered to be adverse with respect to relations between masses and elites. On the contrary, Pye argued that it was essential that these relations not be passive, that the mass not adopt an "uncritical and childlike trust in the rulers and in all forms of higher authority."[117] Although "all political cultures must deal with attitudes toward power," Pye noted, such attitudes ought not be slavish.[118] Given the overall nature of interpretations of Political Development, as a process, such statements had a disingenuous quality.

The notion of "participation crises" was based on an assumption of the inequality of relations between masses and elites and of the greater vulnerability of the latter. Defined as "a conflict that occurs when the governing elite views the demands or behavior of individuals and groups seeking to participate in the political system as illegitimate,"[119] such a stance accepted the vantage point of elites as the normative basis of evaluation concerning the validity of participatory demands. The description of what constituted such "crises" left little room for the implementation of that specific set of attitudes that Pye considered desirable. In fact, the perception of social changes as accelerating the number of participants and demands was accompanied by the belief that such participants were outside the perimeter of elite political culture and, for that reason, untrustworthy. The results were frightening to elites.

> The sudden expansion of new participatory demands is one factor that warrants systematic attention. A very rapid large scale increase in political participation often creates a crisis situation because it frightens the existing elite so that it responds with repression; it strains the resources of the state, particularly of newly formed political systems with limited administrative capabilities and financial resources; and because there is a tendency for new participants, who have not been socialized into a civic order with established rules for influencing public authority, to use violence and civil disobedience.[120]

The judgment as to the acceptability of new participants' demands was in the hands of those who risked being displaced as a result of such increased participation. Hence the logic of the position that future participants be screened lest their views prove incompatible with the existing system. Socialization was a prerequisite for participation. But participation, in this account, assumed the character of a legitimizing function.

In his discussion of the "development syndrome," J. S. Coleman reviewed some of the "sequences and crises" involved in participatory demands with respect to "new patterns of integration and penetration," "resource distribution," and the "resolution of problems of identity and legitimacy."[121] In a passage that was at once blunt and eloquent, Coleman recognized that the "passion for equality" was related to "the humiliating and infuriating inequalities that historically have characterized the relationship between the former colonial countries and the West. Protest against what they feel to have been their debasement by the West is reinforced by their own tendency to lack self-confidence. This fusion of sentiments—rebelliousness and insecurity—is an extraordinarily powerful revolutionary element in their quest for equality.[122] But the passion was divisive. To ignore demands for equality was virtually impossible. To accede to them courted instability. Political elites were caught in a situation that prohibited easy solutions. "Governing elites are vulnerable to egalitarian demands not only because they are statists whose continued legitimacy depends heavily upon distributive output and goal achievement, . . . but also because they are prisoners of the modern egalitarian ideologies that they articulated in their quest for control over central state power."[123]

Political Development and Participation

The predicament described by Coleman was central to the Development/participation question. And participation was central to the credibility of Development theories claiming to be democratic. In reviewing the literature on Political Development, it becomes clear that with few exceptions Development was defined in terms of equality, democracy, and participation. At the same time, qualifications attached to such definitions undermined their formal intent. These qualifications were identified in discussions of the meaning of Political Development, in the different usages of the term that evolved, and in the accompanying arguments associated with such diverse definitions.

In spite of these variations, they contained support for a similar "resolution" of the problems identified with the contradictions of Development. That resolution was to be found in the increasing tendency to identify the actors in the process as vulnerable and unprepared to take on the responsibilities of political change and reform, thus justifying the tutorial approach. At the same time, evidence of such alleged lack of experience was explained in psychological terms associated with the transitional process itself. Under the circumstances, it appeared that increasing participation was not so much directly rejected as consciously postponed in deference to the difficulties of Third World leaders and societies. In the same spirit, it appeared that support for increased political participation had not been withdrawn but was merely set aside for a more propitious time when the unsteadying effects of the transition process would have abated and the Third World leaders involved would be more prepared to deal with their effects. The approach assumed a fanciful view of history and social change. But there was nothing fanciful about its intent.

Definitions of Participation and Development

One after another, writers on Political Development and Modernization acclaimed equality, participation, and democracy as inextricably bound with certain forms of social and political transformation. Shils was unambiguous about the definition of "modernity" that he described as accepted by Third World leaders. It was a dynamic process "concerned with people, democratic and egalitarian, scientific, economically advanced, sovereign and influential."[124] The modern state was defined accordingly as one in which "'the people' are not merely objects of the care and solicitude of their rulers but they are as 'the nation,' also alleged to be the source of inspiration of these rulers."[125] Some years later, Coleman and Lerner contributed to the *International Encyclopedia of the Social Sciences* (1968) on matters related to the meaning of Modernization. For Coleman, the term included "secularization; commercialization; industrialization; increased material standards of living; diffusion of literacy, education, and mass media; national unification; and the expansion of popular involvement and participation."[126] In his turn, Lerner, writing on a different aspect of the subject, agreed that it was widely held to include not only measures for sustaining economic growth, but also a "measure of public participation in the polity—or at least democratic representation in defining and choosing policy alternatives."[127]

Definitions geared to explaining Political Development adopted the same broad interpretations. The shift from "widespread subject status to an increasing number of contributing citizens, with an accompanying spread of mass participation, a greater sensitivity to the principles of equality, and a wider acceptance of universalistic laws,"[128] figured as a common definition of the transition process. However, in 1966, Pye claimed that the usage of the term was nothing short of eclectic. In *Aspects of Political Development*, he produced nearly a dozen different definitions of the subject, proof of a lack of substantive agreement on its limits.[129] But the list of definitions was, in reality, considerably shorter. The differences existed along a continuum on which two fundamental approaches to the subject were contrasted. One directly identified Development with economic growth; the second identified it with democracy. In between, variations of interest and significance amplified these positions. Pye's description of these alternative definitions and his interpretation of the dominant view disclosed the fix to which Development theories led when confronted with the question of participation.

The identification of Development with economic change, Pye claimed, was at the same time too narrow and too broad. Development, dealt with in terms of the diffusion of values and norms, raised problems of ethnocentrism. On the other hand, Development defined in terms of "the operation of a nation state," with its administrative and legal dimensions (considered as separate definitions) and its emphasis on "institution building and citizenship development" (also identified as separate definitions), was more acceptable.[130] The state-building and nation-building dimensions of Development evoked terms such as "mass mobilization and participation," Pye noted. These terms were meaningful for leaders of formerly colonized states who conceived of Political Development as "a form of political awakening whereby former subjects become active and committed citizens."[131] And then there was the linkage between Development and democracy, a combination that was viewed as problematic. It might arouse accusations by Third World states, reluctant to accept democratic reforms or systems, against U.S. policymakers. (This argument appeared two years later in the discussion of Title IX at the MIT conference discussed earlier.)

Without reviewing all the possible usages of Political Development listed by Pye, it was clear from his exposé that the question of Development and democracy was of particular importance. In a detailed discussion Pye explained that such a connection had to be defended against those who regarded democracy as leading to inefficiency and therefore undermining of Development—the implication being that the term had meaning as a reference to economic growth.[132] On the other hand, it had to be qualified vis-à-vis those who tended to minimize the difficulties involved. What were these difficulties? The maintenance of stability; the control of change where Development was rapid; the absence of trained administrators.

Stability was defined as a product of "change that is rationally directed toward satisfying the social needs of the maximum possible proportion of the population, while instability is associated with change that fails to gratify the social demands of the people and leaves an increasing proportion frustrated."[133] In those societies where change was rapid, increasing politicization was a by-product viewed as promoting unrealistic political expectations that could scarcely be met by less than competent administrators. Rapid change, then, accelerated the propensity toward instability. In formerly colonized countries, the departure of colonial administrators was seen as a factor that contributed to the pitfalls of the transition process. Most societies in the process of change, according to Pye, were deficient in several respects. They lacked a "social mechanism" to adjudicate changing patterns of values, interests, and their relationship to "the pattern of power" as well as to a properly functioning bureaucracy.[134] Under the circumstances, political stability was jeopardized, given the absence of administrative talent as well as experienced political leadership.[135]

The "gap" was another problem, exacerbating the political inefficiency at work. Following the line of argument found in *The Civic Culture* and "Political Order and Political Decay," Pye claimed that internal conditions prohibited the establishment of voluntarist associations and that the absence of these interfered with the progressive development of political systems. Adding to the conditions making for instability and administrative difficulties, then, the condition of the populace now became the subject of attention. The shift signified a turning from the analysis of political process to personalities and political cultures. In "transitional countries," Pye maintained, "the processes of modernization and industrial growth have not as yet proceeded to the stage in which the social structure is sufficiently differentiated and the population adequately specialized to create a wide range of specific interests with quite definite but still limited political objectives."[136] In such countries, the processes of political change were described as hampered by the rapidity of change and the demands of the politicized elements.

> To simply open the door to the ever wider popular participation in politics of illiterate and insecure citizens can easily destroy any possibility for orderly government. In the developing areas there is a genuine problem of establishing effective administrations and as shown in later chapters, the threats of insurgency and revolutionary violence are endemic in many transitional societies. There is a need for firm rule if societies are going to advance toward definite goals.[137]

The argument reproduced aspects of the analyses of mass society encountered earlier. The rationale for a tutorial approach was implicit in the allegation that the "open society" would be threatened by increasing participation, particularly since participants were described as "illiterate and insecure." Their involvement in politics—given the operative definition of politics—was perceived as destabilizing. Was the problem to be located in the entry of large numbers of demanding participants? Or was it the practice of politics that was conceived as the source of political instability?

Participation, Politics, and Statism

The participation question had both a quantitative dimension and a qualitative one. (Both addressed the issues raised earlier.) The fear of increasing numbers threatened the adequacy of political institutions to contain the demands of those numbers. However, the concern aroused by the prospect of this crush stemmed not from numbers alone but from fear of a different view of politics associated with participatory pressures.

> A continuing source of potential crisis is environmental change that increases the relevant population for political activity. As processes of social mobilization take place, more and more people define more and more problems as political. Thus, if one could accurately measure some of these dimensions over time, one would probably find in most of the developing nations that the proportion of the population defining issues as political is constantly rising. If the response to these rising expectations requires a new pattern of institutionalization, a crisis exists.[138]

This statement was made by Verba. Several years earlier, in *The Civic Culture*, the matter of keeping politics in its place, considered a talent of the British, was underscored. Introduced with a certain wry humor, it addressed the fears of Development theorists.

Statism, defined in the language of Development to refer to regimes supporting a high level of state planning, was regarded as unacceptable. It was viewed as an example of dangers to which pressures for change might lead. At the same time, it was seen as promoting excessive politicization. Arguments concerning statism differed somewhat in their emphasis. LaPalombara, for example, expressed concern that private enterprise, which he regarded as the most desirable form of economic life, would be discouraged in Third World states where a national bourgeoisie and an entrepreneurial class were frowned upon.[139] Further, he emphasized the association of "economic liberalism . . . with the emergence of political liberalism in the West."[140] If the former was not promoted, what hope would there be for the emergence of the latter? he inquired. Statist regimes were worrisome for their failure to contribute to such conditions, in LaPalombara's estimate.[141] Another argument was proposed by Coleman in *Crises and Sequences*. There, he emphasized the "primacy of the polity" in Third World regimes—a position held to be intolerant of alternative patterns of "development that would lead to greater differentiation and autonomy in nongovernmental institutional spheres or in non-bureaucratic parts of the political system."[142] Citing Shils, Coleman underlined the proposition that such states conduct policies that aim "to create socialistic, governmentally initiated, controlled, or operated enterprises, because they assume that the initiative for productive economic activity is lacking in the population."[143] The results inhibited democratic development because of the intra-elite conflicts that were a by-product of such statist policies, according to Coleman.[144] They led to "mobilization"-type regimes, which, in turn, reflected the paradoxical position of political elites who were described as imprisoned by conflicting demands and pressures. In sum, the "passion for equality," accepted as part of a set of demands that the political elites could not infringe upon, led to internal conflicts among their competitors.

The definition of the "development syndrome" summed up the transformative capacity of capitalist development, without alluding to internal contradictions or predicaments. As Coleman explained,

> Our conception of the political development process is a continuous interaction among the processes of structural *differentiation*, the imperatives of *equality*, and the integrative, responsive, and adaptive *capacity* of a political system. The interaction of these three dimensions constitutes what we have termed the "development syndrome." Political development, in these terms, is seen as the acquisition by a political system of a consciously sought, [sic] and a qualitatively new and enhanced political capacity as manifested in the successful institutionalization of (1) new patterns of *integration* and *penetration* regulating and containing the tensions and conflicts produced by increased differentiation, and (2) new patterns of *participation* and resource *distribution* adequately responsive to the demands generated by the imperatives of equality. The acquisition of such a performance capacity, is, in turn, a decisive factor in the resolution of the problems of identity and legitimacy.[145]

Development, in this view, was a process whose legitimacy was based on criteria determined by existing political elites. Their vantage point was at the source of the processes described in the functionalist language that some Development theorists adopted. Regardless of the particular expression assumed by such definitions, their meaning was clear. The risk-laden processes of social and political change—and, notably, of politicization and participation—were to be contained by institutional and political means legitimized by those in power.

The "Logic" Versus the Politics of Development Theories

In the next few years, works on Development written in similar conceptual frameworks reaffirmed the same view of politics and participation. Some significant changes in emphasis occurred, however. Certain contradictions, far from being either ignored or set aside, were underlined. Moreover, conclusions often latent or disguised in other works were directly confronted. In the essay on "Political Development" by Huntington and Dominguez (1975), *No Easy Choice* by Huntington and Nelson (1976), *Participation and Political Equality* by Verba, Nie, and Kim (1978), and the second edition of *Comparative Politics* by Almond and Powell (1978), the view of participation, its definition, and political implications, while generally compatible with that outlined earlier, had certain distinctive aspects that affected the overall discussion of the subject. Huntington and Dominguez, for example, affirmed that the basis of "mass political partici-pation" was located in a concept of citizenship in which all were decreed as possessing "certain minimal equal rights and responsibilities to participate in the state. Socioeconomic modernization thus implies a political culture and outlook that, in some measure, legitimizes and hence facilitates political participation."[146] The taxonomy of states and political conditions bearing on the timing, expression, and significance of increased political participation did not alter this position or the underlying sense of political difficulty implicit in its implementation. As Huntington noted in his chapter on the United States in *The Crisis of Democracy* (1975), democracy itself was at the root of this problematic condition. The participation crisis in American society was described as a factor in the increasing "vulner-ability of democratic government," which in turn was a function of the "internal dynamics of democracy itself in a highly educated, mobilized, and participant society."[147]

In *No Easy Choice*, Huntington and Nelson suggested that four models of Development might be considered as possible options for Third World Development. Each involved a different political strategy in alliance with a particular form of economic growth. The bourgeois pattern led to changes that confronted governments with the choice of either technocratic or populist forms of Development. The autocratic path was identified as unpopular for regimes not willing to accept the political consequences of such a course. The technocratic model, however, had problems of its own. It implied a repression of popular participation in the name of controlled Development policies. The populist model, on the other hand, was rejected by the authors because it depressed economic growth and was thus interpreted as leading to the intensification of social conflict. Although increased participation was common to populist regimes, low-level economic growth was viewed by the authors as undermining the benefits accruing to those increasingly active participants. The results, according to this interpretation, *decreased* the capacity of government and therefore *increased* instability. The underlying assumption—with respect to Development, economic growth, and participation—was that the first two were of higher priority and that both were prerequisites to participation with stability.

Having indicated their belief that Development theories, as traditionally interpreted, were irrelevant and/or misleading with respect to the analysis of political change, Huntington and Nelson appeared to be counseling a total break with such traditional explanations. But if the form of their analysis differed from that of earlier Development theorists, the substance of their argument was by no means foreign to conventional theories. The difference lay in the extent to which Development theorists were prepared both to identify Development with economic growth and to place questions of participation and democracy in a secondary position. And while the conventional theories reviewed in this text largely avoided adopting the first position openly, their interpretations supported the arguments implicit in it.

In the second edition of *Comparative Politics* (1978), Almond and Powell revealed how close their view of the meaning of Development was to the Huntington/Nelson interpretation. Participation was viewed as an addition to socioeconomic change, as a phase of state formation that followed on the achievement of a certain level of political change. Thus, Almond and Powell maintained that "state building and economy building are logically prior to political participation and material distribution, since power sharing and welfare sharing are dependent on there being power and welfare to share."[148] If there was an inherent contradiction in Development, it was between what the authors referred to as the "logic of development" as opposed to the "politics of development." The first assumed the process to be rational; the second pointed to the unmanageable dimensions that rendered it vulnerable to popular demands. As they observed, "while the logic of development would suggest a prior period of state and economy building, the politics of development compel a simultaneous confrontation of participant and distributive demands and expectations that are the most compelling of all."[149]

Almond and Powell referred to Huntington and Nelson's work sympathetically. But their own resolution of the contradiction did not take exactly the same form as that of the authors of *No Easy Choice*. In fact, it reproduced the manner of dealing with the internal contradictions of Development theories offered in earlier examples. The emphasis was shifted from process to actors; from systemic contradictions to those offered by political cultures and their participants. The conclusion offered by Almond and Powell was that "the social and political structures and cultures in these areas do not produce the kinds of political elites and bargaining culture in which progressives, seeking to combine free institutions with equitable growth, are able to draw conservatives, who are fearful of revolution, into an alliance in which they are prepared to adopt substantial social reforms."[150] The fixing of blame on political cultures that were not supportive of "bargaining cultures" appeared to mitigate somewhat the blunt nature of the Huntington/Nelson formula. But it hardly clarified the meaning of "free institutions" and their relationship with "equitable growth," much less the possible reasons for which such arrangements might with difficulty satisfy the political elites, progressives, and conservatives of the states involved. It was a matter of will and poor experience, such interpretations implied.

Almond and Powell, neither one primarily concerned with matters of Third World Development, were not the only ones to adhere to this view of the matter. In a meeting of exceptional interest held at MIT in the fall of 1979,[151] a number of scholars interested in problems of Third World change met to hear a discussion by Charles Lindblom, author of *Politics and Markets*. What made the session interesting was that many of those who participated were leaders in the field of Development studies. Lindblom's presentation dealt not with the Third World but with more general problems raised by the expansion of capitalist market systems—notably, their relationship with democracy and equality.

In short, Lindblom forced a confrontation with the contradictions that plagued theories of Political Development. He pointed to the tendency of social scientists to avoid dealing with such issues. He criticized their "separatist" habits and their pretense that it was possible or even legitimate to isolate the political dimensions of economic arrangements; whether they occurred in the United States or abroad. He insisted that it was essential to come to grips with the non-neutrality of capitalist market systems. He further argued that the disenfranchisement of significant sectors of the population, in whatever country it occurred, was not something that could be ignored.

With no exception that appeared in the transcript of the ensuing discussions, Lindblom's presentation was viewed as a form of transgression against the scholars' unwritten code. His insistence on the relationship of "politics to markets," and on the adverse character of that relationship insofar as democracy was involved, inspired little enthusiasm from the academic exponents of Political Development. The argument that the "political costs" of such systems merited the highest consideration, separate from the economic growth that various forms of capitalist market systems generated, aroused no visible support. Treated as a messenger of bad news, Lindblom was met with a suspicious if not entirely unfriendly questioning of his adherence to market systems. He did not succeed in arousing concern "that markets require the kinds of political constraints, particularly the inegalitarian obstructions to democracy."

But it is of some interest, in the light of the present study, that the response to these questions was blunt. This response was not expressed through the justificatory arguments encountered in the preceding pages. There was little need, apparently, in closed and friendly circles, to elaborate a psychological portrait of Third World Development to justify defense of the economic system that Lindblom was, in effect, accused of questioning. The underlying problem, as one participant remarked, was a fairly simple one. It was basically a matter of taste. Some preferred economic growth whereas others leaned more to egalitarianism.

The fundamental questions raised by Lindblom, as well as the responses they generated, are directly relevant to the arguments that supported the enterprise of Political Development studies and found expression in its justificatory theories. That these arguments should have been reproduced thirty years after the emergence of Development studies—with a change in style and format, but with little disguise—suggests something about their viability. To be sure, among radical critics of Development studies and elitist theories of democracy, Lindblom's presentation would have been less controversial than commonplace. But this serves to situate the conservative character of Lindblom's respondents as well as the conservative character of theories of Political Development. It is a reminder of what interpretations of Political Development themselves reveal—namely, the ease with which questions of democracy can be set aside in the name of another form of Development.

Epilogue

No author completes a work without experiencing a sense of dissatisfaction, missed opportunities, important arguments left unsaid, vital issues inadequately explored. All of this applies in the present case. Still, enough has been written here to warrant asking what it is that this exercise has demonstrated. What does one know on uncovering the various layers of experience congealed in formal Political Development studies? What does this particular social construction of knowledge reveal?

An exploration of the roots of Political Development doctrine, for one, demonstrates the series of interconnected relationships—intellectual, political, ideological—that constitute an integral part of the discourse on Development. These relationships, in turn, illuminate the conditions that gave rise to Development studies, as well as the conditions that affected the formulations of Development theories. They also disclose the affinity and the intimacy that exist between Development doctrine and conservative interpretations of democratic theory, which have generally preoccupied a different group of intellectuals. The connection is useful. But it touches only the outer, most apparent part of Development theories and interpretations. The same connection has another meaning at a deeper level. Development doctrine reproduces and amplifies the inconsistencies at the source of contemporary liberal democratic theories. And these inconsistencies explain the frustration and deadlock that characterize debates on the meaning of Development and its most sensitive aspect—its relationship to democracy. It is crucial, then, to emphasize this connection. It demystifies the formal claim to democracy that definitions of Political Development contain. Moreover, it exposes the preparedness of Development theorists to resolve the conflicts at the source of these inconsistencies by means of interpretations that undermine or jettison the connection between Political Development and democracy.

The exercise is not a gratuitous one. The justificatory function of Development studies has been indispensable in providing a theoretical mask for the support of authoritarian views of social and political change in the Third World. That such a function assumes widespread support for Development doctrine makes it all the more imperative to consider.

But to understand the continuity of the assumptions common to Development theories it is not enough to situate them in relation to foreign policy. Nor is it sufficient to compare the results of conventional analyses of political change with the experience of Third World states. The deconstruction of Development doctrine suggests other paths of explanation. It redirects attention to the several interrelated layers of experience that underlie Development theories. That experience is part of the legacy of a conservative view of political change elaborated by social scientists to make sense of the First World and then applied to the conditions of the Third. The sequence has intellectual as well as political implications. Among other things, it serves as a reminder that Development doctrine is deeply rooted in contemporary political thinking and that it is more revealing of a particular dimension of American political thinking than it is of Third World societies in transition. From this perspective, then, those who have relied on the paradigms of Development studies to understand the nature of Third World societies will have learned something of their own political tradition instead.

Notes

Introduction

1. For details, see Zachary Lockman, *Field Notes: The Making of Middle East Studies in the United States* (Palo Alto: Stanford University Press, 2016), pp. 194–196.

2. "Some friends and critics were persuaded that the study of conventional interpretations of Political Development was a dead issue, arguing that its exponents were by now spiritually dead and intellectually silent." Irene Gendzier, *Managing Political Change: Social Scientists and the Third World* (Boulder: Westview Press, 1985), p. xii. By coincidence I recently heard from someone else who had submitted a 600-page dissertation that anticipated some of Gendzier's analysis, and who faced the same objections, less successfully in this case. He gave up his search for a position in political science and went back to school for a law degree. See William Arthur Barnes, "Development Theory and Ideology: The Triumph of the Modern Middle Class in Theory and Practice," 2 Volumes, PhD Dissertation, Political Science, University of Michigan, 1979.

3. For evidence of Gendzier's influence see Nils Gilman, *Mandarins of the Future: Modernization Theory in Cold War America* (Baltimore: Johns Hopkins University Press, 2003), and the review that defines her as a founder of the field by Joseph Morgan Hodge, "Writing the History of Development (Part 1: The First Wave)," *Humanity* 6, 3 (Winter 2015), pp. 429–463, and "Writing the History of Development (Part 2: Longer, Deeper, Wider)," *Humanity* 7, 1 (Spring 2016), pp. 125–174. Gendzier will take up the Hodge essay in the pages to follow, but readers should keep in mind that Hodge is not writing about today's development practitioners or the new, post-9/11 projects, rationales, and advocates of intervention. He is concerned with *historiography*, that is, with scholars since Gendzier who, like her, have studied early Cold War development projects and theories. It has become an academic specialization in its own right. As is typical of articles of this kind, Hodge outlines some directions for future research that, to simplify, would look beyond U.S. government records (and professors) to study colonial development ideas and practices as well as Cold War Soviet and Chinese versions. That said, Hodge gets Irene Gendzier's biographical details—a liberal political science "insider" who sought policy reforms—howlingly wrong!

4. Joy Rohde, *Armed with Expertise: The Militarization of American Social Research During the Cold War* (Ithaca: Cornell University Press, 2013).

5. John Hobson, *The Eurocentric Conception of World Politics: Western International Theory, 1760–2010* (Cambridge: Cambridge University Press, 2012).

6. Ibram Kendi, *Stamped from the Beginning: The Definitive History of Racist Ideas in America* (New York: Nation Books, 2016), pp. 2–3.

7. See Robert Vitalis, "The Lost World of Development Theory," *Perspectives on Politics*, 14, 4 (December 2016), pp. 1158–1162.

8. Rohde, *Armed With Expertise*, pp. 150–155.

1. The "New Look" in Development Studies

1. February 10, 2016, http://humanityjournal.org/issue6-3/writing-the-history-of-development-part-1-the-first-wave/ by Joseph Morgan Hodge; and for the second part, March 25, 2016 (http://humanityjournal.org/issue7-1/writing-the-history-of-development-part-2-longer-deeper-wider/ by Joseph Morgan Hodge.

2. Hodge, writing-the-history-of-development, Part 1.

3. Examples of works cited by Hodge consider the following: David Engerman, Nils Gilman, Mark H. Haefele and Michael E. Latham, eds., *Staging Growth, Modernization, Development and the Global Cold War* (Amherst: University of Massachusetts Press, 2003); David Ekbladh, *The Great American Mission, Modernization and the Construction of an American World Order* (Princeton: Princeton University Press, 2010); Nils Gilman, *Mandarins of the Future, Modernization Theory in Cold War America* (Baltimore: The Johns Hopkins University Press, 2007); Michael E. Latham, *Modernization as Ideology, American Social Science and "Nation Building" in the Kennedy Era* (Chapel Hill: The University of North Carolina Press, 2000); Frederick Cooper, *Colonialism in Question, Theory, Knowledge, History* (Berkeley: University of California Press, 2005).

4. Consider the record of the hearings of the Subcommittee on International Organizations and Movements of the Committee on Foreign Affairs of the House of Representatives, December 6, 1965, as discussed in Irene Gendzier, "Play it Again, Sam: The Practice and Apology of Development," *New Political Science*, 20, 2, 1998, n. 79, p. 177.

5. Hodge, writing-the-history-of-development, Part 1.

6. Ibid.

7. Ibid. See also Nils Gilman's discussion of "Modernization Theory, Old and New," in *Mandarins of the* Future, pp. 270–273; and Kees Van Der Pijl, *The Discipline of Western Supremacy: Modes of Foreign Relations and Political Economy, III* (London: Pluto Press, 2003), p. 213, for a discussion of "The Crisis of International Relations."

8. Hodge, writing-the-history-of-development, Part 2.

9. Ibid.

10. Fukuyama's views on the importance of the moral realm are briefly discussed in Gendzier, "Play it Again, Sam," 164–165.

11. Frederick Cooper, commentary on Hodge, writing-the-history-of-development-part-2.

12. Jonathan D. Ostry, Prakash Loungani, and Davide Furceri, "Neoliberalism: Oversold?" (International Monetary Fund, Finance and Development, June 2016).

13. Thomas Piketty, *The Economics of Inequality*, trans. by A. Goldhammer (Cambridge: Harvard University Press, 2015).

14. Ibid., p. 799.

15. Klare cited in Gendzier, "Play it Again Sam," p. 177.

16. James Peck, *Washington's Asia, The National Security World, the Cold War, and the Origins of Globalism* (Amherst and Boston: University of Massachusetts Press, 2006), p. 10.

17. Ibid., p. 223.

18. Kees Van Der Pijl and Michael Barker, "Foundations of Social Change: An Interview with Kees Van Der Pijl," www.newleftproject.org/index.php/site/caegories/C5), Education.

19. Gabriel Almond and Sidney Verba, *The Civic Culture* (Boston: Little, Brown and Co., 1989), p. 343; and see further discussion in Gendzier, "Play it Again Sam," 168–169.

20. Samuel P. Huntington, Michael Crozier and Joji Watanuki, *The Crisis of Democracy* (New York: New York University Press, 1975).

21. Anne McClintock, "The Angel of Progress: Pitfalls of the Term 'Post-colonialism,'" in Patrick Williams and Laura Chrisman, *Colonial Discourse and Post-Colonial Theory, A Reader* (New York: Columbia University Press, 1994), p. 299.

22. Vivek Chibber, *Postcolonial Theory and the Specter of Capital*, Verso, London, 2013, p. 12.

23. Robert Vitalis, *White World Order, Black Power Politics* (Ithaca and London: Cornell University Press, 2016).

24. See page 107 of this volume.

25. Zachary Lockman, *Contending Visions of the Middle East: The History and Politics of Orientalism*, 2nd edition (Cambridge: Cambridge University Press, 2010), p. 134; see also Zachary Lockman, *Field Notes: The Making of Middle East Studies in the United States* (Stanford: Stanford University Press, 2016).

26. Lockman, *Contending Visions*, p. 134.

27. See this volume, pp. 126–129.

28. Consider some of the following books and articles, organized according to general theme and or states about which individual authors write:

    Regional in scope: Omar Dahi, "The UN, the Economic and Social Commission for West Asia, and Development in the Arab World," in Karim Makdisi and Vijay Prashad, *The United Nations and the Arab World* (Oakland, CA: University of California Press, 2016); Omar Dahi, "Understanding the Political Economy of the Arab Revolts," *MERIP* 259; Walid Hamdan, "The International Labour Organization and Workers' Rights in the Arab Region: The Need to Return to Basics," in Makdisi and Prashad, *The United Nations and the Arab World*.

    Algeria: Rachid Tlemcani, "Le Coup de Force Permanent en Algerie. Armée, Elections et Islamisme," *Maghreb-Machrek*, 221, 2015.

    Tunisia and Egypt: Joel Beinin, *Workers and Thieves: Labor Movements and Popular Uprisings in Tunisia and Egypt* (Stanford: Stanford University Press, 2016); Alaa Al Aswany, *On the State of Egypt: What Made the Revolution Inevitable* (New York: Vintage Books, 2011).

    Lebanon: Fawaz Traboulsi, *A History of of Modern Lebanon* (London: Pluto Press, 2012).

    Gaza: Sara Roy, *The Gaza Strip: The Political Economy of De-Development* (Institute for Palestine Studies, 2016).

    Saudi Arabia: Robert Vitalis, *America's Kingdom: Mythmaking on the Saudi Oil Frontier* (Stanford: Stanford University Press, 2007).

    Iran: Ervand Abrahamian, *The Coup: 1953, the CIA, and the Roots of Modern US–Iranian Relations* (New York: The New Press, 2013); "Why the Islamic Republic Has Survived," *MERIP* 250.

29. See I. Gendzier, *Notes From the Minefield: United States Intervention in Lebanon and the Middle East, 1945–1958* (New York: Columbia University Press, 1997, 2006);

and I. Gendzier, *Dying to Forget: Oil, Power, Palestine and the Foundations of U.S. Policy in the Middle East* (New York: Columbia University Press, 2015; 2016).

30. *Dying to Forget*, pp. 177–180.

31. Sean M. Lynn-Jones, "Why the United States Should Spread Democracy," Discussion Paper 98-07 (Harvard University, Center for Science and International Affairs, March 1998), p. 1.

32. Perry Anderson cited in Anders Stephanson, "American Foreign Policy and its Thinkers: Summary and Introduction," *Diplomatic History*, 39, 2, April 2015, 359.

33. Andrew J. Bacevich, *Washington Rules: America's Path to Permanent War*, (New York: Metropolitan Books, Henry Holt and Co., 2010), p. 12.

34. Van Der Pijl, *Discipline of Western Supremacy*, p. 216.

35. Thomas Carothers, *Critical Mission: Essays on Democracy Promotion*, (Washington DC: Carnegie Endowment for International Peace, 2004), p. 2.

36. Noam Chomsky, *Failed States* (New York: Metropolitan Books, Henry Holt and Co., 2006), p. 102.

37. Thomas Carothers, "Global Ten," Carnegie Endowment for International Peace, November 29, 2012.

38. Van Der Pijl, *Discipline of Western Supremacy*, p. 215.

39. Larry Diamond, "Promoting Democracy in the 1990s: Actions and Instruments, Issues and Imperatives," December 1995, A Report to the Carnegie Commission on Preventing Deadly Conflict, Carnegie Corporation of New York, www.carnegie. org/.../ccny_report_1995_promoting.pdf.

40. David P. Forsythe, "Democracy, War, and Covert Action," *Journal of Peace Research*, 29, 4, August 1992, 385–395; cited in Sean M. Lynn-Jones, "Why the United States Should Spread Democracy," p. 7.

41. Thomas Risse, "US Power in a Liberal Security Community," in G. John Ikenberry, ed., *America Unrivaled: The Future of the Balance of Power* (Ithaca and London: Cornell University Press, 2002), p. 261.

42. Carothers, *Critical Mission*, p. 167.

43. Thomas Carothers, ed., *Promoting the Rule of Law Abroad: In Search of Knowledge* (Washington DC: Carnegie Endowment for International Peace, 2006), p. 328.

44. Carothers cited in Chomsky, *Failed States*, p. 150.

45. Thomas Carothers and Marina Ottaway, eds., *Uncharted Journey: Promoting Democracy in the Middle East* (Washington, DC: Carnegie Endowment for International Peace, 2005), p. 4.

46. Ibid., p. 5.

47. Thomas Carothers, "The Democracy Crusade Myth," appears in the symposium, "Debating Democracy," *The National Interest*, July–August 2007, p. 8.

48. Ibid., p. 11.

49. "Carothers Replies," in Paula J. Dobriansky, "Democracy Promotion: Explaining the Bush Administration's Position (2003)", in Carothers, *Critical Mission*, p. 79.

50. Carothers and Ottaway, *Uncharted Journey*, p. 208.

51. Carothers, *Critical Mission*, pp. 5, 81–82.

52. Ibid., p. 82.

53. Carothers, *Promoting the Rule of Law Abroad*, p. 177.

54. Ibid., p. 7.

55. Carothers, *Critical Missions*, p. 79.

56. Carothers, *Promoting the Rule of Law Abroad*, p. 327.

57. Thomas Carothers, "Global Ten," Carnegie Endowment for International Peace, November 29, 2014.

58. Ibid.

59. James Copestake, "Whither development studies? Reflections on its relationship with social policy," Bath Papers in International Development and Wellbeing, Working Paper no. 36, December 2014, p. 8, www.bath.ac.uk/cds.

60. See this volume, pp. 57–58.

61. Ellen Herman, "Project Camelot and the Career of Cold War Psychology," Christopher Simpson, ed., *Universities and Empire, Money and Politics in the Social Sciences During the Cold War* (New York: The New Press, 1998).

62. See the discussion of "Social Science Research and the National Security," in this volume, p. 61.

63. Ibid.

64. Ibid., p. 62.

65. Zaheer Baber, "Modernization Theory and The Cold War," *Journal of Contemporary Asia*, 31, 1 (2001), p. 72.

66. George Leopold, March 11, 2016, "DARPA looks to tag social media, big data to probe causes of social unrest," https://defensesystems.com/articles 2016/03/11/darpa. The quotations that follow are taken from this text.

2. Making Connections

1. See, for example, the works of A. N. Agarwala and S. P. Singh, eds., *The Economics of Underdevelopment* (London: Oxford University Press, 1958); G. M. Meier, *Leading Issues in Development Economics* (New York: Oxford University Press, 1964); D. Lehmann, ed., *Development Theory* (London: Frank Cass, 1979), especially the chapters by D. Seers and E. W. Nafziger. In addition, consult B. Higgins, *Economic Development* (New York: W. W. Norton and Company, 1959); G. M. Meier and R. E. Baldwin, *Economic Development, Theory, History, Policy* (New York: John Wiley, 1957); G. Myrdal, *Economic Theory and Underdeveloped Countries* (London: Gerald Duckworth, 1957); R. Prebisch, "The Economic Development of Latin America and Its Principal Problems," *Economic Bulletin for Latin America* 7, no. 1 (1962); W. W. Rostow, *The Stages of Economic Growth* (London: Cambridge University Press, 1960); A. O. Hirschman, *The Strategy of Economic Development* (New Haven, Conn.: Yale University Press, 1958).

2. I. Adelman and C. T. Morris, *Economic Growth and Social Equity in Developing Countries* (Stanford, Calif.: Stanford University Press, 1973); D. Seers, "The Limitations of the Special Case," *Bulletin of the Oxford Institute of Economics and Statistics* 25 (1963); K. Griffin, *Underdevelopment in Spanish America—An Interpretation* (Cambridge, Mass.: MIT Press, 1969); T. W. Schultz, *Transforming Traditional Agriculture* (New Haven, Conn.: Yale University Press, 1964); M. Lipton, "The Theory of the Optimizing Peasant," *Journal of Development Studies 4* (1968).

3. C. B. Macpherson, *Democratic Theory: Essays in Retrieval* (Oxford: Clarendon Press, 1973), p. 170.

4. P. A. Baran and E. J. Hobsbawm, "The Stages of Economic Growth: A Review," in C. K. Wilber, ed., *The Political Economy of Development and Underdevelopment* (New

York: Random House, 1973); Higgins, *Economic Development,* p. 373; G. Myrdal, *Asian Drama* (New York: Pantheon, 1968), Vol. 3, p. 1855.

5. The following volumes constitute one of the major series of studies on Political Development. The list is arranged chronologically. (1) L. Pye, ed., *Communications and Political Development* (Princeton, N.J.: Princeton University Press, 1963); (2) J. LaPalombara, ed., *Bureaucracy and Political Development* (Princeton, N.J.: Princeton University Press, 1963); (3) R. E. Ward and Dankwart A. Rustow, eds., *Political Modernization in Japan and Turkey* (Princeton, N.J.: Princeton University Press, 1964); (4) J. S. Coleman, ed., *Education and Political Development* (Princeton, N.J.: Princeton University Press, 1965); (5) L. Pye and S. Verba, eds., *Political Culture and Political Development* (Princeton, N.J.: Princeton University Press, 1965); (6) J. LaPalombara and M. Weiner, eds., *Political Parties and Political Development* (Princeton, N.J.: Princeton University Press, 1966); (7) L. Binder, J. S. Coleman, J. LaPalombara, L. Pye, S. Verba, and M. Weiner, *Crises and Sequences in Political Development* (Princeton, N.J.: Princeton University Press, 1971); (8) C. Tilly, ed., *The Formation of National States in Western Europe* (Princeton, N.J.: Princeton University Press, 1975); and (9) R. Grew, ed., *Crises of Political Development in Europe and the United States* (Princeton, N.J.: Princeton University Press, 1978).

6. J. Ocampo and D. Johnson, "The Concept of Political Development," in J. Cockroft, A. Gunder Frank, and D. Johnson, eds., *Dependence and Underdevelopment* (Garden City, N.Y.: Anchor Books, Doubleday and Company, 1972), p. 400; C. B. Macpherson, "Reflections on the Sources of Development Theory," in M. Stanley, ed., *Social Development: Critical Perspectives* (New York: Basic Books, 1972). I am grateful to Professor Macpherson for having brought this article to my attention. R. Packenham, *Liberal America and the Third World: Political Development Ideas in Foreign Aid and Social Science* (Princeton, N.J.: Princeton University Press, 1973). Among the radical and liberal critiques of Development that are relevant to this review, consider the following: A. Gunder Frank, "Sociology of Development and Underdevelopment of Sociology," in Cockroft, Frank, and Johnson, *Dependence and Underdevelopment;* S. Bodenheimer, "The Ideology of Developmentalism: American Political Science's Paradigm-Surrogate for Latin American Studies," *Berkeley Journal of Sociology,* 1970; M. Kesselman, "Order or Movement? The Literature of Political Development as Ideology," *World Politics* 26, no. 1 (October 1973); H. Bernstein, in Lehmann, *Development Theory,* D. Cruise O'Brien, "Modernization, Order and the Erosion of a Democratic Ideal: American Political Science, 1960–1970," in ibid.; A. R. Willner, "The Underdeveloped Study of Political Development," *World Politics* 16, no. 3 (April 1964); R. Bendix, "Tradition and Modernity Reconsidered," in R. Bendix, ed., *Embattled Reason* (New York: Oxford University Press, 1970); A. Mazrui, "From Social Darwinism to Current Theories of Modernization," *World Politics* 21, no. 1 (October 1968); R. F. Hopkins, "Securing Authority: The View from the Top," *World Politics* 24, no. 2 (January 1972); R. B. Pratt, "The Underdeveloped Political Science of Development," *Studies in Comparative International Development* 8, no. 1 (Spring 1973); D. C. Tipps, "Modernization Theory and Comparative Study of Societies: A Critical Perspective," *Comparative Studies in Society and History* 15, no. 2 (March 1973).

7. This criticism now constitutes a voluminous body of literature. Some of the most useful reviews of the main tendencies to be found in the debates on development

are discussed in A. Brewer, *Marxist Theories of Imperialism* (London: Routledge and Kegan Paul, 1980); D. Goodman and M. Redclift, *From Peasant to Proletarian, Capitalist Development and Agrarian Transition* (Oxford: Blackwell, 1981); J. Taylor, *From Modernization to Modes of Production: A Critique of the Sociologies of Development and Underdevelopment* (London: Macmillan, 1979); I. Roxborough, *Theories of Underdevelopment* (Atlantic Highlands, N.J.: Humanities Press, 1979); and W. B. Hansen and B. Schulz, "Imperialism, Dependency and Social Class," *Africa Today* 28, no. 3, 1981; *Latin American Perspectives* 8, nos. 3, 4, issues 30, 31 (Summer-Fall 1981); I. Oxaal, T. Barnett, D. Booth, eds. *Beyond the Sociology of Development* (London: Routledge and Kegan Paul, 1975), pp. 50–85.

8. For a consideration of differences and internal criticisms, see the essays by H. Bernstein, "Sociology of Underdevelopment vs Sociology of Development?" in Lehmann, *Development Theory*, C. Leys, "Underdevelopment and Dependency: Critical Notes," *Journal of Contemporary Asia* 7, no. 1 (1977); Bill Warren, *Imperialism: Pioneer of Capitalism* (London: NLB and Verso Editions, 1981), which includes the essay entitled "Myths of Underdevelopment," to which the following responded: A. Emmanuel, "Current Myths of Development"; and P. McMichael, J. Petras, and R. Rhodes, "Industry in the Third World," *New Left Review*, no. 85 (May-June 1974).

9. Bernstein, "Sociology of Underdevelopment," p. 97.

10. Given their importance in the literature on Political Development, it is instructive to read the essays by Shils and Binder in L. Binder, ed., *Politics in Lebanon* (New York: John Wiley and Sons, 1966). For criticisms of conventional interpretations of contemporary analyses of Lebanon and Iran, see the following: A. Hourani, "Ideologies of the Mountain and the City," in R. Owen, ed., *Essays on the Crisis in Lebanon* (London: Ithaca Press, 1976); M. C. Hudson, *The Precarious Republic Revisited: Reflections on the Collapse of Pluralist Politics in Lebanon* (Washington, D.C.: Institute of Arab Development, Center for Contemporary Arab Studies, Georgetown University, 1977); F. Halliday, "Why the Experts Were Wrong," *Gazelle Review*, no. 6 (1979); E. Said, *Covering Islam* (New York: Pantheon Books, 1981).

11. H. A. Kissinger, *Years of Upheaval* (Boston: Little, Brown, 1982), pp. 672–673.

12. See the references in Note 6 of this chapter.

13. See the references in Notes 21, 25, and 26 of Chapter 6 of this text. In addition, consider C. Lindblom's presidential address before the American Political Science Association, "Another State of Mind," *American Political Science Review* 76 (1982), pp. 9–21; see also C. Lindblom, "The Market as Prison," *Journal of Politics* 44, no. 2 (May 1982); and J. Manley's discussion and references in "Neo-Pluralism: A Class Analysis of Pluralism I and Pluralism II," *American Political Science Review* 77, no. 2 (1983), pp. 368–388.

14. This phrase is taken from the title of C. E. Lindblom's book, *Politics and Markets* (New York: Basic Books, 1977).

15. C. B. Macpherson, *The Political Theory of Possessive Individualism* (Oxford: Oxford University Press, 1962), p. 269.

3. Discourse on Development

1. National Security Council 162/1, a report to the NSC by the NSC Planning Board entitled "Review of Basic National Security Policy" (October 19, 1953). Microfilm

reprint of declassified documents made available by University Publications of America, Inc., Frederick, Maryland.

2. National Security Council 5705/5, "Review of Basic National Security Policy: Foreign Economic Issues Relating to National Security" (April 3, 1957). Microfilm reprint of declassified documents made available by University Publications of America, Inc., Frederick, Maryland.

3. Cited in G. Kolko, *The Politics of War* (New York: Vintage Books, 1968), p. 252.

4. Dean Acheson's statement appears in his testimony before the November 30, 1944, session of the House Subcommittee on Foreign Trade and Shipping of the Special Committee on Post-War Economic Policy and Planning, 78th Congress, 2nd session, 1944, p. 1081.

5. R. F. Mikesell, *United States Economic Policy and International Relations* (New York: McGraw-Hill, 1952), p. 192. See also the recent work by R. Mikesell, R. Kilmarx, and A. Kramish, *The Economics of Foreign Aid and Self-Sustaining Development* (Boulder, Colo.: Westview Press, 1983). For a general critique of the international economic organizations—of particular interest with respect to Third World states— see C. Payer, *The Debt Trap* (New York: Monthly Review Press, 1974) and Payer, *The World Bank* (New York: Monthly Review Press, 1982).

6. Mikesell, *United States Economic Policy and International Relations*, pp. 192–193.

7. A. Berle, cited in W. LaFeber, *America, Russia, and the Cold War, 1945–1975*, 3rd ed. (New York: John Wiley and Sons, 1976), p. 52.

8. Dean Acheson, *Present at the Creation* (New York: W. W. Norton and Company, 1969), p. 219.

9. Cited in LaFeber, *America, Russia, and the Cold War, 1945–1975*, p. 55.

10. The "Message of the President of the United States," presented before a joint session of the U.S. Senate and House of Representatives on March 12, 1947, is reprinted in U.S. Congress, House of Representatives, "Assistance to Greece and Turkey," Report no. 314, 80th Congress, 1st session. Also consult "Aid to Greece and Turkey," in Senate Report no. 1017, 80th Congress, 2nd session.

11. Mikesell, *United States Economic Policy and International Relations*, p. 245.

12. The Inaugural Address of the President, January 20, 1949, appears in the proceedings of the 81st Congress, 1st session, Doc. no. 5 (Washington, D.C.: Government Printing Office, 1949). For an interpretation reflecting the views of the administration, see the discussion on Point IV in *Major Problems of United States Foreign Policy, 1949–1950* (Washington, D.C.: Brookings Institution, 1949), p. 292.

13. *Major Problems of United States Foreign Policy, 1950–1951* (Washington, D.C.: Brookings Institution, 1950), p. 121.

14. G. Gray, *Report to the President on Foreign Economic Policies* (Washington, D.C.: Government Printing Office, November 10, 1950), p. 49.

15. B. W. Cook, *The Declassified Eisenhower* (Garden City, N.Y.: Doubleday and Company, 1981), p. 307.

16. Ibid., p. 308.

17. Ibid.

18. R. P. Stebbins, *The United States in World Affairs, 1959* (New York: Harper and Brothers, 1960), p. 88. [Published for the Council on Foreign Relations.]

19. U.S. Congress, House of Representatives, Tax Exempt Foundations, report of the Special Committee to Investigate Tax Exempt Foundations and Comparable Organizations, 83rd Congress, 2nd session on H. Res. 217 (December 16, 1954).

20. U.S. Congress, Development of Technical Assistance Programs, report to the Committee on Foreign Relations, Subcommittee on Technical Assistance Programs, 83rd Congress, 2nd session (November 22, 1954).

21. "Economic Development of Underdeveloped Countries," statement by Paul G. Hoffman, January 4, 1957, in *Department of State Bulletin* [hereafter referred to as DSB] XXXVI, no. 920 (February 11, 1957), p. 237.

22. Ibid., p. 238.

23. Ibid.

24. Vice-President Nixon, "Private Investment and the Economic Challenge," address to the International Industrial Development Conference in San Francisco, California, reported in *DSB* XXXVII, no. 958 (October 15, 1957), p. 705.

25. Ibid.

26. F. O. Wilcox, "Address to the American Association of University Women," June 27, 1957, reported in *DSB* XXXVII, no. 942 (July 15, 1957), p. 108.

27. Ibid.

28. Secretary of State John F. Dulles, Senate Special Committee to Study the Foreign Aid Program, April 8, 1957, reported in *DSB* XXXVI, no. 931 (April 29, 1957), pp. 677–678.

29. Rockefeller Brothers Fund, *Foreign Economic Policy for the Twentieth Century* [Special Studies Project Report III, America at Mid-Century Series] (Garden City, N.Y.: Doubleday and Company, 1958), p. 33.

30. Ibid., p. 17.

31. Ibid., p. 19.

32. Ibid., p. 40.

33. Ibid.

34. F. O. Wilcox, "The United States and the Challenge of the Underdeveloped Areas of the World," address to Wayne State University Conference, May 1, 1959, reported in *DSB* 40, no. 1039 (May 25, 1959), p. 751.

35. Rockefeller Brothers Fund, *Foreign Economic Policy for the Twentieth Century*, p. 69.

36. P. Sweezy, "Obstacles to Economic Development," in C. Feinstein, ed., *Socialism, Capitalism and Economic Growth*, essays presented to Maurice Dobb (Cambridge: Cambridge University Press, 1967), p. 195.

37. Rockefeller Brothers Fund, *Foreign Economic Policy for the Twentieth Century*, p. 44.

38. Under Secretary of State Dillon to House Foreign Affairs Committee, March 24, 1959, reported in *DSB* 40, no. 1036 (May 4, 1959), p. 643.

39. Under Secretary of State Dillon in an address before the 6th Annual Conference on International Economic and Social Development, April 30, 1959, reported in *DSB* 40, no. 1038 (May 18, 1959), p. 698.

40. President John F. Kennedy Inaugural Address, January 20, 1961, reported in *DSB* 44, no. 1128 (February 6, 1961), p. 175.

41. Ibid.

42. A. Stevenson, "The Search for Balanced Economic and Social Development," *DSB* 45, no. 1157 (August 28, 1961), p. 364.

43. Acting Secretary Chester Bowles, address before the Methodist National Convocation on Christian Social Concerns, April 26, 1961, reported in *DSB* 45, no. 1142 (May 15, 1961), p. 706.

44. Ibid., p. 708.

45. Under Secretary of State Chester Bowles, "Building Just Societies in a Decade of Development," address to Ministerial Session of the thirteenth meeting of the consultative committee on Cooperative Economic Development in South and Southeast Asia (Columbo Plan) at Kuala Lumpur, Malaya, November 15, 1961, reported in *DSB* 45, no. 1172 (December 11, 1961), p. 990.

46. Cited in D. Wall, *The Charity of Nations: The Political Economy of Foreign Aid* (New York: Basic Books, 1973), p. 69.

47. Ibid., p. 42.

48. M. T. Klare, *War Without End* (New York: Vintage Books, 1972), p. 33.

49. Ibid., p. 36.

50. M. T. Klare and C. Arnson, *Supplying Repression: U.S. Support for Authoritarian Regimes Abroad* (Washington, D.C.: Institute for Policy Studies, 1981).

51. Cited in Klare, *War Without End*, p. 44.

52. D. Galula, *Counterinsurgency Warfare* (New York: Frederick A. Praeger, 1964), Ch. 1; J. S. Pustay, *Counterinsurgency Warfare* (New York and London: The Free Press, Collier-Macmillan Publishers, 1965); D. Blaufarb, *The Counterinsurgency Era: U.S. Doctrine and Performance* (New York: The Free Press, Collier-Macmillan Publishers, 1977); E. Ahmad, "Revolutionary Warfare and Counterinsurgency," in N. Miller and R. Aya, eds., *National Liberation* (New York: The Free Press, 1971), pp. 172–175.

53. T. Hoopes, *The Limits of Intervention* (New York: David McKay Company, 1969), pp. 14–15.

54. Blaufarb, *The Counterinsurgency Era*, p. 70.

55. Pustay, *Counterinsurgency Warfare*, p. 33. The same point is made without the medical analogy in Galula, *Counterinsurgency Warfare*.

56. N. Chomsky and E. S. Herman, *The Washington Connection and Third World Fascism: The Political Economy of Human Rights*, Vols. 1 and 5 (Boston: South End Press, 1979); Klare and Arnson, *Supplying Repression*, pp. 22–23; R. McGehee, "The CIA and the White Paper on El Salvador," *Nation* (April 11, 1981), pp. 423–424.

57. "Objectives of the United States Economic Assistance Programs," prepared by the Center for International Studies at MIT for the U.S. Senate Committee to Study Foreign Aid Programs, S. 5290 (January 1957), p. 1 [hereafter referred to as MIT 1957/U.S. Senate Foreign Aid].

58. Ibid., p. 22.

59. Ibid., p. 24.

60. "The Operational Aspects of United States Foreign Policy," prepared by the Maxwell Graduate School of Citizenship and Public Affairs at Syracuse University for the Committee on Foreign Relations of the U.S. Senate (November 11, 1959), p. 33.

61. Ibid., p. 15; see also "The Principal Ideological Conflicts, Variations Thereon, Their Manifestations, and Their Present and Potential Impact on the Foreign Policy of the United States," report prepared by the Center for International Affairs at Harvard University, for the Committee on Foreign Relations of the U.S. Senate (August 1959).

62. "The Operational Aspects of United States Foreign Policy," p. 13.

63. Ibid., p. 14.

64. National Security Council 5719/1, NSC Operations Coordinating Board report entitled "U.S. Policy Toward South Africa South of the Sahara Prior to Calendar Year 1960" (March 21, 1958).

65. "Economic, Social, and Political Change in the Underdeveloped Countries and Its Implications for United States Policy," report prepared at the Center for International Studies, Massachusetts Institute of Technology, for the Committee on Foreign Relations, U.S. Senate, submitted January 31, 1960 [hereafter referred to as MIT 1960/Committee on Foreign Relations].

66. Ibid., p. 63.

67. Ibid.

68. Ibid., p. 72.

69. Ibid., p. 74.

70. Ibid.

71. Ibid.

72. Ibid.

73. Ibid., p. 75.

74. "The Operational Aspects of United States Foreign Policy," p. 33.

75. Ibid., p. 36.

76. MIT 1960/Committee on Foreign Relations, p. 77.

77. Ibid.

78. Ibid., p. 78.

79. Ibid.

80. Ibid., p. 79.

81. Ibid.

82. Blaufarb, *The Counterinsurgency Era*, p. 317, n. 40. It appears that the footnote reference on p. 72 of this text has been omitted.

83. W. W. Rostow, "Guerrilla Warfare in Underdeveloped Countries," in M. Raskin and B. Fall, eds., *The Vietnam Reader* (New York: Vintage Books, 1965), pp. 108–116. In-text references to this address are taken from this source.

84. See the discussion in A. M. Schlesinger, Jr., *A Thousand Days* (Greenwich, Conn.: Fawcett Crest, 1965).

85. C. Maechling, Jr., "Counterinsurgency, Yes—But with Controls," *Washington Post* (February 12, 1981), p. 19.

86. S. P. Huntington, "Instability at the Non-Strategic Level of Contact," Study Memorandum No. 2 (Washington, D.C.: Institute for Defense Analysis, Special Studies Group, October 6, 1961), pp. 21–22.

87. Ibid., p. 22.

88. Ibid., p. 28.

89. Ibid.

90. Ibid., p. 33.

91. Ibid.

92. Ibid., p. 36.

93. Ibid., p. 35.

4. Transparent Boundaries:
From Policies to Studies of Political Development

1. "Economic, Social, and Political Change in the Underdeveloped Countries and Its Implications for United States Policy," prepared at the request of the Senate

Committee on Foreign Relations by the MIT Center for International Studies (January 31, 1960).

2. A report to the National Security Council by the Under Secretary of State entitled "A Plan for National Psychological Warfare," NSC 74 (July 10, 1950).

3. H. D. Lasswell, "The Relation of Ideological Intelligence to Public Policy," *Ethics* 53 no. 1 (October 1942), p. 29. An abridged version of this article appears in D. Marvick, ed., *Harold D. Lasswell on Political Sociology* (Chicago: University of Chicago Press, 1977).

4. Ibid., p. 25.

5. Ibid., p. 26.

6. Ibid.

7. Ibid.

8. Ibid., p. 27.

9. Ibid., pp. 27–28.

10. D. Lerner, *Sykewar* [Psychological Warfare Against Germany, D-Day to V. E. Day] (New York: George Stewart Publishers, 1949), p. 318. For further information on Lerner's work and its relationship to *The Passing of Traditional Society*, see I. L. Gendzier, "Notes Toward a Reading of 'The Passing of Traditional Society,'" *Review of Middle East Studies*, no. 3.

11. D. Lerner and H. D. Lasswell, eds., *The Policy Sciences* (Stanford, Calif.: Stanford University Press, 1951).

12. Criticisms of this approach appear in W. Ilchman and N. T. Uphoff, *The Political Economy of Change* (Berkeley: University of California Press, 1969), p. 257, n. 3. For an update of the position, see G. D. Brewer and R. D. Brunner, eds., *Political Development and Change, A Policy Approach* (London and New York: The Free Press, Collier-Macmillan Publishers, 1975); and H. D. Lasswell, D. Lerner, J. Montgomery, *Values and Development: Appraising Asian Experience* (Cambridge, Mass.: MIT Press, 1976); see especially the articles by Lasswell and Brewer and the opening essay.

13. D. Lerner with I. de Sola Pool and G. K. Schueller, *The Nazi Elite* (Stanford, Calif.: Stanford University Press, Hoover Institute Series, 1951).

14. D. Lerner, "International Coalition and Communications Content: The Case of Neutralism" (Special issue on international communications research, edited by L. Lowenthal), *Public Opinion Quarterly* 16 (1952–1953), pp. 681–688.

15. D. Lerner, *The Passing of Traditional Society* (Glencoe and London: The Free Press and Collier-Macmillan Publishers, 1958).

16. G. Almond, "Western European Politics and American Policy," Memorandum No. 26 (New Haven, Conn.: Yale Institute of International Studies series, March 15, 1948); see also G. Almond, "The Christian Parties of Western Europe," *World Politics* 1, no. 1, 1948.

17. Almond, "Western European Politics and American Policy," p. 43.

18. G. Almond, ed., *The Struggle for Democracy in Germany* (New York: Russell and Russell, 1965). See the preface and two articles by Almond: "Resistance and Repression Under the Nazis," written with W. Kraus, and "The Social Composition of the German Resistance," also written with Kraus. It is useful to note that this work originally appeared in 1949, published by the University of North Carolina Press at Chapel Hill.

19. G. Almond, *The American People and Foreign Policy* (New York: Harcourt Brace and Company, 1950), p. 17.

20. Ibid., p. 159.

21. Ibid., p. 193.

22. Ibid., p. 235.

23. Ibid.

24. B. W. Cook, *The Declassified Eisenhower* (Garden City, N.Y.: Doubleday, 1981), p. 177.

25. U.S. Congress, House of Representatives, Report 4 with Part IX of hearings on "Winning the Cold War: The U.S. Ideological Offensive," prepared by the Subcommittee on International Organizations and Movements of the Committee on Foreign Affairs (Washington, D.C.: Government Printing Office, 1966), p. 1 [hereafter referred to as *BSNS*].

26. Ibid.

27. Ibid., p. 5R.

28. Ibid., p. 34.

29. Ibid., p. 141.

30. Ibid., p. 72.

31. Ibid., p. 119.

32. Ibid., p. 34.

33. Ibid.

34. Ibid., p. 129.

35. Ibid., p. 152.

36. See citation in Klare, *War Without End*, p. 78.

37. The debate over Title IX is discussed in D. Hapgood, ed., *The Role of Popular Participation in Development*, report on a conference on the Implementation of Title IX, Foreign Assistance Act (Cambridge, Mass.: MIT Press, 1969), June 24-August 2, 1968.

38. J. Peck, "The Roots of Rhetoric: The Professional Ideology of America's China Watchers," in E. Friedman and M. Selden, eds., *America's Asia: Dissenting Essays on Asian-American Relations* (New York: Vintage Books, 1971), p. 51.

39. Fairbank, cited in Peck, ibid., p. 51; see also Note 53, p. 64.

40. L. Pye, *Guerrilla Communism in Malaya* (Princeton, N.J.: Princeton University Press, 1956), p. 345.

41. Ibid., p. 357.

42. MIT 1960/Committee on Foreign Relations, p. 1.

43. Ibid.

44. Ibid., p. 11.

45. Ibid., p. 12.

46. C. Johnson, *Revolutionary Change* (Boston: Little, Brown and Company, 1966), p. 66.

47. S. S. Wolin, "The Politics of the Study of Revolution," *Comparative Politics* 5, no. 3 (April 1973), p. 345.

48. Ibid.

49. On Project Camelot, see *BSNS* in its entirety; I. L. Horowitz, ed., *The Rise and Fall of Project Camelot*, rev. ed. (Cambridge, Mass.: MIT Press, 1974); I. L. Horowitz, *Ideology and Utopia in the United States, 1956–1976* (New York: Oxford University Press, 1977); I. L. Horowitz and J. E. Katz, *Social Science and Public Policy in the*

United States (New York: Praeger Publishers, 1975); Klare, *War Without End;* and for the more general question of objectivity in research, N. Chomsky, *American Power and the New Mandarins* (New York: Vintage Books, 1969).

50. *BSNS*, p. 32.

51. Ibid., p. 3R.

52. Ibid., p. 5.

53. Ibid.

54. Ibid., pp. 20–21.

55. Ibid., p. 62.

56. Senator Fulbright's views are cited in Horowitz, *The Rise and Fall of Project Camelot*, p. 197.

57. Department of State, Foreign Affairs Research Council, "A Report on the First Three Years" (August 1968), p. 1.

58. *BSNS*, p. 48.

59. M. Klare, *The University-Military-Police Complex* (Berkeley, Calif.: North American Congress on Latin America, 1977), pp. 49–62.

60. *BSNS*, p. 39. On "civic action," see the work by W. F. Barber and C. N. Ronning, *Internal Security and Military Power: Counterinsurgency and Civic Action in Latin America* (Columbus: Ohio State University Press, 1966).

61. Some examples of this approach and its variations may be found in S. Fisher, ed., *The Military in the Middle East* (Columbus: Ohio University Press, 1963); M. Janowitz, *The Military in the Political Development of New Nations: An Essay in Comparative Analysis* (Chicago: University of Chicago Press, 1964); M. Janowitz, ed., *The New Military, Changing Patterns of Organization* (New York: Russell Sage Foundation, 1964) [see the Bibliographic Guide in this latter text for additional sources on this subject]; E. Lieuwen, *Armies and Politics in Latin America* (New York: Frederick A. Praeger, 1960); S. P. Huntington, ed., *Changing Patterns of Military Politics* (New York: The Free Press, 1962); and for a more recent review that includes critical essays on the general approach, K. Fidel, ed., *Militarism in Developing Countries* (New Brunswick, N.J.: Transaction Books, 1975). See also the very different analysis offered by R. First, *Power in Africa* (New York: Pantheon Books, 1970), which discusses army interventions against the background of the politics of the state.

62. J. J. Johnson, *The Role of the Military in Underdeveloped Countries* (Princeton, N.J.: Princeton University Press, 1962).

63. L. Pye, "Armies in the Process of Political Modernization," ibid., p. 88.

64. Ibid.

65. L. Pye, "Southeast Asia and American Policy," address to the National War College, Center for International Studies at MIT, Cambridge, Mass. (March 6, 1959), pp. 18–19.

66. L. Pye, "Armies in the Process of Political Modernization," in Johnson, *The Role of the Military,* L. Pye, "The Roots of Insurgency and the Commencement of Rebellions," Princeton University Symposium on Internal War, Center for International Studies at MIT, Cambridge, Mass. (June 1962).

67. E. A. Shils, "The Military in the Political Development of the New States," in Johnson, *The Role of the Military,* p. 31.

68. MIT 1960/Committee on Foreign Relations, p. 45.

69. Ibid., p. 46.

70. Pye, "The Roots of Insurgency and the Commencement of Rebellions," p. 37.

71. M. Millikan and D. L. M. Blackmer, eds., *The Emerging Nations* (Boston: Little, Brown and Company, 1961), pp. 113–114.

72. Ibid., p. 120.

73. Klare, *War Without End*, p. 108.

74. J. LaPalombara, ed., *Bureaucracy and Political Development*, (Princeton, N.J.: Princeton University Press, 1963), p. 21.

75. Millikan and Blackmer, *The Emerging Nations*, p. 133.

76. Ibid.

77. I. L. Horowitz, "Militarization, Modernization and Mobilization: Third World Development Patterns Reexamined," in Fidel, *Militarism in Developing Countries*, p. 301.

78. M. Janowitz, *The Last Half Century, Societal Change and Politics in America* (Chicago: University of Chicago Press, 1978), p. 166.

79. Klare and Arnson, *Supplying Repression* p. 9.

80. Ibid., p. 11.

81. S. P. Huntington, *Political Order in Changing Societies*, (New Haven, Conn.: Yale University Press, 1968), p. 4.

82. Ibid., p. 194.

83. Ibid., pp. 192–193. For another description of the effects of U.S. military power in the postwar era, written from a compatible perspective albeit a less apologetic one, see L. Bloomfield and A. Liess, *Controlling Small Wars: A Strategy for the '70s* (New York: Alfred A. Knopf, 1969), pp. 394, 400–401.

84. S. P. Huntington, *Political Order*, p. 193.

85. Ibid., p. 359.

86. MIT 1960/Committee on Foreign Relations, p. 41.

87. Ibid., pp. 13–14.

88. Ibid., p. 19.

89. Ibid., p. 21.

90. Ibid., p. 34.

91. Ibid., p. 36.

92. Ibid., p. 37.

93. Ibid., p. 38.

94. Ibid.

95. Ibid., p. 39.

96. Ibid.

97. Ibid., p. 48.

98. Ibid., p. 49.

99. E. R. Morss and V. A. Morss, *U. S. Foreign Aid: An Assessment of New and Traditional Development Strategies* (Boulder, Colo.: Westview Press, 1982), p. 21.

100. U.S. Congress, House, Committee on Foreign Affairs, "Title IX: Utilization of Democratic Institutions in Development," Report No. 15, 750, 89th Congress, 2nd session (1966).

101. Ibid.

102. D. Hapgood, ed., *The Role of Popular Participation in Development* (Cambridge, Mass.: MIT Press, Center for International Studies, 1969), p. 44.

103. Committee on Foreign Affairs, Title IX; as an illustration of this position, see Sec. 281 of the amendment in the appendix.

104. Hapgood, *The Role of Popular Participation*, p. 19.

105. Ibid., pp. x, 54.

106. Ibid., p. 49.

107. Ibid., p. 56.

108. See the comments by K. Griffin on the implications of this approach to Development, and particularly agricultural change, in *The Political Economy of Agrarian Change*, 2nd. ed. (London: Macmillan Press, 1979), p. 204.

109. Hapgood, *The Role of Popular Participation*, p. 28.

110. Ibid., p. 62.

111. Ibid.

112. Ibid.

113. Ibid.

5. Defining the Parameters of Discourse

1. R. W. Friedrichs, *A Sociology of Sociology* (New York: The Free Press, 1970), p. 17.

2. S. P. Huntington, *American Politics: The Promise of Disharmony* (Cambridge, Mass.: Belknap Press of Harvard University Press, 1981), p. 169.

3. D. Bell, "The Cultural Contradictions of Capitalism," in D. Bell and I. Kristol, eds., *Capitalism Today* (New York: Basic Books, 1970), p. 24.

4. B. W. Cook, *The Declassified Eisenhower* (Garden City, N.Y.: Doubleday, 1981), p. vii.

5. V. S. Navasky, *Naming Names* (New York: Viking Press, 1980).

6. See S. Diamond, "The FBI in the Yard: Hoover Goes to Harvard," *Nation* (October 24, 1981); S. Diamond, "McCarthyism on Campus: Extra College Kids Scoop Press," *Nation* (September 19, 1981); S. Diamond, "Veritas at Harvard," *New York Review of Books* (April 28, 1977) and the response by M. Bundy, *New York Review of Books* (May 26, 1977); and E. W. Schrecker, "McCarthyism at Harvard: A Tentative Survey," Radcliffe Institute Working Paper (n.d.). McCarthyism and the intellectuals is the subject of M. P. Rogin's book *The Intellectuals and McCarthy* (Cambridge, Mass.: MIT Press, 1967); it is also treated in a number of the essays collected in D. Bell, ed., *The Radical Right* (Garden City, N.Y.: Doubleday, 1964).

7. E. A. Purcell, Jr., *The Crisis of Democratic Theory* (Lexington, Ky.: University Press of Kentucky, 1973), p. 137.

8. A. Schlesinger, Jr., *The Vital Center* (Boston: Houghton Mifflin, 1949).

9. See the *Partisan Review* [hereafter referred to as *PR*] symposium on "Our Country and Our Culture" (May-August 1952). This symposium was published in several issues of the journal.

10. See the interview with N. Mailer in *PR* (May-June 1952) and that with C. W. Mills in *PR* (July-August 1952).

11. See the interview with J. Burnham in *PR* (May-June 1952), p. 290.

12. See the interview with C. W. Mills in *PR* (July-August 1952), p. 446.

13. See the interview with P. Rahv in *PR* (May-June 1952), p. 309.

14. See the interview with J. Burnham in *PR* (May-June 1952), p. 290.

15. G. Almond, *The Appeals of Communism* (Princeton, N.J.: Princeton University Press, 1954), pp. 246–247.

16. Ibid., pp. 201–202, n. 10.

17. E. A. Shils, *The Torment of Secrecy* (Glencoe, Ill.: The Free Press, 1956), p. 162.

18. Ibid., pp. 82–86.

19. Ibid., p. 126.

20. Ibid., p. 15.

21. Ibid., p. 16.

22. Ibid., p. 227.

23. C. Lasch, "The Cultural Cold War: A Short History of the Congress for Cultural Freedom," C. Lasch, ed., *The Anatomy of the American Left* (New York: Alfred S. Knopf, 1969), pp. 100–102; J. Dittberner, *The End of Ideology and American Social Thought, 1930–1960* (Ann Arbor, Mich.: UMI Research Press, 1979), p. 126.

24. Comment by Dr. J. Margolin, cited in the proceedings of the *Indian Congress for Cultural Freedom* (Bombay: Kanda Press, 1951), p. 74.

25. R. H. Rovere, "A Reporter at Large," *New Yorker* (November 8, 1958), p. 174.

26. *The Congress for Cultural Freedom* (June 1950-December 1955), p. 10.

27. See the comment on Burnham and Indian independence in G. Orwell, *The Collected Essays, Journalism and Letters of George Orwell*, vol. 4 (England: Penguin Books, 1970), p. 368.

28. Cited in *Indian Congress for Cultural Freedom*, p. 82.

29. *Cultural Freedom in Asia*, the proceedings of a conference held at Rangoon, Burma, on Feb. 17, 18, 19, and 20, 1955 and convened by the Congress for Cultural Freedom and the Society for the Extension of Democratic Ideals (Rutland, Vt.: Charles E. Tuttle Company, 1956).

30. Ibid., p. 185.

31. Ibid., p. 14.

32. E. A. Shils, "Letter From Milan, The End of Ideology?" *Encounter* 5, no. 5 (November 1955), p. 52.

33. Ibid., p. 53.

34. Ibid.

35. Ibid.

36. Ibid., p. 54.

37. Ibid., p. 56.

38. Ibid., p. 58.

39. Ibid.

40. Ibid., p. 55.

41. Ibid.

42. Ibid.

43. Ibid.

44. Ibid.

45. D. Macdonald, "No Miracle in Milan," *Encounter* 5, no. 6 (December 1955), pp. 74.

46. J. K. Galbraith, *The Nature of Mass Poverty* (Cambridge, Mass.: Harvard University Press, 1979), p. 36.

47. Shils, "Letter from Milan," p. 58.

48. Ibid., p. 57.

49. Cited in E. H. Berman, "The Extension of Ideology: Foundation Support for Intermediate Organizations and Forums," *Comparative Education Review* (February 1982), p. 62.

50. Rovere, "A Reporter at Large," p. 176.

51. K. A. B. Jones-Quartey, "The Institutions of Public Opinion in a Rapidly Changing Africa," *Proceedings of the International Conference on Representative Government and National Progress*, Ibadan, Nigeria (1959).

52. Ibid.

53. *Democracy in the New States* [Rhodes Seminar Paper] (New Delhi, India: Office for Asian Affairs, Congress for Cultural Freedom, 1959); introduction by Prabhakar Padhye.

54. Ibid., p. 125.

55. Ibid., p. 126.

56. Ibid., p. 128.

57. Ibid., p. 7.

58. Ibid., p. 9.

59. Ibid., p. 21.

60. *Africa, The Dynamics of Change*, proceedings of a Conference on Representative Government and National Progress Organized by the Congress for Cultural Freedom and the Department of Extra Mural Studies, University College, March 16–22, 1959 (Ibadan, Nigeria: Ibadan University Press, 1963), p. 1.

61. Ibid., p. 2.

62. Ibid., pp. 71–85.

63. Ibid., p. 63.

64. Ibid., p. 41.

65. Ibid., p. 182.

66. Ibid., p. 194.

67. Ibid., p. 180.

68. G. Almond, *Political Development: Essays in Heuristic Theory* (Boston: Little, Brown, 1970), pp. 19–20.

69. See the preface in C. Geertz, ed., *Old Societies and New States* (New York: The Free Press; London: Collier-Macmillan Publishers, 1963), p. v.

70. For an overview of the mass society debate, see E. V. Walter, "'Mass Society': The Late Stages of an Idea," *Social Research* 31, no. 4 (Winter 1964); L. Coser, "Comments on Bauer and Bauer," *Journal of Social Issues* 16 (1960); S. M. Lipset, "The End of Ideology and the Ideology of the Intellectuals," in J. Ben David and T. Nichols Clark, eds., *Culture and Its Creators* [Essays in honor of E. A. Shils] (Chicago: University of Chicago Press, 1977).

71. D. Bell, "America as a Mass Society: A Critique," in D. Bell, *The End of Ideology*, rev. ed. (New York: The Free Press, 1962).

72. T. Parsons and W. White, "Commentary," in R. Bauer and A. Bauer, "America, Mass Society and Mass Media," *Journal of Social Issues* 16, no. 3 (1960), p. 67. In addition to the article by D. Bell cited in note 71 above, see his article entitled "Notes on Authoritarianism and Democratic Leadership," in A. W. Gouldner, ed., *Studies in Leadership* (New York: Harper and Brothers, 1950). For some of Shils's essays on the subject, see the following: "The Theory of Mass Society" and "The Stratification Systems of Mass Society" in E. A. Shils, *Center and Periphery: Essays in Macrosociology* (Chicago: University of Chicago Press, 1975); and "Daydreams and Nightmares" and "Mass

Society and its Intellectuals" in E. A. Shils, *The Intellectuals and the Powers and Other Essays* (Chicago: University of Chicago Press, 1972).

73. See the collection in B. Rosenberg and D. M. White, eds., *Mass Culture* (Glencoe, 111.: The Free Press, 1957); M. Horkheimer, "Art and Mass Culture," *Studies in Philosophy and Social Science* 9 (1941); M. Horkheimer and T. W. Adorno, "The Culture Industry: Enlightenment as Mass Deception," in Horkheimer and Adorno, eds., *Dialectic of Enlightenment* (New York: Herder and Herder, 1947).

74. C. Lasch, "Mass Culture Reconsidered," *Democracy* (October 1981), p. 11.

75. Shils, "Daydreams and Nightmares," p. 258.

76. Shils, "The Theory of Mass Society," p. 98.

77. Shils, "Daydreams and Nightmares," p. 255.

78. Shils, "The Study of the Primary Group," in D. Lerner and H. D. Lasswell, eds., *The Policy Sciences* (Stanford: Stanford University Press, 1951), p. 49.

79. Shils, "Daydreams and Nightmares," pp. 258–259.

80. Ibid.

81. Ibid., p. 259.

82. Shils, "The Contemplation of Society in America," in A. Schlesinger, Jr., and M. White, eds., *Patterns of American Thought* (Boston: Houghton and Mifflin, 1963), p. 401.

83. Shils, "Letter from Milan," p. 56.

84. Bell, *The End of Ideology*, p. 13.

85. Ibid., p. 14.

86. Ibid.

87. Ibid.

88. Ibid., p. 38.

89. Ibid., p. 31.

90. D. Bell, "The Cultural Contradictions of Capitalism," in D. Bell and I. Kristol, eds., *Capitalism Today* (New York: Basic Books, 1970), p. 25.

91. Ibid., p. 26.

92. Bell cited in an interview recorded in Dittberner, *The End of Ideology*, p. 316.

93. Ibid., p. 335 (Bell cited in interview).

94. S. M. Lipset, *Political Man* (Garden City, N.Y.: Doubleday, 1960).

95. W. Kornhauser, *The Politics of Mass Society* (Glencoe, Ill.: The Free Press, 1959), p. 13.

96. Ibid., p. 159.

97. Ibid., p. 39.

98. Ibid., p. 43.

99. Ibid.

100. Ibid., p. 47.

101. Ibid., p. 227.

102. Ibid., p. 229.

6. The Academic Translation: Liberal Democratic Theory and Interpretations of Political Development

1. See the works cited in Note 6 of Chapter 2.

2. See the works cited in Notes 13 and 14 of Chapter 2. Of particular interest in this respect is the discussion to be found in the articles by Manley and in Lindblom's 1981

presidential address before the American Political Science convention of the same year, both of which indicate the extent and depth of dissatisfaction with conventional democratic and pluralist theories within the establishment.

3. G. Almond, "Comparative Political Systems," *Journal of Politics* (August 1956); G. Almond and B. Powell, *Comparative Politics: A Developmental Approach* (Boston: Little, Brown, 1966), and the 2nd edition, *Comparative Politics: System, Process and Policy* (Boston: Little, Brown, 1978); G. Almond and S. Verba, *The Civic Culture* (Boston: Little, Brown, 1963), and by the same authors, the anthology that they co-edited, *The Civic Culture Revisited* (Boston: Little, Brown, 1980); L. Pye, *Aspects of Political Development* (Boston: Little, Brown, 1966); S. P. Huntington, "The Change to Change," *Comparative Politics* 3, no. 3 (April 1971); and S. P. Huntington and J. Dominguez, "Political Development," in F. I. Greenstein and N. W. Polsby, eds., *Handbook of Political Science*, Vol. 3 (Reading, Mass.: Addison-Wesley, 1975). It should be noted that Huntington and Dominguez express criticism about various trends in political science, although I argue in the course of this text that Huntington's interpretation of political change is well within the framework of mainstream theory. Among other political scientists who wrote on Political Development and who expressed dissenting views on the subject are J. LaPalombara, "Macrotheories and Microapplications in Comparative Politics," *Comparative Politics* 1, no. 1 (October 1968); and D. Rustow, "Modernization and Comparative Politics," *Comparative Politics* 1, no. 1 (October 1968).

4. C. E. Merriam, *New Aspects of Politics* 3rd ed. (Chicago: University of Chicago Press, 1970) [originally published in 1925].

5. R. A. Dahl, "The Behavioral Approach in Political Science: Epitaph for a Monument to a Successful Protest," in N. Polsby, R. Dentler, P. Smith, eds., *Politics and Social Life* (Boston: Houghton Mifflin, 1963), p. 16.

6. H. Eulau, *Micro-Macro Political Analysis* (Chicago: Aldine Publishing Company, 1969), p. 151.

7. G. Almond and S. J. Genco, "Clouds, Clocks and the Study of Politics," *World Politics* 29, no. 4 (July 1977), p. 489.

8. See the work by E. H. Berman, *The Influence of the Carnegie, Ford, and Rockefeller Foundations on American Foreign Policy* (Albany: State University of New York Press, 1983); E. H. Berman, "Foundations, United States Foreign Policy and African Education, 1945–1975," *Harvard Educational Review* 49, no. 2 (May 1979), and for a response by foundation representatives, see the same issue; E. H. Berman, "The Extension of Ideology: Foundation Support for Intermediate Organizations and Forums," *Comparative Education Review* (February 1982), pp. 48–68; R. F. Amove, ed., *Philanthropy and Cultural Imperialism: The Foundations at Home and Abroad* (Boston: G. K. Hall and Co., 1980).

9. C. Wagley, "The Study of World Areas: A Report on the National Conference," *Items* 2, no. I (March 1948), p. 5; M. Singer, "The Social Sciences in Non-Western Studies," *Annals of the American Academy of Political and Social Science* 356 (November 1964).

10. SSRC, "Research in Comparative Politics," *American Political Science Review* 47, no. 3 (September 1953), pp. 641–675.

11. Ibid., p. 649.

12. Ibid.

13. D. Truman, *The Governmental Process* (New York: Alfred A. Knopf, 1951); R. Dahl, *A Preface to Democratic Theory* (Chicago: University of Chicago Press, 1956); R. Dahl, *Who Governs?* (New Haven, Conn.: Yale University Press, 1961); R. Dahl, "Procedural Democracy," in P. Laslett and J. Fishkin, eds., *Philosophy, Politics and Society* (New Haven, Conn.: Yale University Press, 1979); R. Lane, *Political Life* (Glencoe, Ill.: The Free Press, 1959); R. E. Lane and D. O. Sears, *Public Opinion* (Englewood Cliffs, N.J.: Prentice-Hall, 1964); V. O. Key, Jr., *Public Opinion and American Democracy* (New York: Alfred A. Knopf, 1961); E. E. Schaatschneider, *The Semisovereign People* (Hinsdale, Ill.: Dreyden Press, 1975). The contribution to this literature by G. Almond and S. Verba, *The Civic Culture* (Boston: Little, Brown, 1963) is discussed at greater length in the pages that follow.

14. W. C. Runciman, *Social Science and Political Theory* (London: Cambridge University Press, 1971), p. 95.

15. J. A. Schumpeter, *Capitalism, Socialism and Democracy* (New York: Harper and Brothers, 1942), p. 269.

16. B. Berelson, P. Lazarsfeld, and W. McPhee, *Voting* (Chicago: University of Chicago Press, 1954).

17. H. B. White, "The Processed Voter and the New Political Science," *Social Research* (1961); P. Converse, "Public Opinion and Voting Behavior," in F. Greenstein and N. Polsby, eds., *Handbook of Political Science*, Vol. 4 (Reading, Mass.: Addison-Wesley, 1975); D. Ippolito, T. G. Walker, and K. Kolson, *Public Opinion and Responsible Democracy* (Englewood Cliffs, N.J.: Prentice-Hall, 1976); see also the articles and references cited in Note 21 below that take issue with the liberal analysis. Among recent expositions that build on the views expressed in such analyses, see N. H. Nie, S. Verba, J. R. Petrock, *The Changing American Voter* (Cambridge, Mass.: Harvard University Press, 1976).

18. Almond and Verba, *The Civic Culture*, p. 338.

19. Schaatschneider, *The Semisovereign People*, p. 102.

20. Ibid.

21. For critical assessments of contemporary liberal democratic theories, consider the following: P. Bachrach, *The Theory of Democratic Elitism* (Boston: Little, Brown, 1967); W. Connoly, ed., *The Bias of Pluralism* (New York: Atherton Press, 1969); G. Duncan and S. Lukes, "The New Democracy," *Political Studies* 11, no. 2 (June 1963); J. Habermas, "Legitimation Problems in the Modern State," in J. Habermas, *Communication and the Evolution of Society* (Boston: Beacon Press, 1979); A. Levine, *Liberal Democracy: A Critique of Its Theory* (New York: Columbia University Press, 1981); C. E. Lindblom, *Politics and Markets* (New York: Basic Books, 1977); C. McCoy and J. Playford, *Apolitical Politics* (New York: Thomas Y. Crowell Co., 1967); C. B. Macpherson, *Democratic Theory: Essays in Retrieval* (Oxford: Clarendon Press, 1973); C. B. Macpherson, *The Life and Times of Liberal Democracy* (Oxford: Oxford University Press, 1979); C. B. Macpherson *The Political Theory of Possessive Individualism* (Oxford: Oxford University Press, 1962); C. B. Macpherson, *The Real World of Democracy* (Oxford: Oxford University Press, 1972); R. Miliband, *The State in Capitalist Society* (New York: Basic Books, 1969); the articles by L. Panitch and E. M. Wood in J. Saville and R. Miliband, eds., *The Socialist Register* (New York: Monthly Review Press, 1981); A. Wolfe, *The Limits of Legitimacy* (New York: The Free Press,

1977); and R. P. Wolff, "Beyond Tolerance," in R. P. Wolff, B. Moore, Jr., and H. Marcuse, *A Critique of Pure Tolerance* (Boston: Beacon Press, 1965).

22. Duncan and Lukes, "The New Democracy."

23. Bachrach, *The Theory of Democratic Elitism.*

24. Macpherson, *The Democratic Theory*, p. 78.

25. Bachrach, *The Theory of Democratic Elitism;* P. Bachrach, ed., *Political Elites in a Democracy* (New York: Atherton Press, 1971); McCoy and Playford, *Apolitical Politics;* J. Roland Pennock and H. W. Chapman, eds., *Participation in Politics* (New York: Lieber-Atherton, 1975).

26. C. Pateman, *Participation and Democratic Theory* (Cambridge: Cambridge University Press, 1970); see especially the chapter entitled "Recent Theories of Democracy and the 'Classical Myth.'"

27. Duncan and Lukes, "The New Democracy," p. 177.

28. Bachrach, *The Democratic Theory of Elitism*, p. 32.

29. Pateman, *Participation and Democratic Theory*, p. 17.

30. G. Almond, "The Intellectual History of the Civic Culture Concept," in G. Almond and S. Verba, eds., *The Civic Culture Revisited* (Boston: Little, Brown, 1981). In the same volume, see C. Pateman, "The Civic Culture: A Philosophic Critique."

31. Macpherson, *Democratic Theory*, p. 185.

32. Macpherson, *The Life and Times of Liberal Democracy*, p. 79.

33. See the references in Note 3 of this chapter and the "Introduction" and "Conclusion" by G. Almond and J. S. Coleman, respectively, in their jointly edited work, *The Politics of the Developing Areas* (Princeton, N.J.: Princeton University Press, 1960).

34. G. Almond and G. B. Powell, *Comparative Politics: A Developmental Approach* (Boston: Little, Brown, 1966), p. 6.

35. Almond and Powell in ibid., p. 8.

36. The phrase is by Richard J. Bernstein, *The Restructuring of Social and Political Theory* (Philadelphia: University of Pennsylvania Press, 1978), p. 42.

37. G. Almond, *Political Development: Essays on Heuristic Theory* (Boston: Little, Brown, 1970), p. 249.

38. G. Almond, "Political Development: Analytical and Normative Perspectives," *Comparative Political Studies* 1, no. 4, (January 1969), p. 448.

39. G. Almond, "Comparative Politics and Political Development, an Historical Perspective," presented before the Joint Seminar on Political Development of Harvard and MIT (October 26, 1983), unpublished paper.

40. J. LaPalombara, "Decline of Ideology: A Dissent and an Interpretation," *American Political Science Review* 60, no. 1 (March 1966), p. 5.

41. J. LaPalombara, "Macrotheories and Microapplications in Comparative Politics," *Comparative Politics* 1, no. 1 (October 1968), p. 59.

42. D. Rustow, "Modernization and Comparative Politics," in ibid., pp. 37–51.

43. Ibid., pp. 39, 48.

44. See J. LaPalombara, "The Comparative Roles of Groups in Political Systems," *Items* 15, no. 2 (June 1961). I am indebted to Professor LaPalombara for having made this report available to me.

45. S. P. Huntington, "The Change to Change," *Comparative Politics* 3, no. 3 (April 1971).

46. Ibid., p. 284.

47. S. P. Huntington, "Political Science, American Area Studies, and Their Paradigms of American Politics," in L. Pye, ed., *Political Science and Area Studies: Rivals or Partners?* (Bloomington: Indiana University Press, 1975), p. 59.

48. Almond and Genco, "Clouds, Clocks and the Study of Politics."

49. Ibid., p. 497.

50. Almond and Verba, *The Civic Culture*, p. x.

51. Ibid., p. 6.

52. Ibid., p. 3.

53. Ibid., p. 7.

54. See the conclusion to Almond and Powell, *Comparative Politics*, 2nd ed. 1978.

55. Almond and Verba, *The Civic Culture*, p. 11.

56. Ibid., p. 13.

57. Ibid., p. 85.

58. Ibid., p. 136.

59. Ibid., p. 134.

60. Ibid., p. 190.

61. Ibid., pp. 190–191.

62. Ibid., p. 191.

63. Ibid., p. 343.

64. Ibid., p. 346.

65. Ibid., p. 206.

66. Ibid., p. 204.

67. Ibid., p. 346.

68. Ibid., p. 227.

69. Ibid., p. 231, n. 11.

70. Ibid., p. 366.

71. M. Foucault, "The Discourse on Language," *The Archaeology of Knowledge*, trans, by A. M. Sheridan Smith (New York: Pantheon Books, 1972), p. 226.

72. G. Almond, "Political Development: Analytical and Normative Perspective," *Comparative Political Studies* 1, no. 4 (January 1969), p. 459.

73. D. Cruise O'Brien, "Modernization, Order and the Erosion of a Democratic Ideal: American Political Science, 1960–1970," in D. Lehmann, ed., *Development Theory* (London: Frank Cass, 1979), p. 51.

74. S. Verba, "Sequences and Development," in L. Binder, J. S. Coleman, J. LaPalombara, L. Pye, S. Verba, and M. Weiner, eds., *Crises and Sequences in Political Development* (Princeton, N.J.: Princeton University Press, 1971), p. 283.

75. S. P. Huntington, "The Change to Change," *Comparative Politics* 3, no. 3 (April 1971), p. 311; see also S. P. Huntington and J. Nelson, *No Easy Choice* (Cambridge, Mass.: Harvard University Press, 1976), p. 20.

76. Huntington, "The Change to Change," p. 309.

77. Ibid., p. 311.

78. Verba, "Sequences and Development," p. 283.

79. Ibid., p. 307.

80. Ibid., p. 308.

81. J. C. Davies, "Where From and Where To?" in J. W. Knudson, ed., *Handbook of Political Psychology* (San Francisco, Calif.: Jossey-Bass Publishers, 1973), p. 18.

82. J. W. Knudson, "Personality in the Study of Politics," in ibid., p. 54.

83. D. Lerner, *The Passing of Traditional Society* (Glencoe, 111., and London: The Free Press and Collier-Macmillan Publishers, 1958), p. 78.

84. Ibid., p. 85.

85. Ibid., p. 47.

86. Ibid., p. 78.

87. Ibid., p. 50.

88. Ibid.

89. Ibid., p. 286.

90. Ibid., p. 362.

91. I. W. Zartman, "Political Science," in L. Binder, ed., *The Study of the Middle East* (New York: John Wiley and Sons, 1976), p. 272.

92. Compare the attributes of the index appearing in B. Singer and D. Wills, "Political Extremists in Iran," *Public Opinion Quarterly* 16 (1952–1953) p. 696, with those listed in Lerner, *The Passing of Traditional Society*, pp. 369–370.

93. Lerner, *The Passing of Traditional Society*, pp. 372–373.

94. Ibid., p. 374.

95. K. Deutsch, "Social Mobilization and Political Development," *American Political Science Review* 55, no. 3 (September 1961). For an introduction to the literature on social and political mobilization, see J. P. Nettl, *Political Mobilization: A Sociological Analysis of Methods and Concepts* (New York: Basic Books, 1967).

96. Deutsch, "Social Mobilization," p. 505.

97. Ibid., p. 493.

98. Ibid., p. 483.

99. Ibid., p. 494.

100. Ibid.

101. K. Mannheim, *Man and Society in an Age of Reconstruction: Studies in Modern Social Structure* (London: Routledge and Kegan Paul, 1940), p. 44.

102. K. Mannheim, *Freedom, Power, and Democratic Planning* (New York: Oxford University Press, 1950), p. 303.

103. Mannheim, *Man and Society*, p. 63.

104. Among critics of the traditional / modernity dualism, some of whom were well-known contributors to the literature of Modernization and Development, are the following: S. N. Eisenstadt, "Breakdowns of Modernization," *Economic Development and Cultural Change* 12 [hereafter referred to as *EDCC*] (July 1964); S. N. Eisenstadt, "Review Article: Some New Looks at the Problems of Relations Between Traditional Societies and Modernization," *EDCC* 11, no. 3 (April 1963); G. Almond, "Introduction," in Almond and Coleman, *The Politics of the Developing Areas*; LaPalombara, "Distribution" in Binder et al., *Crises and Sequences;* J. Gusfield, "Tradition and Modernity, Misplaced Polarities in the Study of Social Change," *American Journal of Sociology* 72 (January 1967); R. Bendix, "Tradition and Modernity Reconsidered," *Comparative Studies in Society and History* 9 (April 1967). Criticism of the abuse of this dualism was also common to radical criticisms of Development theories, including those cited in Note 6 of Chapter 2 of this text.

105. E. A. Shils, *Political Development in the New States* (The Hague: Mouton and Co., 1962), p. 31.

106. Ibid., p. 31–32.

107. E. A. Shils and M. Young, "The Meaning of the Coronation," in *Sociological Review* 1, no. 2 (1953); see also the reply by N. Birnbaum in *Toward a Critical Sociology* (London: Oxford University Press, 1971), pp. 57–80.

108. Shils, *Political Development in the New States*, p. 28.

109. Ibid., p. 17.

110. Ibid., p. 30.

111. Ibid., p. 8.

112. C. Geertz, "The Judging of Nations," *Archives Europeennes de Sociologie* 18, no. 2 (1977), p. 252.

113. Shils, *Political Development*, p. 48.

114. Ibid., p. 50.

115. Ibid.

116. Ibid., p. 31.

117. G. Almond, "Introduction: A Functional Approach to Comparative Politics," in G. Almond and J. S. Coleman, *The Politics of Developing Areas* (Princeton, N.J.: Princeton University Press, 1960), p. 53, n. 37.

118. Ibid., p. 4.

119. S. E. Finer, "Almond's Concept of 'The Political System': A Textual Critique," *Government and Opposition* (Winter 1969–1970), p. 5; Marion Levy, Jr., *Moderniza-tion and the Structure of Societies* (Princeton, N.J.: Princeton University Press, 1966), p. 316; C. Pateman, "The Civic Culture: A Philosophic Critique," in Almond and Verba, *The Civic Culture Revisited*, pp. 66–70.

120. Almond, "Introduction," p. 25.

121. Ibid., p. 7.

122. Ibid., p. 31.

123. Ibid.

124. Ibid., p. 33.

125. Ibid., p. 34.

126. Ibid.

127. Ibid., p. 35.

128. Ibid.

129. Ibid., p. 43.

130. Almond and Powell, *Comparative Politics*, 2nd ed. (1978), p. 392.

131. For an earlier text that merits comparison, see S. P. Huntington "Conservatism as an Ideology," in *American Political Science Review* 51, no. 2 (June 1957).

132. S. P. Huntington, "Political Order and Political Decay," in S. P. Huntington, *Political Order in Changing Societies* (New Haven, Conn.: Yale University Press, 1968), p. 86.

133. Ibid., p. 6.

134. Ibid., p. 28.

135. Ibid., p. 24.

136. Ibid., p. 27.

137. Ibid., p. 28.

138. Ibid.

139. Ibid., pp. 31–32.

140. Ibid., p. 31.

141. Ibid., p. 33.

142. Ibid., p. 35.

143. Ibid., p. 36.
144. Ibid.
145. Ibid., p. 45.
146. Ibid., p. 46.
147. Ibid., p. 21.
148. Ibid., p. 37.
149. Ibid., p. 55.
150. Ibid.
151. Ibid.
152. Ibid., p. 57.
153. Ibid., p. 59.
154. Ibid., p. 80.
155. Ibid., pp. 80–81.
156. Ibid., p. 81.
157. Ibid., p. 82.
158. Ibid., p. 83.

7. The Impossible Task of Theories of Political Development

1. S. P. Huntington, *Political Order in Changing Societies* (New Haven, Conn., and London: Yale University Press, 1968), pp. 58–59.
2. G. Almond, review of B. Moore, Jr.'s *Social Origins of Dictatorship and Democracy*, in *American Political Science Review* 61, no. 3 (September 1967), p. 769.
3. Ibid.
4. C. Tilly, ed., *The Formation of National States in Western Europe* (Princeton, N.J.: Princeton University Press, 1975), p. 73.
5. C. B. Macpherson, *The Political Theory of Possessive Individualism* (Oxford: Oxford University Press, 1962), p. 269.
6. Ibid., p. 221.
7. Ibid., p. 269.
8. Ibid.
9. Ibid., p. 221.
10. Ibid.
11. Ibid., pp. 221–222.
12. Ibid., p. 232.
13. Ibid., p. 232.
14. Ibid., p. 244.
15. Ibid., p. 246.
16. Ibid., p. 245.
17. Ibid., p. 247.
18. For a commentary on the relationship between market systems and personality, see the many articles by R. Lane, including "Market and Politics: The Human Product," *British Journal of Political Science* 11, part 1 (January 1981).
19. Lindblom, *Politics and Markets* (New York: Basic Books, 1977), p. 232.
20. G. Almond in G. Almond and S. Verba, eds., *The Civic Culture Revisited* (Boston: Little, Brown, 1980), pp. 13–14.

21. Ibid., p. 13.
22. See the appreciation of Lasswell in G. Almond, *Political Development: Essays in Heuristic Theory* (Boston: Little, Brown, 1970).
23. H. D. Lasswell, "World Politics and Personal Insecurity," (p. 24.) in H. D. Lasswell, C. Merriam, and T. V. Smith, eds., *A Study of Power* (Glencoe, 111.: The Free Press, 1950).
24. H. D. Lasswell, *Psychopathology and Politics* (Chicago: University of Chicago Press, 1977), p. 8.
25. Ibid., pp. 75–76.
26. Ibid., p. 153.
27. Ibid., p. 203.
28. P. Schrag, *Mind Control* (New York: Pantheon Books, 1978).
29. Ibid., p. 196.
30. Ibid., p. 197.
31. Ibid., p. 194.
32. Ibid.
33. Ibid., pp. 202–203.
34. Ibid., p. 203.
35. See B. Crick, *The American Science of Politics* (Berkeley, Calif.: University of California Press, 1967), p. 208; and for a recent laudatory assessment of Lasswell, see R. M. Merelman, "Harold D. Lasswell's Political World: Weak Tea for Hard Times," *British Journal of Political Science* 11, part 4 (October 1981).
36. Lasswell, *World Politics and Personal Insecurity*, p. 282.
37. Pye, *Aspects of Political Development* (Boston: Little, Brown, 1966), p. 61.
38. Ibid.
39. Ibid.
40. M. Weber, *The Protestant Ethic and the Spirit of Capitalism*, trans, by T. Parsons (New York: Charles Scribner's Sons, 1958), pp. 58–59.
41. Ibid., p. 60.
42. Ibid., p. 30.
43. Ibid., p. 68.
44. Ibid., p. 70.
45. Ibid., p. 183.
46. M. Rodison, *Islam and Capitalism* (New York: Pantheon Books, 1973), pp. 77–78.
47. S. N. Eisenstadt, *The Protestant Ethic and Modernization* (New York: Basic Books, 1968).
48. B. Hoselitz, ed., *The Progress of Underdeveloped Areas* (Chicago: University of Chicago Press, 1952), p. 8.
49. Ibid., p. vi.
50. A. Gunder Frank, "Sociology of Development and Underdevelopment of Sociology," in J. D. Cockroft, A. Gunder Frank, and D. Johnson, eds., *Dependence and Underdevelopment* (Garden City, N.Y.: Doubleday, 1972), Ch. 12.
51. E. E. Hagen, *On the Theory of Social Change* (Homewood, 111.: Dorsey Press, 1962), p. 55.
52. Ibid., p. 193.
53. Ibid., p. 86.

54. J. J. Spengler, "Theory, Ideology, Non-Economic Values and Politico-Economic Development," in J. J. Spengler and R. Braibanti, eds., *Traditions, Values and Socio-Economic Development* (Durham, N.C.: Duke University Press, 1961), p. 53.

55. T. Parsons, *Social Structure and Personality* (London: Collier-Macmillan Publishers, 1970), p. 80.

56. Ibid., pp. 91–92.

57. See G. Almond and S. Verba, *The Civic Culture* (Boston: Little, Brown, 1963), pp. 11, 16; Almond in Almond and Verba, *The Civic Culture Revisited*, p. 26; G. Almond and G. B. Powell, *Comparative Politics* (Boston: Little, Brown, 1966), p. 23; L. Pye and S. Verba, eds., *Political Culture and Political Development* (Princeton, N.J.: Princeton University Press, 1965)—both the Introduction and Conclusion, in particular; and, from a critical perspective, C. Pateman, "Political Culture, Political Structure and Political Change," *British Journal of Political Science* 1, part 3 (July 1971).

58. D. Lerner, "International Coalitions and Communications Content: The Case of Neutralism" [special issue on international communications research], *Public Opinion Quarterly* 16 (Winter 1952–1953), p. 684.

59. Ibid., p. 687.

60. The description appears in an essay that situates Development studies in the context of Western intellectual history. See L. Binder, "Crises of Political Development," in L. Binder et al., *Crises and Sequences in Political Development* (Princeton, N.J.: Princeton University Press, 1971), p. 37.

61. See L. Pye, "Identity and the Political Culture," in ibid.

62. L. Pye, *Guerrilla Communism in Malaya* (Princeton, N.J.: Princeton University Press, 1956), p. 348.

63. L. Pye, "The Non-Western Political Process," in H. Eckstein and D. Apter, eds., *Comparative Politics* (New York and London: The Free Press and Collier-Macmillan Publishers, 1963), p. 657.

64. Ibid., p. 658.

65. L. Pye, *Politics, Personality and Nation Building* (New Haven, Conn.: Yale University Press, 1962; 4th printing, 1966), p. 5.

66. Ibid., p. 41.

67. Ibid., p. 85.

68. Ibid., p. 86.

69. Ibid.

70. Ibid., p. 96.

71. Ibid., p. 55.

72. "To exaggerate the picture somewhat for the sake of clarity, it can be said that the Burmese tend to seek in life those warm and close personal associations they occasionally experienced with their mothers, but their behavior is governed by the expectation that any human relationship may hold great dangers. The basic outlook is that people can be easily provoked to hostile responses. Behind every sign of friendliness there always lies the possibility of precisely the opposite pattern of behavior. And in an even more complex fashion, the acculturation process tends to reinforce a sense of distrust toward precisely those who would appear to be anxious to help, for helping is the same as controlling" (quoted from ibid., p. 126).

73. Ibid., p. 139.

74. Ibid., p. 150.

75. Ibid., p. 156.

76. Ibid., p. 157.

77. L. Pye, "Identity and the Political Culture."

78. L. Pye, "Introduction: Political Culture and Political Development," in Pye and Verba, *Political Culture and Political Development*.

79. S. Verba, "Conclusion: Comparative Political Culture," in ibid., p. 529.

80. The interpretation of political change in terms of political culture produced uneven results. See, for example, the following essays: R. Scott, "The Established Revolution," and D. Levine, "Ethiopia: Identity, Authority, and Realism," both in ibid.

81. Verba, "Conclusion," p. 545.

82. Ibid.

83. Ibid.

84. A. Inkeles, "Participant Citizenship in Six Developing Countries," *American Political Science Review* 63, no. 4 (December 1969), p. 1123. In the same text Inkeles noted a further qualification of the approach taken by the authors of *The Civic Culture*. On the basis of research carried out by his own team, Inkeles observed that "the participant citizen is not also consistently non-anomic, non-hostile, and satisfied with the performance of his government. Rather, we must say 'it depends' on the country—and no doubt, on the segment of the population being studied, as well."

85. E. J. Hobsbawm, *Primitive Rebels* (Manchester: Manchester University Press, 1959); E. J. Hobsbawm, *Bandits* (London: Weidenfeld and Nicolson, 1969).

86. George Rudé, *The Crowd in the French Revolution* (London: Oxford University Press, 1959).

87. Ibid., 5.

88. See the comments on interpretations of "elite" in C. E. Black, *The Dynamics of Modernization* (New York: Harper and Row, 1966), p. 62; see also J. LaPalombara and M. Weiner, *Political Parties and Political Development* (Princeton, N.J.: Princeton University Press, 1966), pp. 432–433, for a discussion of political tutelage that applies to the treatment of Political Development and elites in the analyses of Development studies.

89. E. A. Shils, *Political Development in the New States* (The Hague: Mouton and Co., 1962), pp. 36–37, n. 3.

90. Ibid.

91. J. S. Coleman, "Conclusion: The Political Systems of the Developing Areas," in G. Almond and J. S. Coleman, eds., *The Politics of Developing Areas* (Princeton, N.J.: Princeton University Press, 1960), p. 556.

92. E. A. Shils, "Intellectuals in the Political Development of the New States," in E. A. Shils, *The Intellectuals and the Powers and Other Essays* (Chicago and London: University of Chicago Press, 1972), p. 386.

93. See the interpretations on this subject by Sidney Verba in S. Verba, "Assumptions of Rationality and Non-Rationality in Models of the International Systems," *World Politics* 14, no. 1 (October 1961), p. 116.

94. T. P. Thornton, "Communist Attitudes Toward Asia, Africa, and Latin America," in C. Black and T. Thornton, eds., *Communism and Revolution* (Princeton, N.J.: Princeton University Press, 1964), p. 266.

95. Shils, *Political Development in the New States*, p. 21.

96. Ibid.
97. F. W. Riggs, "Bureaucrats and Political Development: A Paradoxical View," in J. LaPalombara, ed., *Bureaucracy and Political Development* (Princeton, N.J.: Princeton University Press, 1963), p. 166.
98. B. Hoselitz, "Investment in Education and Its Political Impact," in J. S. Coleman, ed., *Education and Political Development* (Princeton, N.J.: Princeton University Press, 1965), p. 561.
99. Ibid., pp. 561–562.
100. Ibid., p. 562.
101. Coleman, "Introduction to Part 3," in ibid., p. 371.
102. Huntington, *Political Order in Changing Societies*, p. 371.
103. Ibid.
104. Ibid., p. 373.
105. Ibid., p. 48.
106. Ibid., p. 49.
107. J. Pustay, *Counterinsurgency Warfare* (New York and London: The Free Press and Collier-Macmillan Publishers, 1965), p. 20.
108. H. D. Lasswell, D. Lerner, and C. E. Rothwell, *The Comparative Study of Elites* (Stanford, Calif.: Stanford University Press, 1952), p. 1.
109. H. D. Lasswell and D. Lerner, eds., *World Revolutionary Elites* (Cambridge, Mass.: MIT Press, 1965), p. 1.
110. S. Verba, "Conclusion."
111. Shils, *Political Development in the New States.*
112. Pye, "Introduction."
113. See M. Weiner, "Political Participation: Crisis of the Political Process," in Binder et al., *Crises and Sequences in Political Development.*
114. See J. S. Coleman, "Development Syndrome: Differentiation—Equality—Capacity," in ibid.
115. Shils, *Political Development in the New States*, p. 86.
116. Pye, "Introduction," p. 16.
117. Ibid., p. 22.
118. Ibid.
119. M. Weiner, "Political Participation: Crisis of the Political Process," in ibid., p. 187.
120. Ibid., p. 193, n. 30.
121. J. S. Coleman, "The Development Syndrome: Differentiation—Equality—Capacity," in ibid., pp. 74–75.
122. Ibid., p. 94.
123. Ibid., p. 96.
124. Shils, *Political Development in the New States*, p. 7.
125. Ibid., p. 8.
126. J. S. Coleman, "Modernization," in D. Sills, ed., *International Encyclopedia of the Social Sciences*, Vol. 10, (1968), p. 385.
127. D. Lerner, in Ibid., p. 387.
128. L. Pye, "Introduction," p. 13.
129. Pye, *Aspects of Political Development*, pp. 33–48.
130. Ibid., p. 38.
131. Ibid., p. 39.

132. Ibid., p. 72.
133. Ibid., p. 75.
134. Ibid., p. 76.
135. Ibid., p. 78.
136. Ibid., p. 81.
137. Ibid., pp. 87–88.
138. S. Verba, "Sequences and Development," in L. Binder et al., *Crises and Sequences in Political Development*, p. 304.
139. J. LaPalombara, "Bureaucracy and Political Development: Notes, Queries, and Dilemmas," in LaPalombara, *Bureaucracy and Political Development*, p. 58.
140. Ibid., p. 57.
141. Ibid., p. 60.
142. Coleman, "The Development Syndrome," p. 89.
143. Ibid., pp. 89–90.
144. Ibid., p. 90.
145. Coleman, "The Development Syndrome," pp. 74–75.
146. S. P. Huntington and J. Dominguez, "Political Development," in F. I. Greenstein and N. W. Polsby, eds., *Handbook of Political Science*, Vol. 3 (Reading, Mass.: Addison-Wesley, 1975), p. 38.
147. S. P. Huntington, M. Crozier, and J. Watanuki, *The Crisis of Democracy* (New York: New York University Press, 1975), p. 115.
148. G. Almond and G. B. Powell, Jr., *Comparative Politics* (Boston: Little, Brown, 1978), p. 363.
149. Ibid.
150. Ibid., pp. 369–370.
151. C. E. Lindblom, "Politics and Markets in Developing Areas," Joint Seminar on Political Development, Harvard University and MIT (September 26, 1979), unpublished transcript.

Index